SPALDING.

BOOK OF RULES
AND
1993 SPORTS ALMANAC

BING BROIDO

Illustrations by Elmer Wexler

MASTERS PRESS

A Subsidiary of Howard W. Sams & Co.

The Spalding Book of Rules and 1993 Almanac

ISSN: 1065-4763

Published by Masters Press (a subsidiary of Howard W. Sams)
2647 Waterfront Pkwy E. Dr, Suite 300, Indianapolis, IN 46214

Credits:

Illustrations of competition areas and officials' signals by Elmer Wexler except those on pages 192 and 193, which are reprinted with the permission of the NCAA.

For A. G. and Phoebe and Henry
—who have the best seats in the upper deck

ACKNOWLEDGEMENTS

The accuracy and most current interpretations of the rules as stated in this book were made possible by the expertise, cooperation and enthusiasm of rules chairmen, association officers, referees, umpires and sports experts. The dedication of these authorities to their sport is reflected on every page.

John Adams

Larry Bergstrom

Robert Brown

Merle Butler

Mark Cord

Robert Cowan

Lance Deckinger

Otto E. Dietrich

Ken Dothee

Bob Dunn

Harold Edmondson

Tom Fleetwood

Pat French

Gene Gill

Randy Gordon

Jeff Hall

Howard Hammer

Jeff Henry

Dwain Hebda

Bob Hersh

Kathy Kelly

Rodney Kenney

Darwin Kingsley

Ed Lawrence

Al Kleinatis

Don Leas

Elmer J. Lehotsky

John Lewis

Dr. Neill Luebke

Gerald Mahoney

Dr. Charles Mallery

Bruce Mathis

Christen Matta

Larry McCaigue

Jim Miles

Hank Nichols

Tom Perry

Skip Phillips

Chuck Quast

Terry Quinn

Vern Roberts

Richard Rose

Kate Spence

Steven B. Stenersen

Jack Thomas

Bob Vehe

Bob Waldman

Steve Waldman

Steve Whitlock

Don Leas

Elmer J. Lehotsky

John Lewis

The book has been greatly enhanced by the product of three all-star talents: Elmer Wexler's superb artwork, Eric Richards' fascinating research, Vincent Mallozzi's all-inclusive compilations.

Special thanks to Al Bender and Ralph Carlson at Spalding for giving me the ball.

Finally, deserved recognition to the team at Masters Press; especially, Tom Bast, Holly Kondras and my editor, Mark Montieth.

ONTENTS

ABOUT THE AUTHOR

H. W. "Bing" Broido is president of a consumer products marketing firm. A graduate of Dartmouth College, he has developed merchandise programs under the sponsorship of many international government and private sector organizations in areas such as art, entertainment, fashion, sports and fitness. Married and the father of three, he is a rules expert, writer, popular speaker and lifelong sports enthusiast.

FOREWORD

This book began when my family was given a badminton set, which we assembled with care and in anticipation of friendly competition. There were no instructions included and the questions soon began. Do you serve underhand or overhand? Do you score like tennis or volleyball or ping pong? How many points must be scored to win a game, and do you have to win by two?

I only had one question: why was everyone asking me about the rules? The confusion about the value of a leaner in horseshoes was nothing compared to the frustrations in croquet. And these were just in family lawn games.

Every individual and team sport has rules of play, but they are not always available when needed and seldom presented in an easy-to-understand format. This book was created as a convenient source of rules information for active sports participants, including young beginners, casual players who enjoy sports but do not have to win to have fun, sports fans who want to better understand how the games are to be played, new entrants, especially women and teenagers, parents and family members, in-person spectators and TV viewers and those responsible for organized sports events.

Complete with perspective graphics, this book is a single-volume, clearly-stated, current reference to the rules and regulations of the most popular competitive American sports.

Spalding has a great sports history dating back to 1876 when Hall of Fame pitcher A.G. Spalding developed the first major league baseball. Spalding also made the first American football, golf ball and clubs, tennis ball and other significant firsts in many sport. About 200 million products enter the consumer market every year carrying the Spalding name for players and enthusiasts at every level: from the official NBA game ball to entry items for children.

Spalding has long been involved in the publishing of books about sports. By the early 1900s, the Spalding Athletic Library had hundreds of titles. Some rules have never changed: it's still 90 feet between the bases in baseball and five of Dr. Naismith's 13 original basketball principles from 100 years ago (such as, the ball may not be advanced by running) are part of the game as it is played today in almost 200 countries. But organized sport is not static; rules change. For example, major laws recently were introduced in soccer to speed up the game and increase spectator appeal; they are included in the text as are illustrations of all of the revised official's signals.

This is a book about understanding, not skills. Knowing how a game is meant to be played will make each sport more enjoyable to both participants and enthusiasts.

I have had extraordinary cooperation from the governing bodies and federations responsible for each of the sports. If more information is needed (such as full rule books and other publications, regional chapters and local groups, events schedule, membership, youth activities, books, program development, education and safety, sponsorships, exhibits), a listing of key organizations is included.

The home team has made this book possible, and it is dedicated to my wife/partner, Lois. The questions of Belinda and Raffael, Lisa and Andy, and Amy generated the project. I hope the answers give Alana and Jack and their generation the basics of sports for years of competition, recreation and pleasure.

GOVERNING BODIES

The national governing bodies of each of the sports included in this book have reviewed the appropriate text and approved its accuracy. The names and addresses of the various associations, organizations, federations, leagues and sources of information on sports rules and regulations follow:

AMATEUR ATHLETIC UNION
3400 West 86th Street
Indianapolis, IN 46268

AMATEUR SOFTBALL ASSOCIATION OF AMERICA
2801 N.E. 50th Street
Oklahoma City, OK 73111

AMATEUR SPEEDSKATING UNION OF THE UNITED STATES
1033 Shady Lane
Glen Ellyn, IL 60137

AMERICAN AMATEUR RACQUETBALL ASSOCIATION
815 North Weber
Suite 101
Colorado Springs, CO 80903

AMERICAN BOWLING CONGRESS
5301 South 76th Street
Greendale, WI 53129-1127

AMERICAN DARTS ORGANIZATION
7603 E. Firestone Blvd.
Suite E6
Downey, CA 90241

AMERICAN PADDLEBALL ASSOCIATION
26 Old Brick Road
New City, NY 10956

AMERICAN PLATFORM TENNIS ASSOCIATION
251 Park Street
Upper Montclair, NJ 07043

THE ATHLETICS CONGRESS
P.O. Box 120
Indianapolis, IN 46206

BASEBALL OFFICE FOR UMPIRE DEVELOPMENT
P.O. Box A
201 Bayshore Drive SE
St, Petersburg, FL 33731

BILLIARD CONGRESS OF AMERICA
1700 S. 1st. Avenue
Suite 25-A
Iowa City, IA 52240

FIELD HOCKEY ASSOCIATION OF AMERICA
1750 East Boulder Street
Colorado Springs, CO 80909

THE LACROSSE FOUNDATION
113 West University Parkway
Baltimore, MD 21210

LITTLE LEAGUE BASEBALL, INC.
P.O. Box 3485
Williamsport, PA 17701

MAJOR LEAGUE BASEBALL
350 Park Avenue
New York, NY 10022

**NATIONAL ARCHERY
ASSOCIATION**
1750 East Boulder Street
Colorado Springs, CO 80909

**NATIONAL BASEBALL
CONGRESS**
300 South Sycamore
Wichita, KS 67203

**NATIONAL BASKETBALL
ASSOCIATION**
645 Fifth Avenue
New York, NY 10022

**NATIONAL COLLEGIATE
ATHLETIC ASSOCIATION**
Nall Avenue at 63rd Street
Mission, KS 66201

**NATIONAL FEDERATION OF
STATE HIGH SCHOOL
ASSOCIATIONS**
11724 Plaza Circle
Kansas City, MO 64195

NATIONAL FOOTBALL LEAGUE
410 Park Avenue
New York, NY 10022

NATIONAL HOCKEY LEAGUE
650 Fifth Avenue
New York, NY 10019

**NATIONAL HORSESHOE
PITCHERS ASSOCIATION**
P.O. Box 7927
Columbus, OH 43207

**NATIONAL SHUFFLEBOARD
ASSOCIATION, INC.**
3816 Norbrook Drive
Upper Arlington, OH 43220

**UNITED STATES AMATEUR
CONFEDERATION OF ROLLER
SKATING**
4730 South Street
Lincoln, NE 68506

**UNITED STATES BADMINTON
ASSOCIATION**
1750 East Boulder Street
Colorado Springs, CO 80909

**UNITED STATES BOCCE
FEDERATION**
2239 Orange Street
Martinez, CA 94553

**UNITED STATES CROQUET
ASSOCIATION**
500 Avenue of the Champions
Palm Beach Gardens, FL
33418-9990

**UNITED STATES CYCLING
FEDERATION**
1750 East Boulder Street
Colorado Springs, CO 80909

UNITED STATES DIVING
Pan American Plaza
Suite 430
Indianapolis, IN 46225

**UNITED STATES FIGURE
SKATING ASSOCIATION**
20 First Street
Colorado Springs, CO 80906

UNITED STATES GOLF ASSOCIATION
Golf House
Far Hills, NJ 07931

UNITED STATES GYMNASTICS FEDERATION
Pan American Plaza
Suite 300
201 S. Capitol Avenue
Indianapolis, IN 46225

UNITED STATES HANDBALL ASSOCIATION
930 N. Benton Avenue
Tucson, AZ 85711

UNITED STATES OLYMPIC COMMITTEE
1 Olympic Plaza
Colorado Springs, CO 80909

UNITED STATES PADDLE TENNIS ASSOCIATION
189 Seeley Street
Brooklyn, NY 11218

UNITED STATES SAILING ASSOCIATION
Box 209
Newport, RI 02840

UNITED STATES SOCCER FEDERATION
U.S. Soccer House
1801-1811 South Prairie
Chicago, IL 60616

UNITED STATES SQUASH RACQUETS ASSOCIATION
23 Cynwyd Road
Bala-Cynwyd, PA 19004

UNITED STATES SWIMMING, INC.
1750 East Boulder Street
Colorado Springs, CO 80909

UNITED STATES TABLE TENNIS ASSOCIATION
1750 East Boulder Street
Colorado Springs, CO 80909

UNITED STATES TENNIS ASSOCIATION
1212 Avenue of the Americas
New York, NY 10036

UNITED STATES VOLLEYBALL ASSOCIATION
3595 East Fountain Blvd.
Colorado Springs, CO 80910-1740

UNITED STATES WATER POLO, INC.
Pan American Plaza
201 S. Capitol Avenue
Indianapolis, IN 46255

USA BASKETBALL
1750 East Boulder Street
Colorado Springs, CO 80909

USA BOXING
1750 East Boulder Street
Colorado Springs, CO 80909

USA HOCKEY
4965 North 30th Street
Colorado Springs, CO 80919

USA WRESTLING
AAU House
3400 West 86th Street
Indianapolis, IN 46268

History

The use of the bow and arrow for warfare and hunting dates back to prehistoric times. The ancient Egyptians and Greeks practiced recreational archery. The Turks developed a curved bow in the A.D. 900s, but it was soon displaced in medieval warfare by the crossbow — a sophisticated missile-like weapon. The use of the longbow — and later the straight bow — was common in England and Scotland until the end of the 16th century. The English kings insisted on compulsory practice with equipment they supplied and this became the basis for archery as a sport. The Finsbury Archers of London, who held tournaments in the 17th and 18th centuries, trace their origin to a grant from Henry VIII in 1537.

In the United States, where the bow and arrow had long been the primary weapon for Native Americans, the first archery group was formed in Philadelphia in 1879.

The National Archery Association is the governing body for the sport. Archery was part of the Olympics in the early 1900s. It was suspended for many years and then re-introduced for men and women in 1972.

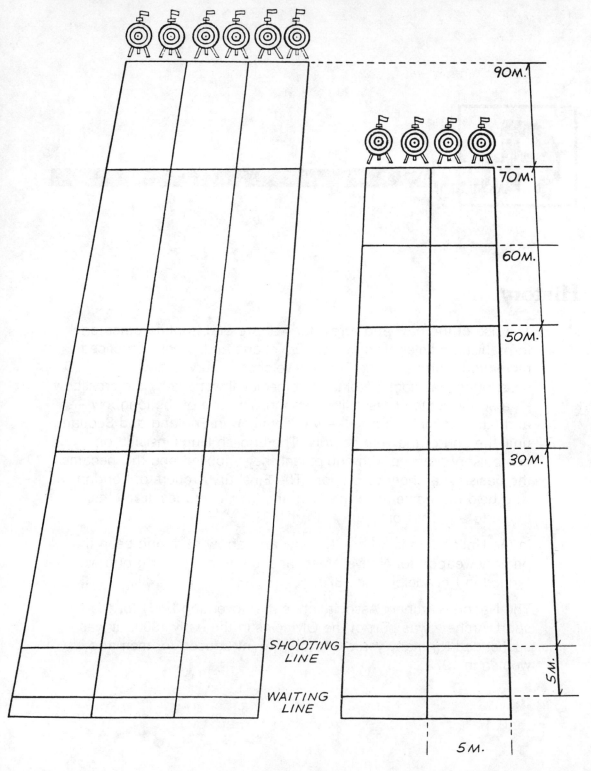

SHOOTING
LINE

WAITING
LINE

90M.

70M.

60M.

50M.

30M.

5M.

5M.

Object of the Game

Each player shoots a number of arrows from different distances at a target marked with scoring rings. The highest total score wins.

Playing Field

The archery field is divided into lanes that are at right angles to the shooting line and may contain one, two or three targets. Shooting is from south to north. Male and female archers are separated by a clear lane. Men shoot 36 arrows at each distance of 30, 50, 70 and 90 meters (34½, 56, 78 and 99 yards). Women shoot the same number at 30, 50, 60 and 70 meters (34½, 56, 67 and 78 yards).

Equipment

The **target** is made of straw mat or other available material and is covered with a paper or canvas face. It comes in two sizes, as follows:

- 80 centimeters (32 inches) in diameter for shots from 30 and 50 meters
- 122 centimeters (48 inches) for longer distances

The **target face** is divided into five concentric color zones arranged from the center outward: gold (or yellow), red, blue, black and white. Each color is divided by a thin line into two zones of equal width, making 10 scoring zones of equal width.

The 122-centimeter face has a 12.2-centimeter (4¾ inches) diameter gold circle; other colors are 6.1 centimeters (2⅜ inches) wide.

The 80-centimeter face has an eight-centimeter (3¼ inches) diameter gold circle; other colors are four centimeters (1½ inches wide).

The target face is mounted on a **buttress** (support) that is made of any material that will not damage the arrows on impact.

Bows can come in any standard form (although not a crossbow) and material with a single bowstring and adjustable arrowrest.

Arrows can be any style, length and weight as suits the archer. They should be marked with the archer's name or initials on the shaft; all arrows used should have the same color pattern.

Accessories include quiver (holder for arrows), finger protectors, gloves, bowsight and related items.

Dress is casual. Archers should wear white attire, with some color. All targets are numbered, and archers should wear their target numbers.

Procedure

Matches can be played between individuals or teams, usually consisting of three players each. Play proceeds as follows:

- The archers draw for targets
- The archers stand with one foot on each side of the shooting line or with both feet on the shooting line
- The bow is held in one hand; the string is pulled back and released by the fingers of the other hand, shooting the arrow.
- Official practice is conducted before the start of the competition; archers may shoot as many arrows as they want
- Each archer shoots an *end* of three or six arrows. The maximum time for each end of three is 2½ minutes; for six it is four minutes.

A *round* is an agreed-upon number of arrows, a series of ends, that the archers shoot in rotation at the set distances.

For example, men and boys 18 years and older shoot 36 arrows from 90 and 70 meters to a 122-centimeter face, then shoot 36 arrows from 50 and 30 meters to an 80-centimeter face.

Shooting moves from the longest to the shortest distance or vice versa, at the decision of the tournament director.

No arrows can be touched until all scores are recorded.

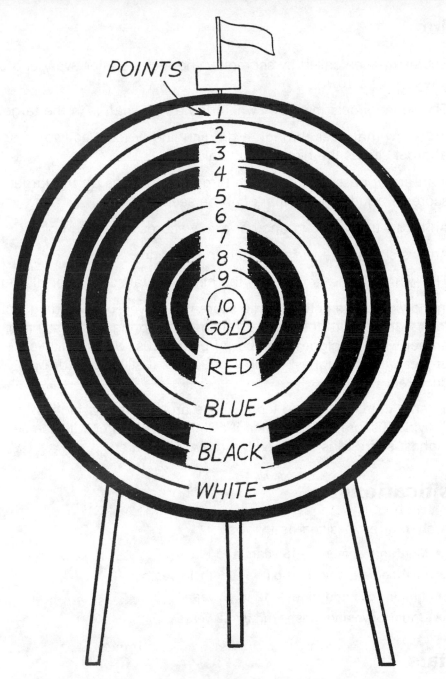

POINTS

1
2
3
4
5
6
7
8
9
10
GOLD

RED

BLUE

BLACK

WHITE

White: outer, 1 point; inner 2 points

Black: outer, 3 points; inner, 4 points

Blue: outer, 5 points; inner, 6 points

Red: outer, 7 points; inner, 8 points

Gold: outer, 9 points; inner, 10 points

Scoring

Scores may be called by scorers or the archers after every end of three or six arrows.

The score is determined by where the arrow shaft is in the target.

An arrow that goes through a dividing line or touches two colors on a target scores the higher point value.

If an arrow passes through the target or bounces off the target, it scores if an identifying mark can be seen.

An arrow that lands in another arrow scores the same points.

Arrows shot in the wrong target do not score.

The winner is the archer with the highest total score after all rounds.

In individual competition, a tie score is resolved by awarding victory to the archer with the highest number of scoring hits; if still tied, the archer with the highest number of *golds* (10s) wins; if still tied, the archer with the highest number of 9s win; if still tied, a draw is declared.

In team competition, the team whose archer has the highest individual score is the winner; if still tied, the archer with the second highest score wins; if still tied, a draw is declared.

Classifications

Archers are classified as follows:

- Men and women — 18 years and older
- Intermediate boys and girls — 15 to 18 years
- Junior boys and girls — 12 to 15 years
- Cadet boys and girls — under 12 years

Officials

Archery officials include a tournament director, scorers and assistants.

History

Badminton's roots are in 5th century B.C. China. It evolved from a game of kicking a small feathered object, a **shuttlecock**. A variation was played in England in the 14th century. English officers learned **poona** in India, which was later played at Badminton, the country home of the Duke of Beaufort, in 1873. The game took its new name from that estate. The term **to serve** comes from when English royalty played badminton and a servant hit the shuttlecock into play at the start of each game and after every point.

English settlers brought the sport to America; documentation shows it being played at colonial Williamsburg. The first badminton club in the U.S. was opened in New York in 1878. Participants at that time wore tuxedos and long dresses. Growth was rapid in the 1920s and 1930s. The game was popular in Hollywood — celebrity players included James Cagney, Bette Davis, Ginger Rogers, Douglas Fairbanks and many others. Today, badminton is one of the world's most active participation games and was introduced as a full-medal Olympic sport in 1992.

The United States Badminton Association is the national governing body that promotes the sport and designs programs to develop the skills of players at all levels.

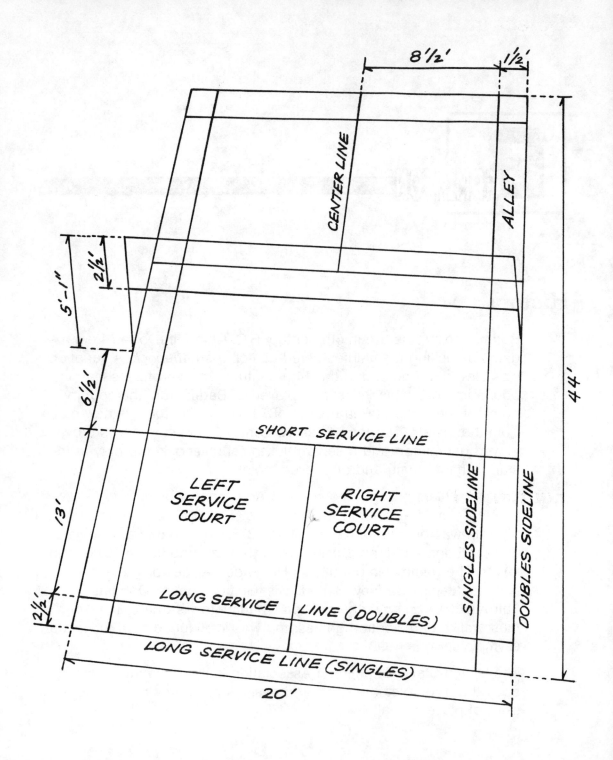

Object of the Game

Two or four players using rackets try to hit a feathered object (shuttlecock) over a high net so that it lands inside the opposite court and cannot be hit for a successful return. The highest score wins.

Playing Field

The court is 17 × 44 feet for singles and 20 × 44 feet for doubles.

The *short service line* is 6 feet, 6 inches from the net.

The *long service line* for doubles is 13 feet behind the short service line.

The *long service line* for singles is 2 feet, 6 inches behind the long service line for doubles, which is 22 feet from the net. This also is the back boundary line.

The *singles side line* is 1 foot, 6 inches inside the doubles sideline.

The *center line* is at midcourt, between the short service and back line.

The *net* is made of cord, is 30 inches deep and is five feet from its top to the floor at center court (5 feet, 1 inch at the posts).

Equipment

The **racquet** can be made of various materials. It should have crossed strings and a flat hitting surface, and has a maximum length of 26¾ inches.

The **shuttlecock** (also called the *shuttle* or *birdie*) contains 14 to 16 feathers or a plastic mesh extending 2¾ inches from a cork or synthetic base. It weighs approximately ⅕ ounce.

Dress is informal, similar to tennis.

General Rules

Games are played between individuals or pairs. The serving team is called the *in* side; the other side is **out**.

Only the serving side can score. The server earns a point if the receiver is unable to return the shuttle within the boundaries.

Game length

Games are played to varying point totals, as follows:

- Men's singles and all doubles: 15 points
- Women's singles: 11 points
- One-game match of any type: 21 points

The length of a game can be extended by a scoring option called *setting* when the score is tied near the end of a game.

In a 15-point game, when the score is tied at 13, the set to win is five (raising the winning score to 18). At 14-all, the set is three.

In an 11-point game, when the score is tied at 9, the set is three; at 10-all, the set is two.

In a 21-point game, when the score is tied at 19, the set is five; at 20-all, the set is three.

The first player/team to reach 13 or 14 points (or 9, 10, 19 or 20, depending on the length of the game) can choose to play to the regular end point total or to set the game for an additional number of points if the score becomes tied.

After the game is set, the score becomes 0-0 (*love-all*) and the first side to reach the set number — 5, 3 or 2 points — is the winner. The final score is the total number of points scored, including the set.

A match is the best of three games.

Procedure

Players spin a racquet or toss a coin to determine the start of play. The winner chooses between serving first or the end of the court from which to receive.

Play is non-stop with five minutes rest between the second and third games.

Players change ends after each game and halfway through the third game.

Serving/returning

Service is made from within the serving player's court, not from behind the back line. The shuttle must be hit underhand into the service court diagonally opposite the server.

The server and receiver must both be in their service courts and the receiver must be ready.

All returns must be made before the shuttle hits the ground.

A shuttle that lands on the marking line is considered in-bounds.

The server calls the score after each point.

In singles play:

> The service areas are bounded by a short service line, a singles long service line and singles sidelines. The outside alleys are not inbounds. If the score adds up to 0 or an even number, the serve is made from the right service court; if the score is an odd number, the serve is made from the left service court.

In doubles play:

> The service areas are bounded by a short service line, a doubles long service line and doubles side lines. The server winning the first point continues serving, changing service courts for each point (the receiving players do not switch) until failing to score.

> Service then changes to the opponent in the right service court, who keeps serving as long as points are scored. When the new server fails to score, the partner takes over and serves from

alternate courts to alternate opponents until failing to score. Service then returns to the original pair and each serves in turn. The receiving side must prevent both servers from scoring to regain service.

After the service is returned by the player in the service court diagonally opposite the server, any player can hit the shuttle.

Faults

A *fault* is any error that ends play, whether occurring during service, the receipt of service or the *rally* (an exchange that decides a point). A fault committed by the serving side gives the serve to the opponent; a fault by the receiving side gives the point to the server.

Service faults include the following violations:

- The shuttle does not cross the net or lands in the wrong court
- The shuttle is not hit on its base
- The shuttle is higher than the server's waist when hit
- The shuttle is hit in an overhand motion
- The server is outside the service court, has a foot or feet off the ground, or steps on any line
- The server misses the shuttle while attempting to serve

A receiving fault occurs when:

- The receiving player does not stand in the correct service court or moves before the serve is made

Faults that can be committed during rallies include the following:

- The shuttle touches the ground inbounds
- The shuttle does not go back over the net
- The shuttle falls outside the court
- The shuttle is hit more than once by a player and/or partner before it is returned over the net
- A player touches the net with his body or racquet
- A player reaches over the net to hit the shuttle
- A player is hit by the shuttle
- A player blocks the opponent's play

Note: It is not a fault if the shuttle is played around a post.

Lets

A *let* occurs when a point does not count and must be replayed. It is called by an umpire or agreed upon by the players.

A let includes the following violations:

- Serves taken out of turn
- Serves taken before the receiver is in place
- Rallies won after serving from the wrong court
- Simultaneous faults by both sides
- The shuttle becoming stuck in the net after crossing

Note: It is not a let if the shuttle hits the top of the net while passing over it; play continues.

Officials

An umpire in a raised chair at the net controls the game and may be helped by line and service judges.

History

The beginnings of baseball may trace back to a game played in England during the Middle Ages — stoolball. A batter tried to hit a pitched ball before it reached an upside-down milk stool. If the ball was hit, the batter ran around three stools and back to the "home stool." Beginning in the 17th century, British children played *rounders* which had a diamond-shaped field with bases on the corners and many elements that are directly related to baseball. One major difference was the way a runner was put out; the fielders threw the ball at the runner and "plugged" him.

When the colonists brought rounders to America in the early 1700s, it became known as *town ball* because every village seemed to play with its own local rules. The first reference to *base ball* was in an illustrated 18th century book published in England and then printed in America.

A.G. Spalding (whose Hall of Fame bronze plaque reads, in part, "organizational genius of baseball's pioneer days") suggested in 1905 that a commission be appointed to discover the true origins of the sport. The group's report declared that Abner Doubleday, a West Point cadet, invented the game at Cooperstown, N.Y. in 1839. Historians now credit Alexander Cartwright, a surveyor, for first developing standard rules in 1845. Many of his original regulations are still part of the game: the dimensions of the infield, three strikes,

14

three outs, foul balls defined, nine players to a side and base runners tagged out instead of being hit by a thrown ball. The first game played under the new rules was in June, 1846. By 1858 there was an association of amateur players and games were played for nine innings instead of 21 runs to win.

The Civil War (Doubleday was a General) helped baseball become the national pastime as soldiers from the east taught the game to others from different parts of the country. The first all-professional team was the 1869 Cincinnati Red Stockings and an association of professional players was formed two years later. Pitching was still underhand and no gloves were used. The National League — a group of eight clubs, not players — was established in 1876 and the American League (renamed from the Western League) began in 1900.

Today, thousands of teams compete in America's most popular outdoor sport. Apart from the professional Major and Minor Leagues, games are played — day and night — by amateurs and semi-pros on sandlots and other public spaces, in schools at all levels and in numerous programs for younger players (such as, American Legion, Babe Ruth and Little League). The National Baseball Congress maintains a standard of excellence in amateur baseball and serves as the governing body for affiliated teams and officials across the world.

Baseball is a major international sport. American missionaries introduced the game to Japan in the 1870s; A.G. Spalding led baseball's first around-the-world tour in 1886. It has been played in Mexico and Cuba since the late 1800s and is greatly popular in Latin America, Canada, Taiwan and several European countries. Baseball became an official Olympic sport with the 1992 games.

Object of the Game

Two teams of nine players plus substitutes compete to score *runs* (points) by players safely moving around four bases on a diamond-shaped field. The highest score wins.

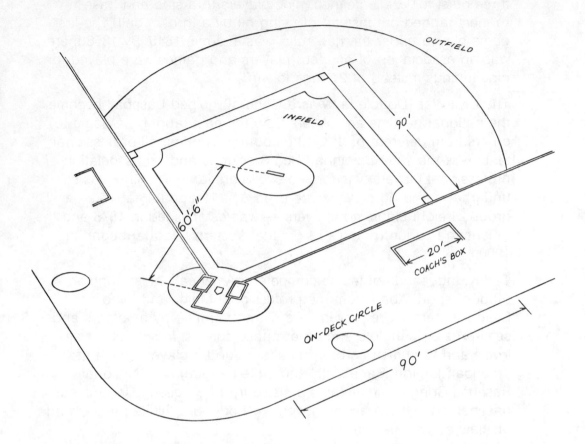

Playing Field

The field of play is shared by an infield and an outfield and is separated into fair and foul territory.

Infield

The *diamond* is a 90-foot square with a base at each corner.

The *bases* include first, second and third base. They are made of canvas, are 15 square inches and up to five inches high. They are fastened in place.

Home plate is made of white rubber, is five-sided and is set flush with the ground. It is 17 inches wide across the edge facing the pitcher, 8½ inches long on each side and 12 inches long on the sides of the point facing the catcher.

The distance between home plate and second base and between first and third base is 127 feet, 3⅜ inches.

The *pitcher's mound* is 18 feet in diameter and is centered 59 feet from the rear of home plate.

The *pitcher's plate* is made of rubber. It is 6 × 24 inches, set on the mound 10 inches above the level of home plate and is 60 feet, 6 inches from the rear point of home plate.

The *batter's boxes* are 4 × 6 feet and six inches from the outside edges of home plate.

The *catcher's box* is 43 inches wide and eight feet long, behind home plate.

The *on deck circle* for the next batter is five feet in diameter and located between each players' bench and home plate.

The *three-foot line* is parallel to and three feet outside the base line starting halfway from home plate and ending beyond first base to guide the runner.

The *coaches' boxes* are 20 × 10 feet and set 15 feet outside the diamond behind first and third bases.

Outfield

The outfield is the wide area of the playing field beyond the diamond and most distant from home plate. The recommended distances are 325 feet or more (250 feet minimum) from the back of home plate to the side boundaries and 400 feet to center field. The boundaries may be changed for different levels of play, age of players and so on.

The *foul lines* extend from home plate past first and third bases to foul poles set at the boundary at the ends of the outfield. *Fair territory* is the playing field within and including the foul lines; *foul territory* is the area outside the foul lines.

Equipment

The **bat** is made of smooth and rounded wood. It has a maximum diameter of 2¾ inches and a maximum length of 42 inches. The handle may be covered with material up to 18 inches long to improve the batter's grip.

The **ball** is made of stitched white horsehide or cowhide. It is 9 to 9¼ inches in circumference and weighs 5 to 5¼ ounces.

The **gloves** are made of leather. The fielders' gloves have four fingers connected to the thumb by a web. They have a maximum height of 12 inches and a maximum width of 7¾ inches. The first baseman's glove, or *mitt*, is padded and has no fingers. It has a maximum height of 12 inches and a maximum width of eight inches. The catcher's mitt has a maximum height of 15½ inches and a maximum circumference of 38 inches.

All players wear the same design and style **uniforms** with numbers at least six inches high on the back. The home team wears white.

Shoes may not have pointed spikes.

For **protective gear**, batters must wear helmets with ear flaps. Catchers wear head protection, throat and body protectors and knee and shin guards.

General Rules

The game is divided into innings, in which each team has a turn *at bat* (to hit the ball) and to be in the field. A regulation game lasts nine innings.

The second half of the ninth inning does not have to be played if the home team has scored more runs than its opponent or only needs a fraction of the inning to score more runs.

If the game is tied, extra innings are played until one team has more runs at the end of a complete inning or until the team batting second scores more runs before a third out.

A game stopped (such as for rain or darkness) counts as complete if five innings have been played or if the team batting second has more runs after four innings than the other team has scored in five. A game is called a tie if it ends after five or more innings with the team scores even. It may be replayed at a later date.

The **home team** is the team on whose field the game is played; the other team is the **visitors**. If the game is played in a neutral setting, one team is made the home team.

The team at bat is allowed three **outs** (batters or base runners are prevented from safely reaching or advancing a base) in an inning. After that, the side is **retired**, its players move to the field and the team that was in the field comes to bat.

One run is scored each time a base runner touches first, second and third base and home plate before the third out of an inning.

Fielders (defensive players), except for the pitcher and the catcher, can stand anywhere in fair territory. The pitcher must start on the pitcher's plate (fair territory) and the catcher in the catcher's box (foul territory). The fielding positions are as follows:

The battery	Infielders	Outfielders
1—pitcher	3—first base	7—left field
2—catcher	4—second base	8—center field
	5—third base	9—right field
	6—shortstop	

In some games, a **designated hitter** (DH) named before the game may bat for the pitcher. The DH is locked into the batting order and cannot play on defense. If the DH becomes a fielder, there is no longer a DH and the pitcher must bat in the place of the fielder taken out of the game. The DH may be replaced by a **pinch hitter** (substitute), who takes that place in the batting order.

A replaced DH may not come back into the game.

Substitutions can be made for any player when the ball is **dead** (out of play.) Players removed may not re-enter the game. A substitute takes a player's place in the **batting order** (the hitting sequence) and can take any position in the field.

Procedure

The manager of each team gives the plate umpire the team's *lineup* (the names of the players at each defensive position and batting order). The visiting team bats first (the *top* of the inning; the second half is the *bottom*) and the home team players take their defensive positions in the field. The plate umpire calls "play" to start the game.

Batting

Players bat in the order listed.

The batter stands inside or on the batter's box lines and tries to hit the ball or otherwise get on base.

The *strike zone* is the rectangular space above home plate between the batter's armpits and knee tops when in a natural batting stance.

A *strike* is called when the batter:

- Swings at a pitch and misses
- *Takes* (does not swing at) a pitch that the umpire determines entered the strike zone
- Hits a *foul ball* (a ball hit into foul territory that is not caught by a fielder); if caught, the batter is out. If the batter already has two strikes and hits a foul ball that is not caught, the strike count stays at two and the ball is dead.
- Hits a *foul tip* (a ball hit directly back to the catcher and caught); the ball is *live* (in play) and any base runner who tries to advance is at risk of being put out
- Is hit by a pitch thrown into the strike zone, or is hit by a batted ball while standing in the box with less than two strikes; the ball is dead.

The batter is out after three strikes.

A *ball* is a pitch called by an umpire that does not pass through the strike zone and is not swung at by the batter.

Four balls allow the batter to go to first base, which is called a *walk* or *base on balls*.

If the batter does not swing at and is hit by a ball pitched outside of the strike zone, the batter goes to first base.

A fair ball is a batted ball that:

- Lands in or is touched by a player in fair territory (infield or outfield)
- Goes over the boundary fence on the fly in fair territory or bounces off a foul pole (both are *home runs* and the hitter goes around all the bases to score)
- Bounces past first or third base on or over fair territory
- First lands in foul territory, then rolls fair into the infield
- Bounces on a base or touches a player or an umpire while in fair territory

A foul ball is a batted ball that:

- Lands in or is touched by a player in foul territory
- Hits the bat or the batter while in the batter's box
- Touches a player or umpire in foul territory
- Rolls into foul territory before reaching first or third base before being touched and comes to rest there

The batter is out, the ball is in play and runners may try to advance if:

- A called or swinging third strike is caught by the catcher
- A third strike foul ball is caught by a fielder in foul territory
- The batter misses at a third strike and is touched by the ball
- There is a third strike with a runner on base and less than two outs
- A fly ball is caught in fair or foul territory (a *pop-up* is a short, high fly ball, a *line out* is hit hard and straight to a fielder)
- The *infield fly rule* (a fly ball hit into the infield with runners on first and second base or first, second and third with less than two outs) is called by umpire; the pitcher and catcher are considered infielders on this play
- The batter *grounds out* (does not reach first before the fielder touches the base or is tagged out)

A batter is out and the ball is dead if:

- A fielder intentionally drops a fly ball or *line drive* (a ball hit on a straight line) with a runner on base and less than two outs
- A *bunt* (a ball not fully swung at but lightly tapped to the infield) goes foul after a second strike
- A ball is hit twice or hit and touches the batter in fair territory after coming out of the batter's box

- The catcher drops a third strike but touches the batter with the ball or throws it to first base before the batter reaches the base
- The batter interferes with a catcher's play at the plate, brings an illegal bat into the box or switches boxes after the pitcher begins to throw
- A base runner interferes with a fielder's play before reaching first base

A batter hits a ball into fair territory in one of the following ways:

- In the air: If the ball is caught by a fielder before it touches the ground or an outfield boundary fence, the batter is out
- On the ground: If the fielder can pick up ball and get it to a teammate at first base (or make the play alone) before the batter arrives, the batter is out

If a ball cannot be caught before touching the ground and cannot be received at first base before the batter arrives, the batter has a *single* base hit and may stay safely at first base or try to run to other bases.

If the defensive team can get the ball to second or third base and *tag* the batter (touch him with the ball or with the ball in the glove) before the batter arrives at a base or between the bases, the batter is out.

A hit that allows the batter to safely reach second base is a *double*; if the batter reaches third base it is a *triple.*

On a home run, the batter runs around all the bases, crosses home plate and scores, as do any teammates already on base. A home run can also be made *inside the park* if the fielders cannot get the ball to home plate in time to tag the batter.

A *grand slam* home run is when the bases are *loaded* (runners on all three bases) and four runs score.

The first batter in an inning is the next in order after the last batter of the previous inning.

Base running

The batter becomes a base runner, with the ball in play, if:

- The ball is hit into fair territory
- Four balls are called
- The catcher drops a third strike with less than two outs and first base unoccupied, or with two outs and first base occupied; the batter is safe if he is not tagged or beats the catcher's throw
- A fielder makes an *error* (mishandles the ball)
- On a *fielder's choice* (a preceding base runner is put out instead of the batter)

The batter goes to first base and the ball is dead if:

- Catcher or fielder interference is called
- A fair ball strikes a base runner or umpire before the ball passes or touches a fielder
- A pitch, not swung at and not a called strike, hits a batter in the box who is trying to avoid it

A runner has a right to be at each base by getting there before being put out and can stay until legally advancing to another base or being *forced* to leave by the batter or another base runner (such as on a batted ball or walk).

The runner must touch all bases, including home plate, in correct order to score.

Two runners cannot be on the same base at the same time. The first to legally arrive is safe; the other runner may be tagged out. If the first runner is forced to advance and two runners are on base, the second runner has legal right to the base.

When the ball is in play, a base runner may progress under the following circumstances:

- A ball is hit into fair territory or thrown into fair or foul territory
- After any fly ball is caught, but the runner must first *tag up* (touch the current base)
- On a *steal* by running to the next base as soon as the ball is pitched; the runner is out if tagged

- After a *wild pitch* (the catcher cannot reach the pitch) or a *passed ball* (the catcher cannot handle the ball)
- A fair ball hits a base runner or umpire after passing a fielder or touches a fielder

A runner advances with no risk of being put out under the following circumstances:

- A batter walks and forces any teammates to move ahead one base
- The umpire calls a *balk* (illegal pitching motion); all runners move up one base
- A ball in play is blocked or overthrown into out-of-play territory or a pitch goes in or past the backstop
- A fielder obstructs a runner and the runner does not run past a base that the umpire feels the runner would have made if not for the obstruction
- A batter hits a home run
- A batter hits a *ground rule double* (the ball bounces over a fair boundary fence or goes into an unplayable area); the batter and base runners are awarded two bases

A runner must return to the base after:

- Each pitch that is not hit by the batter
- A ball is caught on the fly
- A foul ball is not caught
- Batter, runner or umpire interference
- An intentionally dropped infield fly
- A batter is hit by a pitched ball that is swung at and missed

A run does not score if the third out comes from the batter being out before reaching first base or another base runner being forced out.

A base runner is called out if the runner:

- Is forced (made to advance) to another base and the fielder with the ball tags the runner or touches the base before the runner arrives
- Is tagged by a fielder and is not safely standing on base when the ball is in play
- Runs past first base safely, turns toward second and is tagged
- Runs more than three feet outside of a direct line between the bases to avoid being tagged

- Interferes with a player fielding a batted ball or with a thrown ball
- Is involved in a *double play* (two offensive players put out in the same action) or a *triple play* (three runners out)
- Is hit by a fair ball while off base and before it passes any infielder, except the pitcher
- Passes another runner or arrives last while another runner is on a base
- Leaves a base before a fly ball is caught or is tagged before returning
- Misses touching a base and a defensive player tags the runner or base
- Purposely kicks the ball or runs the bases backward to confuse the defense

A base runner is not out if the runner:

- Runs outside the base path to avoid interfering with a fielding attempt
- Is not tagged with the ball firmly held by the fielder
- Touches and runs past first base but returns directly to it (must run past the base into foul territory)
- Is hit with a batted ball while standing on base or with a ball batted past an infielder when there was no opportunity for an out
- Stays on base until a fly ball is touched, then tries to advance (can be tagged out at next base)

Pitching

Eight warm-up pitches are allowed before each inning or to a *relief* (replacement) pitcher during an inning. The pitcher must throw the ball to the catcher within 20 seconds after receiving it.

Pitchers have two legal starting positions. A *windup* includes the following elements:

- The pitcher faces the batter
- The pitcher has one foot (a *pivot* foot) on or touching the pitcher's plate and the other foot free (may be set anywhere)
- Before the pitch, the pivot foot may come off the rubber and the pitcher can throw to any base
- After the pitching motion has begun, the movement must be continuous
- The free foot may take one step forward and backward during the throwing motion, but the pivot foot cannot leave the ground

Pitching from a *set* includes the following elements:

- The pitcher faces the batter from a sideways stance
- The pivot foot must be on the rubber and the free foot in front
- The ball is held in both hands in front of the body
- The pitcher may *stretch* (bring the arms over the head) but must come to a complete stop before throwing the ball

The pitcher may throw to the batter, come off the rubber, or take a step toward and throw to an occupied base.

From a set position, the motion to the plate cannot be broken.

Pitching violations include the following:

- Balls intentionally thrown (*bean balls*) at a batter
- Putting a foreign substance on the ball or purposely damaging a ball
- Throwing a ball to a base while the foot is on the pitcher's plate; pitchers must step off the plate

A *balk* is a pitching violation with runners on base. It includes:

- Pitching when the foot is not in contact with the rubber
- Pitching from the set position without coming to a full stop
- Throwing to a base from the set without first taking a step toward the base
- Pretending to throw to the batter or first base
- Making a quick pitch or not completing a pitch
- Dropping the ball during the pitching motion
- Being charged with a delay of game

Officials

The umpire-in-chief controls the game from behind home plate. His responsibilities include calling balls and strikes, fair and foul balls, all decisions about the batter, and all matters related to the conduct of the game. The field umpires call play on the bases and assist the plate umpire in other judgments.

Many calls (such as "play" and "infield fly") are by voice. The umpire's signals include the following, as illustrated:

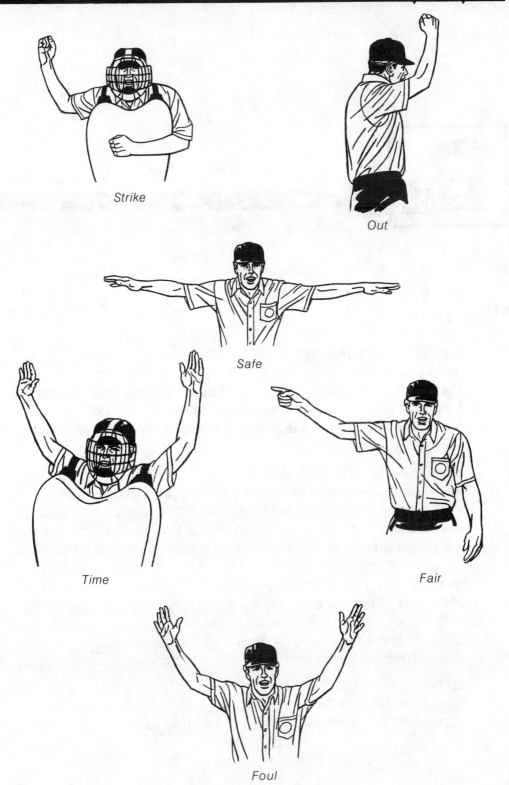

Strike

Out

Safe

Time

Fair

Foul

27

History

Basketball was invented in 1891 by Dr. James Naismith, an instructor at the YMCA Training School in Springfield, Massachusetts. Unlike football and baseball and other sports that evolved over the years from earlier games in other countries, Naismith's game was specifically created to stimulate attendance during the winter.

Several elements contributed to the success of his game as an indoor sport. Running with the ball and hard contact were eliminated. The ball was light and large (for safety and handling) as it would not be hit or kicked. Setting the basket over the heads of the players reduced the body contact normally found near an on-the-ground goal. (Two half-bushel peach baskets attached to the gym balcony 10 feet above the floor gave the game its name and also established a measurement that remains in use.) Women's competition started the next year and has been a major force in the sport from the beginning. A player from the first women's team later married James Naismith.

Spalding made the first basketball and today Spalding is the official ball of the NBA. In 1893, a metal ring with a netted bag was introduced but after each goal the ball had to be released by pulling a chain. (Nets without bottoms were not used until 1913.) Backboards were first installed in 1894 to keep spectators from reaching out to deflect the ball.

The game began with 13 fundamental rules which were expanded over the years. It was originally played with nine on a side because Naismith had eighteen members in his class; five on a side has been standard since 1895. The first college game (Chicago vs. Iowa) was played in 1896 and the first professional game was in 1898. The sport grew in popularity during the next 50 years. Rules were standardized, arenas were built, competition began between teams from different parts of the country and annual tournaments were established for all levels of play. The National Basketball Association was formed in 1949 from a consolidation of earlier leagues. The first black professional played the next season. The televising of college and pro games brought basketball to millions of additional fans. Dr. Naismith's original 13 rules were the foundation of what is now the most popular indoor sport in the world.

USA Basketball is the national governing body for the sport in the United States and is made up of many different organizations, including the Amateur Athletic Union (AAU), the National Basketball Association (NBA), the National Collegiate Athletic Association (NCAA) the National Federation of State High School Associations, and the coaches associations for both men and women. The International Basketball Federation (FIBA) is the sport's world organization formed by 176 national groups.

Note: Rule differences between the NCAA, NBA and FIBA are identified.

Object of the Game

Each team tries to score points by *shooting* (throwing) a ball into a *basket* (goal) while preventing its opponents from scoring. The team that scores the most points wins the game.

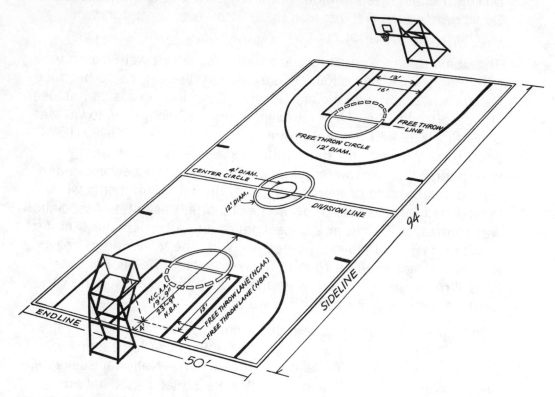

Field of Play

The court dimensions vary according to the level of play, as follows:

- NCAA: 50 × 94 feet
- NBA: 50 × 94 feet
- FIBA: 49 feet, 2½ inches by 91 feet, 10 inches
- High school: 50 × 84

The *basket* is a single orange metal ring with an inside diameter of 18 inches, set 10 feet above the floor, with a white cord net 15-18 inches long.

The *backboard* is a rigid flat surface, either transparent or white, measuring 6 × 4 feet, with a 24 × 18-inch rectangle outlined above the basket. A fan-shaped backboard, approximately 54 × 35 inches, may be used in high school games.

The hardwood floor includes *side lines* and *end lines* according to the size of the court.

A *division line* runs across the center of the court connecting the sidelines.

Two *center circles*, one with a two-foot radius within another with a six-foot radius are at the court's midpoint.

Two *free-throw lanes* are at each end of the court, with one of the following dimensions:

- NCAA: 12 × 19 feet, and a semi-circle with a six-foot radius from the center of the free-throw line
- NBA: as above, but 16 × 19 feet
- FIBA: as above, but widens to 19 feet at the end lines

Four spaces 36 inches apart are along the lane lines.

A *free-throw line* is in front of the lane semi-circles and parallel to the end line, 15 feet from the backboard

A *three-point field goal line* in the shape of a semi-circle is around each basket with the following dimensions:

- NCAA: 19 feet, 9 inches from the center of the basket
- NBA: 23 feet, 9 inches
- FIBA: 20 feet, 6 inches

Two *coaching boxes* are behind the side lines, 28 feet long and extending from each end line

Equipment

The **ball** is round, with an orange pebbled leather or synthetic cover. It has a circumference of 29 to 30 inches and weighs 20 to 22 ounces. The women's ball has a circumference of 25½ to 29 inches and weighs 18 to 20 ounces.

A scoreboard, game clock, shot clock and possession indicator are used.

Players dress in tank tops with numbers in the front and back, shorts, socks and leather shoes with rubber soles.

BASKETBALL

General Rules

Each team has five players on the court, usually a center, two forwards and two guards.

A *point guard* is the primary ballhandler; the *shooting guard* is a top scorer.

Substitutions may be made when the ball is *dead* (out of play) and the game clock is stopped. A substitute reports to the scorer and enters the game after being signaled to by an official.

The ball may be passed, thrown, tapped, rolled or *dribbled* (bounced on the ground with one hand) as a team with the ball moves toward the goal. The ball may not be carried or kicked.

A dribble ends when the player catches the ball with one or both hands, touches the ball with both hands, when an opponent *taps* (tips or strikes the ball) or if the ball becomes dead.

A team's own basket is the one into which its players try to throw the ball; in FIBA, it is the basket defended.

A team's front court is the half of the playing area in which it attacks the goal. The backcourt is the half in which a team defends the goal.

Game length

The length of the game varies according to the level of play, as follows:

- NCAA: two 20-minute halves, 15 minutes between halves
- NBA: four 12-minute quarters, 15 minutes between halves
- FIBA: two 20-minute halves, 10 minutes between halves
- High school: four eight-minute quarters, 10 minutes between halves halves.
- Youth play: four six-minute quarters, 10 minutes between halves

Timeouts

The number of timeouts permitted varies according to the level of play, as follows:

- NCAA: five (one-minute each) per game; one in each overtime
- NBA: seven (90 seconds) per game; one 20-second timeout per half
- FIBA: two (one minute) per half
- High school: four (one minute) per game

Note: In a televised game with three or more TV timeouts in any half, each team is only permitted three timeouts.

Officials may call a timeout for player injury.

Scoring

A goal is made when a live ball goes into the basket from above, remains in the basket or passes through the net.

A *field goal* may be shot from anywhere on the court. Shots from beyond the three-point line count three points, and shots within the three-point line count two points.

A *free throw* (unobstructed try for a goal) is taken from the free throw line as a penalty shot after certain fouls. It counts one point.

The team with the most points at the end of the game wins.

If the score is tied, play continues for as many extra periods as are needed, with a one-minute rest between periods. In the NCAA, NBA and FIBA, overtime periods last five minutes. In high school, they last three minutes.

The game ends when one team has more total points at the end of an extra period.

Timing

Shot clock rule: The team with possession of the ball has a specific amount of time to shoot the ball. The ball must hit the rim to count as a shot attempt. The time varies according to the level of play, as follows:

- NCAA: 45 seconds
- NBA: 24 seconds
- FIBA: 30 seconds

After a failure to shoot, the ball is given out-of-bounds to the opponent and the clock is reset.

Three second rule: No player can stay within the free throw lane in front of the opponents' basket (in the *key* or *paint*) for more than three seconds while the player's own team has possession of the ball, unless the ball is in the air, *rebounding* (bouncing from the backboard or off the basket rim after a missed shot on goal) or dead.

Five second rule (in NCAA and FIBA): Teams have five seconds to get the ball into play after a basket or a free throw or upon gaining possession after an out-of-bounds.

Ten second rule: The team gaining possession of the ball in its backcourt must move it into the frontcourt within 10 seconds.

The game clock starts when the ball:

- Is touched during a jump ball
- Touches a player after a failed free throw
- Touches a player from a throw-in from out-of-bounds

The game clock stops at the end of each period and at a whistle for:

- A violation or foul
- A *held ball* (two opposing players both have their hands firmly on the ball)
- A ball out-of-bounds
- An injury or other reason ordered by officials

- When the shot clock is sounded (if the shot clock sounds while the ball is in the air and the ball hits the rim, the shot clock buzzer is ignored and the game clock keeps running)
- Timeouts

Each period begins when the ball first becomes live; it ends when time expires unless the ball is in flight for a field goal or if there is a foul.

Time is allowed for free throws after a foul is committed at the end of a period.

A score counts if ball is in the air when time runs out.

Procedure

The visiting team chooses which end of the court to play; a coin toss decides on a neutral court.

Teams change ends at halftime, but do not change ends for overtime periods.

The game and any overtimes are started by a jump ball in the center circle. The referee throws the ball into the air between the two opposing centers.

The jumpers stand inside their half of the circle. They cannot tap the ball until it reaches its highest point, catch the ball or touch it more than two times.

The other players must stand outside the circle until the ball is tapped.

If the ball is not tapped and reaches the floor, a jump ball is repeated.

The team that controls the ball moves it forward by player dribbling or passing between teammates and tries to score a goal.

If a basket is made, the opposing team is given possession of the ball out-of-bounds behind its end line. If the shot is missed, the rebound can be captured by either team.

A team's control ends when a shot is taken, the defense recovers the ball or the ball is dead. Neither team controls the ball during a jump ball or while tapping a rebound.

A ball is dead when:

- A goal is made
- A foul or violation occurs
- A free throw is not successful after the first of two free throws or on a throw for a technical foul
- A held ball occurs
- An official's whistle blows
- A shot clock signal sounds
- A period's time expires

The ball is not dead and any score counts if:

- A foul occurs, a whistle is blown or the shot clock or period ends while the ball is in flight toward the basket
- The opponent fouls a player during the shooting motion

The ball becomes live when tapped at a jump ball, on a *throw-in* (the ball put in play from out-of-bounds) or when given to a player for a free throw.

A player receiving a live ball may:

- *Pivot* by keeping one foot in contact with the floor with no limit on the steps taken with the free foot
- Dribble by taking any number of steps as the ball is bounced on the floor with one hand while walking or running, but may not dribble again (*double dribble*) if the ball is held in one or both hands; a second dribble is permitted if the ball is touched by another player or leaves the dribbler's control.
- Pass or hand the ball to a teammate
- Try to score

After a timeout, play is resumed by the team that had control of the ball, by a jump ball or alternating possession (if neither team had control) or a free throw.

Jump ball

In addition to the start of the game or any overtime periods, a jump ball may be called if neither team has control, if the ball goes out of bounds without certainty as to which player last touched it, if two

opponents create personal fouls at the same time and other situations.

Substitutes cannot be made for the jumping players.

Players also jump at held ball situations.

Under the *alternating possession* rule, play continues with one of the teams being given the ball for a throw-in instead of both actually jumping for the ball. The team that did not get control at the game's opening begins the alternating process (teams take turns) with a throw-in from a spot nearest to where the situation occurred. The direction of the possession arrow is reversed at the time of the throw-in. The NCAA uses alternating possession instead of jump balls.

Throw-in

When a team is awarded the ball out of bounds, the official hands the ball to the inbounding player who must throw, bounce or roll it to a teammate on the court within five seconds.

The thrower cannot step on or over the side line or move while releasing the ball. Defensive players cannot cross the boundary line or touch the ball before the throw-in. After a score, the player making the throw-in does not have to stay in a designated spot but may run along the end line.

Free throw

A free throw is an opportunity to score one point by an unhindered shot from behind the free throw line and inside the free throw semi-circle. The shot must be attempted within 10 seconds (NCAA, NBA) or five seconds (FIBA).

The shot attempt starts when the shooter is given the ball and it ends with a basket or an unsuccessful try, when the ball touches a player or the floor or when the ball becomes dead.

The thrower must remain behind the line until the ball touches the basket.

Opponents take the space closest to the basket on either side of the free throw lane.

Teammates of the free throw shooter may take the next positions on each side; the remaining players alternate along each lane line. Only the spaces nearest the basket must be taken. Only the four spaces on each side may be used; all other players must be behind the three-point field goal line and an imaginary extension of the free throw line.

The players at the lane remain in position until the ball is shot; the other players must stay beyond the three-point line until the ball touches the basket rim.

If the shot is good, play restarts by a throw-in from behind the end line. If a shot is unsuccessful and rebounds, play continues from the rebound.

If requested before the play, a substitute can be made for a free-thrower after the first of two or more free throws (NBA) or after the first successful throw (NCAA). The opponent also is allowed one substitute, if requested, to enter the game after the basket. The NCAA allows a substitute at any time the ball is dead, whether requested or not.

Out of bounds

The ball is considered out of bounds and possession is awarded to the team that did not last touch it when:

- A player with the ball touches the floor on or beyond a boundary line
- The ball touches a person or object on or beyond a boundary line

Interference

It is **goaltending** if a player touches the ball during a field goal attempt or free throw while the ball is in its downward flight above the basket until it touches the basket's ring.

A player cannot reach into the basket from below and touch the ball before it enters the space above the ring.

If the defense interferes, a goal is scored and the game is restarted. If the offense interferes, opponents are given a sideline throw-in.

Guarding

When defending a player with the ball, the legal position is to face the opponent and have both feet on the ground; no time or distance is required.

When defending a player without the ball, the defender must give the opponent time and distance (two steps) to avoid contact.

Contact

A player makes contact by holding, pushing, tripping or charging into an opponent

The first player to establish position without contact has priority.

The player that moves into the path of another is responsible for the contact.

A player cannot move into the path of an opponent off the ground.

Each player has the right to *verticality* (the space occupied) and may jump up and raise his arms and hands within that space.

Blocking is contact that interferes with an opponent's movement.

A player may *screen* to delay or prevent an opponent from reaching a position on the court by securing the space before the opponent arrives.

Screening may be done by the offense or defense but with no contact in the attempt to interfere with the movement of the opponent.

Violations

Violations are *infractions* (breaking rules) that do not involve personal contact, including:

- Sending the ball out of bounds
- Running with the ball
- Kicking or punching the ball
- Double dribbling
- Keeping the ball in the backcourt more than 10 seconds

- Not attempting a field goal before the shot clock expires
- Basket interference or goaltending
- Staying in the free-throw lane more than three seconds when a player's own team has possession of the ball
- An opponent crossing the boundary line before the ball does on a throw-in
- A throw-in player (1) leaving the correct position, (2) taking more than five seconds, (3) carrying or handing the ball onto the court, (4) throwing the ball at the basket or (5) touching the ball in the court before it touches another player

When a violation is called, any goal made does not count and the ball is awarded to an opponent for a throw-in from the closest spot on the side line or end line to the infraction or (FIBA only) from the nearest point on a side line.

Fouls

Personal fouls are infractions involving contact with an opponent, whether the ball is in play or not, including the following:

- Holding, pushing, charging or tripping
- Interfering with an opponent's progress by extending the arm, shoulder, hip or knee or by bending in an unnatural body position
- Pushing from behind
- Dribbling into an opponent's path or between opponents or an opponent and a boundary without enough space to avoid contact; if the dribbler gets the head and shoulders past the opponent, the responsibility for contact is on the defender
- Contact with a shooting player
- Rough tactics
- Hitting an opponent with a hand unless to play the ball
- Using the hands to prevent an opponent's movement
- Screening a player closer than one step from the opponent
- Screening a player, then moving in a different direction than the opponent

The offender is charged with a foul.

A player is disqualified and removed from the game after five fouls (NCAA and FIBA) or six (NBA).

A player fouled while shooting is awarded two free throws if the shot misses, or one free throw if the shot is successful.

If the fouled player is on offense but not shooting, the team is awarded a throw-in near the place of the foul.

If the foul is committed by an offensive player, the defense gets possession; no free throws are awarded.

A *penalty situation* occurs after a team commits its limit of personal fouls. The fouled team shoots one or two free throws after every foul for the remainder of the period being played.

During a *one-and-one* foul situation, if the player makes the free throw, a second shot may be taken. The bonus free throw is taken on the seventh team foul per half (NCAA), on the fifth team foul per quarter (NBA) or on the eighth team foul per half (FIBA). In high school, the bonus is awarded on the fifth foul in a half.

A *double personal* is called when two opponents commit personal fouls at the same time.

A foul is charged to each player. Play resumes with a jump ball (NBA, FIBA) or by alternating possession (NCAA).

An *intentional* foul is a deliberate personal foul in which a player does not make a true attempt to play the ball or an opponent. The penalty is two free throws.

A *flagrant* foul is a violent contact that might cause injury.

The penalty is two free throws and the offender is sent to the locker room.

Note: Fighting is a flagrant foul and can bring suspension from future games.

A *multiple* foul occurs when two or more teammates commit personal fouls against the same player at the same time.

Each offending player is charged with a foul; the player fouled receives two free throws. A goal counts if scored and one free throw is awarded.

A *technical* foul is a violation by a nonplayer or a noncontact foul by a player or an intentional or flagrant foul when the ball is dead, including:

- Delay of game
- Taking more timeouts than allowed
- Having more than five team players on the court at one time
- Grasping the basket, except to escape injury
- Goaltending a free throw
- Interfering with the ball after a goal
- Showing disrespect to officials
- Using profanity, obscene gestures or teasing opponents
- Wearing identical or illegal numbers
- Leaving the bench, except to react to a team play
- A coach leaving the box to follow the play or entering the court without permission (the coach may leave the area to confer with officials or, during a timeout, to meet with players near their bench)

If a technical foul is called on a player, two free throws are awarded to the offended team, plus possession of the ball at the division line.

If the technical is called on a coach, substitute or other non- player, two free throws are awarded. (In the NCAA, the offended team also gets possession of the ball at the division line.)

Any player on the non-fouling team may make the free throw; the other players do not line up on the free throw lane.

A second technical is considered flagrant in the NCAA and NBA; in FIBA, it is the third. The player that offends is removed from the game; a coach is ejected from the competition area.

Free throws are awarded as follows:

- NCAA: in a one-and-one situation, a bonus second throw, if the first throw is successful, after the opposing team has nine personal fouls a half
- NBA: two throws for all fouls over four in a regulation time period; after three in each overtime
- NCAA/NBA: two throws if a player is fouled while shooting and a goal missed
- FIBA: two throws after eight opposing team fouls per half

On free throw violations, no point is scored if the violation is by the thrower or teammate; the ball is dead.

On a violation or personal foul, the ball is awarded at the nearest spot out of bounds.

On a violation by the free thrower's opponents, if the throw is good, the goal counts; if not, another throw is taken.

Officials

A referee controls the game and works on the court with one or two umpires, calling fouls or violations and changing positions as the teams move. NBA and NCAA Division I games use three officials.

At the side line, the scorekeepers work the scoreboard and record the play; the timekeeper operates the game clock and the shot clock operator works the shot clock.

NCAA officials' signals

Jump ball

Stop clock

Start clock

Call in substitute

Illegal use of hands

Shot clock violation

Stop clock for foul

Restart shot clock

Pushing/charging

Holding

Technical foul

Blocking

44

Five-second violation (both hands
for 10-second violation)

Intentional foul

Traveling

Illegal dribble

Three-second violation

No score

Player control foul

Direction/possession

Over and back division
line/carrying the ball

45

Goal counts

Points scored (one or two fingers)

Bonus free throw

Official's timeout

Lane violation

Three-point goal good

Three-point field goal attempt

Throw-in; free throw

Double foul

History

Shakespeare's Cleopatra said, "Let's to billiards," which may be literature's best-known reference to the game. Its creation may date to ancient Persia, and it was known as a lawn game in the 12th century. Historic players include Mary, Queen of Scots (who was upset when denied use of her billiard table when in captivity), Marie Antoinette and King Louis XVI of France. Pockets were added to the table by the 1800s, but the original game is still played in many places around the world. Some tables even had obstacles, not unlike the modern bumper pool. Balls were once ivory, but now are made of plastic.

Pool is the popular name for American pocket billiards. Unique in sports, the game was most often played by the two extremes: high society and the lower working class. Today, pool is both a leisure-time game and a competitive sport that crosses all social and economic boundaries. Attractive facilities have opened. Young players, including many women, have become enthusiastic participants. The Billiard Congress of America governs the sport, establishes rules, promotes tournaments and generates a variety of awareness and other activities that have helped make the game one of the 10 most-played in the country.

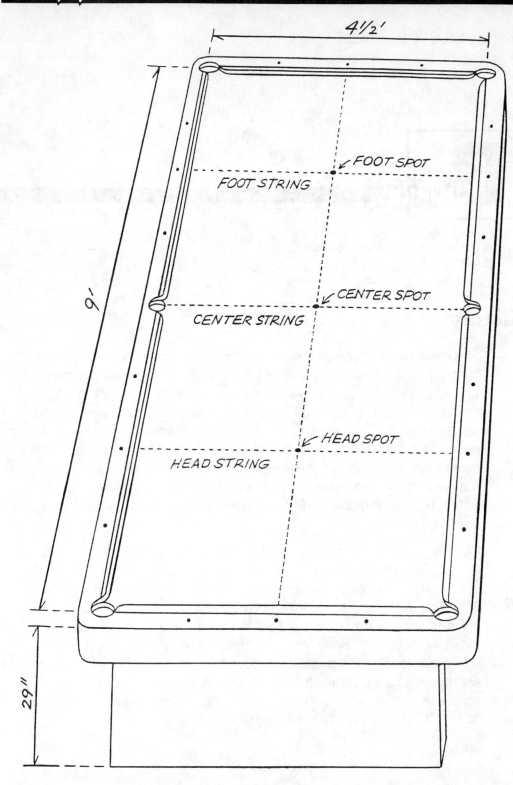

4½'

9'

FOOT SPOT

FOOT STRING

CENTER SPOT

CENTER STRING

HEAD SPOT

HEAD STRING

29"

Object of the Game

A player using a *cue* (wood stick) tries to hit a *cue ball* (white) against *object balls* (numbered and in color) into *pockets* (receptacles) set around a table.

Playing Field

The table is rectangular, twice as long as it is wide. The most popular sizes are 4 × 8 feet and 4½ × 9 feet. The playing surface is approximately 29 inches high and has *cushions* (rubber rails) on all sides. It has a slate base, covered with a green felt-like fabric. It has six pockets, each approximately five inches in diameter, one in each corner and at the center of each side rail.

The *foot rail* is a cushion at one end of the table.

The *foot string* is an imaginary line halfway between the foot rail and the center point of the table.

The *foot spot* is a point marked at the center of the foot string.

The *center spot* is a point marked at the center of the table.

The *head rail* is a cushion at the opposite end.

The *head string* is an imaginary line halfway between the head rail and the center of the table.

The *head spot* is a point marked at the center of the head string.

The *long string* is an imaginary line down the center length of the table.

Equipment

The **cue** is a tapered wooden stick of no specified length or weight, but usually is under 60 inches and 18 to 20 ounces. It has a leather tip.

The **balls** are a hard plastic composition, 2¼ inches in diameter and weighing approximately six ounces.

The **cue ball** is solid white and unnumbered. The **object balls** have varying solid colors (numbers 1 through 8) or have colored stripes (numbers 9 through 15).

The **rack** is a triangular frame used to set up and place the object balls at the start of the game.

The **cue rest** is a mechanical bridge (grooved metal arch on a long handle) that supports the shaft of the cue.

Dress is casual.

General Rules

Games are played between individuals or pairs.

The *break* (opening shot) is decided by *lags*. Each player shoots the cue ball from behind the head string to rebound off the foot rail; the ball may not touch the side rails. The player whose ball comes to rest nearest to the head rail can make the break or play after the opponent.

Object balls are *racked* (arranged) depending on game.

The cue ball may be placed anywhere between the head string and the head rail at the start of play.

Chalk may be put on the cue tip to prevent the cue from slipping off the cue ball if "English" (spin) is applied.

A *stroke* starts when the shooter hits the cue ball with the tip of the cue and lasts until all balls stop rolling.

The first player hits the cue ball from behind the head string to the cluster of object balls. The cue ball may go straight to an object ball or first touch one or more rails. A legal break requires that an object ball be *pocketed* (hit into a pocket) or bounce off a rail. If the break is illegal, the opponent may play the balls as they are or ask the shooter to repeat the break.

Each player's turn is an *inning* and lasts as long as a player pockets balls or until a *foul* (playing violation) occurs. Innings alternate between players. If no foul occurs, the next player plays balls as they lie.

The shooter must call the number of the ball to be pocketed for a score. If the called ball drops, any other balls pocketed from the same shot also count. If the called ball is not pocketed, any balls dropped do not count and are *spotted* (replaced on the table.)

A ball is *In hand* when it has to be set on the table so that play can begin or continue.

A ball that bounces back on to the playing surface from a pocket does not count and is played from where it is on the table. A ball that rolls above a rail and returns to the table is also played from where it rests.

If the called ball *jumps* (lands somewhere other than the playing surface or in a pocket), the inning is over and the ball is spotted. If the called ball is pocketed and another ball jumps, the pocketed ball counts and the jumped ball is spotted.

A ball or balls are spotted if pocketed when:

- The cue ball is also pocketed
- The cue ball did not first hit the called object ball
- The ball(s) were knocked off the playing surface

A single ball is spotted on the foot spot. If more balls must be spotted, they are to be placed one behind the other, beginning with the lowest number, on the long string line between the foot spot and the foot rail.

An object ball is *frozen* if it is against a rail or touching the cue ball. The shooter must hit the frozen ball with the cue ball and pocket the frozen ball or move it to another rail or make the cue ball or another object ball touch a rail. It is a foul if none of these are done.

Officials

A referee judges fair play and a marker keeps the score.

Rules for the three most popular pocket billiards games follow; there are many regional versions.

Straight Pool (14.1 Continuous)

Object of the Game

Players compete to be the first to reach an agreed-upon score (50, 100 or, usually, 150). Each ball legally pocketed counts as one point.

Procedure

The object balls are racked with the 15-ball at the front point of the triangle and over the foot spot. The 1-ball is set in the rear lefthand corner, the 5-ball in the rear righthand corner, the rest of the high numbered balls near the top of the triangle and the lower numbers at the bottom.

On the opening break, the player calls the number of the object ball and the pocket to which it will be played. The shooter must use the cue ball to drop the called ball into the designated pocket or hit the called ball and another ball into a rail.

If neither of these are done, it is a foul and the player loses two points. The opponent may play the balls as they lie or tell the shooter to repeat the break. This continues until a legal break is made or balls are played by the opponent.

It also is a foul if the cue ball from the break shot is pocketed. The shooter loses one point and the opponent becomes the shooter from behind the head string, but plays the balls as they lie.

Other fouls, penalized by loss of point and turn, include the following:

- Hitting any moving balls
- Making the cue ball rise above the playing service by striking it below its center or pushing the cue stick under it
- Jumping the cue ball off the table
- Shooting with both feet off the floor

A player also may call a *safety* (a defensive move to minimize the opponent's chances to score). The player's inning ends when a safety is played, pocketed balls are not scored and any object ball pocketed is spotted.

After 14 balls have been pocketed, the 15th ball and the cue ball remain as they lie and the pocketed balls are re-racked with a space left at the front point. The player who dropped the 14th ball continues to play and may try to pocket the last object ball or call and shoot at the newly grouped object balls. Innings continue with successive 14 balls pocketed, re-racked and broken until a player misses, fouls or scores the points needed to win the game.

A safety is a defensive move in which a player does not call a shot on an object ball but, instead, tries to leave the balls so that an opponent cannot score. This can be done by sending an object ball to a rail or the cue ball to a rail after hitting an object ball. Pocketed balls are spotted. An inning ends after a safety; a one-point penalty is assessed if a safety attempt fails.

A *scratch* is when the cue ball is pocketed at the break or during play or knocked off the table. It causes a one-point penalty and ends the inning. Three scratches in a row adds an additional 15-point penalty.

8-Ball

Object of the Game

Each player or pair tries to be the first to pocket the object balls numbered 1-7 or 9-15 and then the 8-ball.

Procedure

Balls are racked with the 8-ball in the center of the triangle and the first ball of the rack on the foot spot.

The break must either pocket a ball or send at least four object balls off a rail.

Failure to make a legal break is not a foul; the incoming player may play the balls as they lie or have the balls re-racked and take a break shot.

If there is a scratch on the break shot, it is a foul and all balls pocketed are spotted, including the 8-ball. The incoming player places the cue ball behind the head string.

If the 8-ball is pocketed on the break, the breaker may request a re-rack or have the 8-ball spotted and continue shooting. If the breaker scratches, the incoming player may re-rack or have the 8-ball spotted and begin play from behind the head string.

If any object ball is pocketed on the break, a shooter can then play the high (striped) or the low numbered (solid color) balls. If no ball is dropped, an opponent plays balls as they lie, choosing either the high or low numbered group.

In play, a shooter must pocket an object ball or make the cue ball or any object ball touch a rail. Otherwise, it is a foul. If an opponent's ball is pocketed by the shooter, it counts for the opponent. An inning continues until the shooter does not legally pocket an object ball. All seven balls in the series selected (high or low numbers) must be pocketed before the 8-ball.

The shooter must call the pocket for the 8-ball and hit the 8-ball before any other on the table. If the shooter misses, the game continues.

A player loses the game if:

- The 8-ball is pocketed before the other seven
- The 8-ball is dropped into a pocket not called
- A scratch occurs when the 8-ball is pocketed
- The 8-ball is pocketed on an illegal break shot or on the same shot as the last ball in the object group

Individual balls have no value in points and fouls do not create point penalties.

If there is a scratch on the break shot, a player shoots from behind the head string. On all other fouls, the incoming player can place the cue ball anywhere on the table.

The game is over when a player has pocketed all of the striped or solid balls and, then, the 8-ball. The player to win the most games wins the match.

9-Ball

Object of the Game

Players try to be the first to pocket the 9-ball.

Procedure

Nine balls are racked in a diamond shape with the 1-ball on the foot spot and the 9-ball in the center of the group. All balls must be touching.

The 1-ball is the object ball for the break. If missed or not pocketed, the opponent plays the balls as they lie.

Object balls must be played in numerical order; the cue ball must first hit the lowest number on the table before any other ball. If accomplished, any ball that is pocketed counts and the player continues to shoot.

On all fouls, the incoming player can place the cue ball anywhere on the table.

No balls are spotted after a jumped ball or any foul.

The first player to legally pocket the 9-ball wins. The match ends when one player has won a required number of games.

History

Egyptian artifacts from 4000 B.C. depict a game similar to bocce and the game appears in a tomb painting from the Golden Age of Greece. The conquering armies of Alexander the Great spread the forerunner of bocce throughout Asia Minor, North Africa and, along with the Greek colonists, into Italy. It was further spread by the Roman Empire. In the mid-14th century, the Holy Roman Emperor, Charles IV, banned the game so that his subjects could concentrate on war.

History relates that in England, Sir Francis Drake, on learning of the approach of the Spanish Armada while *bowling*, insisted on finishing his game before setting out to battle. James I noted in his *Book of Sports* that *bowls* was one of the few recreations that were allowed on the Sabbath.

In 19th century Italy, bocce flourished with many regional variations, and it was the Italian immigrants who brought bocce to America. The versions of the game that evolved over the years are being combined and standardized. In Europe, the rules are quite different and require special skills. The United States Bocce Federation was organized primarily for the purpose of encouraging amateur competition in the sport by promoting open bocce nationwide and its introduction into school systems.

The rules that follow are the U.S. open/recreational version.

Object of the Game

Two teams of one to four players each roll or throw balls at a smaller target ball. When all balls have been played, points are awarded for balls closest to the target ball.

Playing Field

The standard playing court is 13 × 91 feet. Any smooth, flat surface is suitable, but clay is preferred.

A *center line* runs across midcourt.

A *foot line* extends 12 to 15 feet from each end line. The court is framed with 2 × 10 inch side and back walls.

Note: The end of the court is called the back wall, backboard or back line.

Equipment

Bocce **balls** are 4¼-inch in diameter and weigh about 2.2 pounds. They are made of a synthetic material and are identified by color or other markings.

The **target ball** (also called a *pallino* or *jack*) is made of wood or a synthetic material, and is 1⅜ inches to 2¼ inches in diameter.

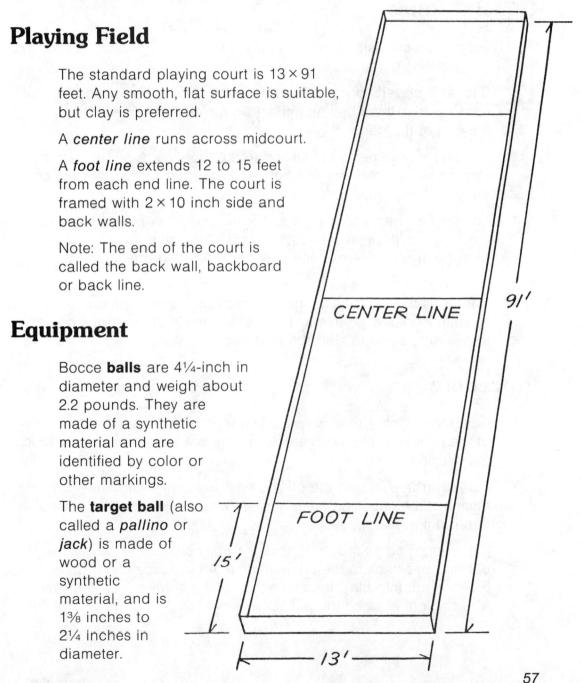

CENTER LINE

91'

FOOT LINE

15'

13'

A tape measure, stick or anything that accurately measures the distance between two objects can be used.

Dress is casual.

General Rules

Each team consists of two or four members. Half of each team stays at each end of the court.

Should a player's bocce ball make contact with the backboard, it is considered a dead ball on impact and is removed from play until the end of the frame.

A player's movements are limited to the foot line. A player cannot step on or over the foot line before releasing the pallino or bocce balls.

Throws can be made from a stationary position or by running up to the foot line. If a player wants to displace an opponent's ball with a hard (fast) roll, several steps may be taken before reaching the foot line.

After a team wins a game, players exchange ends of the court and substitutions may be made. The team winning the previous game tosses the pallino to start the next game.

Procedure

A match begins with a coin flip. The winner may have the first toss of the pallino or choose the color of the balls or the end from which play begins.

If a player fails to toss the pallino past the center line after two attempts, the opposing team has two chances to toss the pallino and put it in play.

If the opposing team fails to toss the pallino past the center line, the pallino goes back to the original team. After the pallino has been properly put into play, the first bocce ball is thrown by the player who originally tossed the pallino.

If the bocce ball hits the backboard, the team must roll again. After a proper roll has been made, the player steps aside and the team does not roll again until the opposing team has either placed one of its balls closer to the pallino or has thrown all of its balls.

The team whose bocce balls are closest to the pallino is called *inside* and the opposing team is **outside**.

When a team gets inside, it stops rolling and lets the outside team play. The team outside throws until it beats (not ties) the opposing ball. This order continues until both teams have rolled all of their bocce balls.

A *frame* is when both teams have played their allotted balls one time down the court.

The team that scored last throws the pallino from the opposite end to begin the next frame.

After the pallino has been tossed past the center line and is in play, it remains in play even if it hits the backboard. If the pallino is knocked out of the court or in front of the center line, it is placed in the middle of the foot line at the playing end of the court.

Scoring

Only the inside team scores.

One point is given for each ball of the inside team that is closer to the pallino than any ball of the opposing team.

If at the end of any frame the closest ball of each team is the same distance from the pallino, the frame ends in a tie; no points are awarded to either team.

The first team to score 12 points wins the match. In some locations, games must be won by two points.

Officials

Referees or participants may keep score and measure the distances between balls.

History

Stone pins and balls dating back to 5200 B.C. have been found in an Egyptian tomb. Other ancient bowling-like games have been traced to such diverse cultures as Polynesia and 4th century Germany, where it seemed to be part of a religious ceremony. By the Middle Ages, stones were rolled toward three to 17 wooden forms as the game spread throughout Europe. The lanes were first roofed over in 1450; that was the true start of modern bowling as an all-weather sport. Henry VIII declared "the game of bowls is an evil . . ." yet Martin Luther is credited with setting nine as the ideal number of pins.

The Dutch brought the game to North America in the 1600s. An area in lower Manhattan is still known as Bowling Green. Washington Irving wrote of bowling in *Rip Van Winkle*. Both Bowling Green in Kentucky and Ohio may have been named for the sport. The nine-pin game was outlawed in Connecticut in the 1840s and it is thought that a pin was added to beat the ban, beginning the now standard 10-pin game.

The American Bowling Congress, formed in 1895, standardized rules and equipment and held its first annual tournament in 1901. Women have long been active players; bowling may have the largest number of female participants of any competitive sport. Automatic pin setters, introduced in the 1950s, made the game faster and

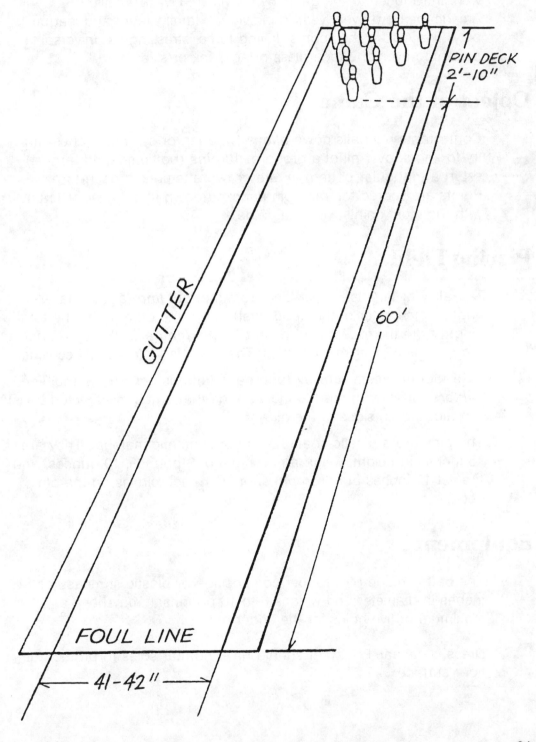

PIN DECK
2'-10"

GUTTER

60'

FOUL LINE

41-42"

stimulated the building of attractive, modern facilities. Many players were introduced to the game by television. Over 60 million Americans bowl every year in individual, family, team and league play. The ABC is the sport's driving force, stressing its universal appeal to everyone regardless of age, sex or size.

Object of the Game

Contestants roll balls down *alleys* (wooden or synthetic lanes) and try to knock over all of a group of 10 *pins* (bottle-shaped targets) set in a triangular pattern in one or two attempts in each turn. Points are scored for each pin knocked down; the player or team with the most points wins the game.

Playing Field

The alley or lane is 60 feet long from the *foul line* (at the players' end) to the center of the *head* (first) pin at the other end. The total length from the foul line to the end of the *pin deck* (the area under the pins) is 62 feet, 10³⁄₁₆ inches. The width is 41 to 42 inches wide.

A 15-foot minimum *runway* (approach lane) is behind the foul line. *Gutters* (grooved lanes 9½ inches wide that catch misdirected balls) run along both sides of the alley.

The pins are a plastic-coated wood or synthetic material. They are 15 inches in height, weigh a maximum of 3 pounds, 10 ounces, and are set 12 inches apart on *pin spots* (2¼-inch circles on the pin deck).

Equipment

The **ball** is made of a rubber composition or plastic. It measures 8½ inches in diameter and weighs 6 to 16 pounds. It may have a maximum of five holes for the finger grip.

Dress is casual. Footwear should have no-mar soles to protect the floor surface.

General Rules

A game may be played between individuals or in teams, up to five on a side.

A game consists of 10 *frames*, a segment in which each player bowls a maximum of two balls. (There are special rules for the 10th frame.)

The ball must be rolled in an underhand motion, and the player cannot touch or cross the foul line. If there is a *foul* (an illegally thrown ball), any pins knocked down by that ball do not count.

Scoring

Every pin knocked over in a frame scores one point; a bonus is awarded if all the pins are knocked over.

A *strike* is when all 10 pins are knocked over by the first ball rolled in a frame. It is noted on the scoresheet by an X in a small box at the upper right corner of the square for the frame bowled. The final score for the frame is not entered until the player rolls two more times. A strike earns 10 points plus the total count (number of pins knocked over) from the next two balls. If the strike is in the last frame, the player gets two extra balls to complete the bonus score. A *double* is two strikes in a row; a *triple* or *turkey* is three. Ten strikes plus two extra balls score 300 points, a *perfect* game.

A *spare* is when all 10 pins or any pins left standing are knocked down by the player's second ball in a frame. It is noted by a slash mark (/) in a small box in the frame's square on the scoresheet. The final score for the frame is entered after the player rolls another ball (the first ball of the next frame.) A spare earns 10 points plus the count from the next ball thrown. If the spare is in the last frame, a player gets one extra ball to complete the bonus score.

If a player leaves pins standing after two balls in a frame, it is a *miss*, a *break* or an *error*.

A *split* is when two or more pins are left standing — but not the head (No. 1) pin — after the first roll and spaced so far apart that they will be hard to knock down with the second ball.

Fouls count as a ball thrown. If the foul is on the first throw, any pins knocked down are reset for the second ball. If all the pins are downed by the second ball, it scores as a spare. If a foul is on the second throw of a frame, only those knocked down by the first ball count.

Pins knocked down that remain in the playing area, including the gutters, are called *dead wood* and must be removed.

Pins knocked down by other pins count.

Pins do not count if they are:

- Downed by a ball that first left the lane
- Downed by a ball rebounding back onto the pin deck
- Knocked out of the alley but return upright
- Knocked over because of mechanical or human interference

The ball counts as a roll in these instances.

Officials

Official or automatic scorers are used in tournaments. A foul judge can look for players stepping on or over the foul line.

Sample Scoresheet

A spare (/) counts 10, plus what is knocked down on the next ball.

A strike (X) counts 10, plus what is knocked down on the next two balls.

Results should be marked in the proper frame box immediately after each ball is bowled.

NAME HDCP.	1	2	3	4	5	6	7	8	9	10	TOTAL
1 ROZ	6 3 / 9	9 - / 18	7 / / 34	6 / / 54	X / 83	X / 102	9 - / 111	7 / / 127	6 2 / 135	7 / 9 / 154	154
2 IRVING	7 / / 20	X / 38	6 2 / 46	X / 74	X / 94	8 / / 110	6 3 / 119	X / 149	X / 178	X 9 - / 197	197
3 BARNEY	X / 20	9 / / 37	7 - / 44	8 / / 63	9 - / 72	8 - / 80	7 / / 100	X / 130	X / 150	6 / X / 170	170

Roz, frame-by-frame:

1. Knocked down six pins with the first ball and three with the second. The ball scores are entered in the small boxes and the total (nine) in the space below.

2. Scored nine on first ball, then a miss. Add to total (now 18).

3. Scored seven then three for a spare. No total entered yet.

4. Scored six, then four for another spare. Add 16 (10+6) to total for frame 3.

5. A strike. Add 20 for total In frame 4.

6. Another strike. No total entered yet.

7. Scored nine, then a miss. Add 29 (10+10+9) in fifth frame, add 19 (10+9) in sixth frame, and add nine for the seventh frame.

8. Scored seven then three for a spare. No total entered yet.

9. Scored six, then two. Add 18 (10+6) for eighth frame and eight for the ninth frame.

10. Scored seven, plus three for a spare, then nine on the bonus ball. Add 19 (10+9) for final total of 154.

Irving — two spares and six strikes, including one on a bonus roll.

Barney — four spares and four strikes, including the bonus.

History

Boxing is one of the oldest of sports; stone carvings of boxers date back 5000 years. It was a favorite sport of the Greeks where fighters, fists covered with leather straps, battled without rounds until one was defeated. In Roman times, the sport became so violent that it was finally banned.

Boxing, as an organized activity, was contested in 18th century England. Rules were established, such as a round continued until one contestant was knocked down; he then had 30 seconds to *square off* (stand one yard from his opponent or be declared the loser). Bare knuckle fighting was the style until 1872. The Marquess of Queensbury endorsed a set of rules that became the basis of modern boxing: three-minute rounds, 10 seconds for a downed boxer to get up or the fight was over, padded gloves. John L. Sullivan, the greatest 19th century American boxer, won the last bare-knuckle championship in 1889 but later lost a title match under the Queensbury rules.

The "golden age" of boxing in the U.S. began in the 1920s with the first million dollar ticket sale; over 100,000 fans saw the second Dempsey-Tunney fight. Since that time, and helped by television exposure, boxers have become major American sports celebrities. Champions have come from many ethnic backgrounds, such as Irish, German, Jewish, Afro-American and Hispanic.

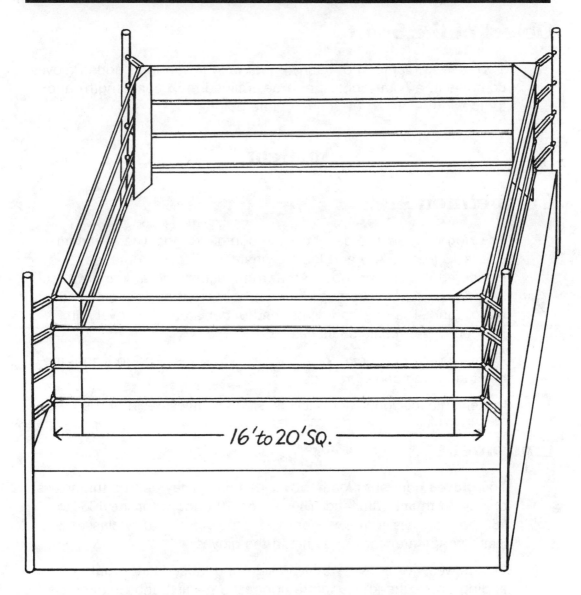

16' to 20' SQ.

Amateur boxing has contributed greatly to the game and was one of the oldest Olympic sports in this country. AAU competitions began in 1896 and the United States Amateur Boxing Federation assumed governing responsibilities in 1978. Among their many functions and activities, the USA Boxing Junior Olympic program was developed to teach competitors to play hard and fair, to win honors and, as occurs, to lose with grace. Its objectives are to involve youngsters, ages 8 to 15, to a wholesome athletic and recreational activity and provide an opportunity to advance in the sport according to their desire and ability.

Object of the Sport

Two *boxers* (fighters) of nearly equal weight wearing padded gloves compete in a *bout* (contest of a determined maximum length) and try to win the match by scoring more points.

Amateur

Competition Area

The *ring* is a roped area where the bout is fought. The minimum size is 16 feet square and the maximum is 20 feet square, as measured inside four ropes. An apron must extend at least two feet beyond the ropes. The ring shall not be more than four feet above the ground. The ring floor is padded under a canvas cover with padded corner posts 58 inches high.

A sound device (a gong, bell, buzzer or horn) is used to signal the beginning and end of rounds.

Implements include water buckets, stools, bottles, resin and sponges.

Equipment

The **gloves** consist of leather over padding. They can be thumbless or have a thumb attached. They weigh 10 ounces for the 106- to 156-pound classes and 12 ounces for the 165 to 201+ classes. Hand wraps are worn underneath the gloves.

Boxers wear a sleeveless athletic shirt and loose-fitting trunks ending above the knees with a contrasting waistband (the beltline should not extend above the waist); soft footwear without heels, a fitted mouthpiece, and a cup-protector. A competitive headguard must be worn. Metal or jewelry, glasses and grease are not permitted. Hair cannot interfere with the boxer's vision.

General Rules

An amateur boxer shall not compete against a professional boxer or any pro athlete. After a boxer becomes a professional in any sport he cannot participate as an amateur.

A tournament usually involves clubs, LBCs (local boxing committees), regions and so on. Winners advance to the next round. Boxers 16 or older must have a minimum of five bouts prior to any LBC tournaments that lead to regional or national championships; this does not apply to the Junior Olympic program.

Each boxer may have one coach and an assistant, but only one can enter the ring between rounds and neither can remain there during the competition.

Medical and safety precautions must be maintained.

Classifications

Boxers are classified by age, as follows:

JUNIOR OLYMPIC

Bantam: 8 to 9 years old; any starting weight, with five-pound increments

Junior: 10 to 11 years old; 15 weights, from 60 to 130 pounds, with five-pound increments

Intermediate: 12 to 13 years old; 18 weights, from 70 to 201 pounds

Senior: 14 to 15 years old; 17 weights, from 80 to 201+ pounds

OPEN: 16 to 32 years old

MASTERS: 33 and over

Boxers are matched by weight categories, as follows:

Light flyweight	106 pounds
Flyweight	112
Bantamweight	119
Featherweight	125
Lightweight	132
Light welterweight	139
Welterweight	147
Light middleweight	156
Middleweight	165
Light heavyweight	178
Heavyweight	201
Super heavyweight	201 and over

Boxers are classified by experience, as follows:

Sub-novice: has not competed in a USA Boxing match

Novice: has competed in 10 or fewer matches

Post-novice/open: has competed in more than 10 matches

The length and number of rounds varies according to the level of competition, as follows:

Division	# of rounds	Length
Masters	3	2 minutes
Open	3	3
Novice & Sub-novice	3	2
Open (feature bout)	5	2
Senior Junior Olympic	3	2
Intermediate J.O.	3	1½
Junior J.O.	3	1
Bantam J.O.	3	1

Officials

The referee is the only person in the ring with the boxers, controls the contest and gives instructions that must be obeyed. The referee's primary concern is the safety of the boxers. The referee checks gloves and dress. The referee uses three commands:

- "Stop" — halt boxing
- "Box" — restart action
- "Break" — boxers must separate and take one step back

The referee gives *cautions* (advises boxer about improper actions without stopping the contest) and *warnings* (stops the bout to tell a boxer that a rule has been broken and notifies the judges). Three cautions for the same type of foul require a warning; the third warning brings automatic disqualification. Fouls include:

- Hitting below the belt, to the back of the neck or to the kidney
- Holding, tripping, kicking or butting with foot or knee
- Blows with the head, shoulder, forearm, elbow or pushing the opponent's head back over the ropes
- Striking with an open glove or the inside of the glove
- Hitting an opponent who is down or on the way up
- A *pivot blow* (a hit made while turning)
- Hitting on the break and before stepping back
- Holding, pushing or shoving

The referee does not act as a judge.

Judges sit at ringside and rate the merits of the contestants. Points are awarded after the end of each round and entered on a scorecard. At the end of a bout, the judges total the points and declare a winner.

Five judges are required but three can be used, except in championship events.

The timekeeper regulates the number and length of the rounds and the time between rounds (one minute) and sounds a signal at the start and end of each round. If one boxer has been knocked down, the timekeeper gives a *count* (calls out numbers 1 to 10 with one second intervals) to the referee.

Procedure

Contestants must weigh in on the day of the bout.

Boxers meet at the ring center, shake hands, then return to their corners.

Rounds begin and end with the timekeeper's signal; fighting must stop at the end of the round.

A boxer is considered *down* if, as the result of a blow or series of blows, he touches the floor with any part of his body or is hanging on the ropes or is outside the ropes or on the ropes but semi-conscious.

In the case of a knockdown, the referee immediately begins to count the seconds (or gets the count from the timekeeper) and indicates each second with a hand movement. The count does not begin until the opponent has gone to a *neutral corner* (either of the two corners not originally used by the boxers) designated by the referee. The opponent cannot continue until the downed boxer has gotten up and the referee commands "box."

When a boxer is down, the bout shall not restart until the referee has reached the *mandatory* count of eight, even if the boxer is ready before then. When a boxer has three mandatory eight counts in the same round or four in a bout, the referee will stop the contest. If a boxer is down for the mandatory eight count, gets up and falls again without being hit, the referee continues counting from eight.

If the boxer cannot get on his feet and upright by the count of 10, the referee stops the contest. *RSCH* is when the referee stops the contest because of head blows; *RSCM* is for medical reasons. (The term *knockout* is not used in amateur boxing.)

When a boxer is down at the end of a round, the referee continues to count. If the count reaches 10 and the boxer is still down, the bout is over.

Should both boxers go down at the same time, counting continues as long as one is still down. If both remain down until 10, the bout is stopped and the winner determined by the points scored prior to the knockdowns.

Amateur boxing is scored on a point system, not by rounds.

A win on points is when one boxer is determined the winner by a majority of the judges based on points awarded in the bout.

During each round, the judges assess the scores of the boxers by counting the number of legal blows. To have scoring value, each blow must land, without being blocked, with the knuckle part of the closed glove on the front or side of the opponent's head or body above the waist. Non-scoring blows include those hit with the side, heel or inside part of the glove or with an open glove or any part other than the knuckle. Blows that land on the arms or connect without any weight from the body or shoulder are also non-scoring.

Twenty points are awarded for each round (no fractions). At the end of each round, the better boxer receives 20 points and the opponent proportionately fewer. If both boxers were equal in the round, each receives 20 points. Extra points are not awarded for a knockdown.

At the end of a contest, if a judge finds the boxers equal in points, a decision is made based on which boxer was more aggressive; next, by who had a better defense; then, who had more style. There are no *draws* (ties).

Decision wins are also by *retirement* (a boxer resigns during or after the rest between rounds), if the referee stops the bout when a boxer is *outclassed* (unfit to continue) or due to injury or other physical reason, if the mandatory count limit has been passed, or by a disqualification.

When the decision is known, the referee raises the hand of the winner.

Professional Boxing

The sport is regulated by athletic commissions in the 42 states that permit professional contests. The laws and rules differ in many ways from the amateur sport and also vary between the individual states.

Major differences include:

- Ring size: usually 18 feet square minimum to 22 feet maximum
- Glove weight: not less than eight ounces
- Headgear: not required

- Bout lengths: 12 rounds
- Scoring: a 10-point *must system*, in which three judges award a maximum of 10 points per boxer in a round based on clean hitting, aggressiveness, defense and ring command; a boxer whose performance is more convincing and decisive (including a knockdown) than the opponent's might win a round 10-8
- Ties are permitted

Other differences include:

- The number of rounds permitted by age; boxers under 19, for example, cannot box more than six rounds
- Additional classes of competition (such as cruiserweight and strawweight)
- Weight limits
- Technical terms (such as *technical knockout* or *TKO* when the referee stops the bout)
- Consequences of major and minor fouls on the scoring

History

Games resembling croquet have been played for 500 years. It came to the United States from England in the 1860s, was taken up by society and soon became popular across the country. Rules were published as early as 1865 in Newport. Lawn tennis was established about the same time, but croquet enthusiasts far outnumbered the tennis players. It was one of the first games played by both sexes.

Croquet was introduced into the Olympics in 1904. Between the two World Wars, the game became a favorite of literary, entertainment and other celebrities. Harpo Marx, Darryl Zanuck, Sam Goldwyn, George S. Kaufman, Alexander Wollcott and W. Averall Harriman are among those honored at the U.S. Croquet Hall of Fame.

Croquet is one of the few sports in which men and women compete on equal terms. As a lawn or backyard game, it is played by millions of Americans. The United States Croquet Association manages the competitive game through its membership and registered clubs. Croquet has been described as a "blend of chess on grass, golf, billiards and war." It is expected that the U.S. will soon become the world's most active croquet-playing nation.

CROQUET

Object of the Game

A player or team competes by hitting balls twice through a layout of *wickets* (hoops) to a center stake. The first side to finish or score the most points wins.

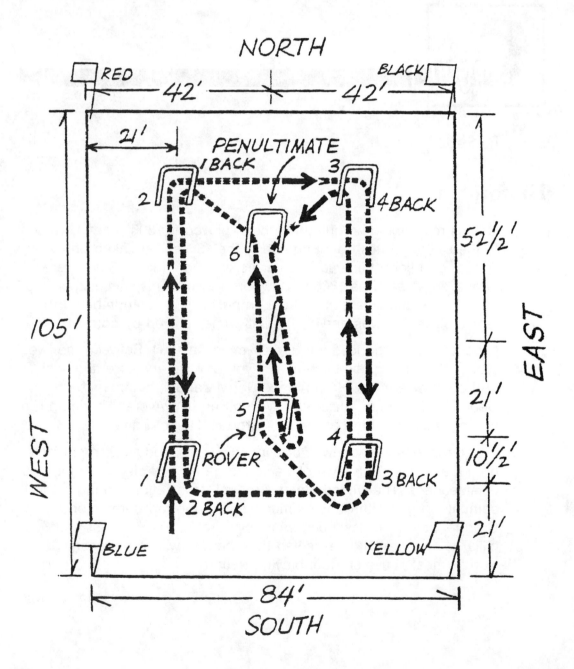

Standard American Six-Wicket

Playing Field

The court consists of a grass rectangle with boundaries marked with white string. It is 105 feet long at the east and west sides and 84 feet at the north and south ends. Smaller courts have a ratio of 5:4.

The *wickets* are round white metal hoops, 12 inches in height when placed in the ground. The *crown* (top) of the first wicket is blue; on the last wicket (the *rover*) it is red.

The *stake* is made of wood, and stands 18 inches in height at the center of the court. It is white with blue, red, black and yellow bands descending in that order to show the order of play.

The corner flags are blue (1), red (2), black (3) and yellow (4).

Equipment

The **mallet** is made of hardwood and is long-handled. It is approximately 30 inches long, with parallel *faces* (ends).

The **balls** are 3⅝ inches in diameter. They are colored blue, red, black or yellow.

The **clips** are the same colors as the balls. They are placed on the wickets to indicate ball direction.

The **deadness board** displays which balls each player cannot hit.

Dress is casual, although white clothing is traditional.

General Rules

The game can be played by two (singles) or four (doubles) people.

One side plays the blue and black balls; the other plays the red and yellow balls.

The order of play: blue, red, black, yellow.

In singles, a player can play either ball of his colors; in doubles, each player uses the same ball during the game.

The player whose turn it is to hit the ball is called the *striker* and gets one shot, unless the striker can hit another ball that player is *alive* on (able to hit other balls) or *score a wicket* by hitting a ball completely through a wicket in the proper order and direction. The striker then becomes alive.

If the striker is alive on a ball and hits it (a *roquet*), the striker gets two free shots.

A *croquet shot* is the first of two extra shots. Players may set their own ball against the other and hit it so that both balls move. After playing the croquet shot, the player takes a *continuation* (free) shot.

The striker that scores a wicket earns a continuation shot, which can be used to go to another hoop or to hit another ball.

After a ball has hit another ball it is *dead* on that ball (cannot hit it again) until the striker's ball has gone through the next wicket and becomes alive again.

If two balls are hit at the same time, the first one hit is the roqueted ball.

A ball that goes out-of-bounds is placed the length of a mallet's head (nine inches) in from where it crossed the boundary.

A ball must be hit, not pushed, with the face end of the mallet head.

A player picks up a clip after scoring one or more wickets and, after the turn ends, puts it on the next wicket to be scored.

A player may pass a turn.

No distracting behavior is permitted during shot play.

Procedure

Before starting, a coin toss permits one side to choose to play blue/black or red/yellow.

The players' turns — a hit or series of hits — alternate, but only one color ball can be played at a time.

Play begins with a single shot from three feet directly behind the first wicket.

Players who have not gone through the number 1 wicket cannot hit balls that have gone through it; balls already through number 1 cannot hit balls not yet through it.

Players attempt to score the first six wickets in a clockwise direction around the court. (See diagram.)

At the number 7 wicket (also called 1-back) players attempt to score the same six wickets in a counter-clockwise direction for a total of 12 points, and then *stake out* (hit the stake) for the thirteenth point.

As each ball scores number 7, the opposing side gets to clear one ball of deadness.

After a ball has scored number 12 (the rover wicket), it becomes a rover and can clear its deadness on all balls by going through any wicket in any direction. Once cleared, a rover cannot hit the last ball on which it was dead until it first hits a different ball. A rover ball cannot hit a ball twice in the same direction.

The winner is the first side to reach 26 points, or to score the most points in a timed game. A player or side wins after both balls have gone through the 12 wickets (six wickets passed, each twice) and hit the stake. One point is scored for stroking the ball through a wicket plus one point for hitting the stake. Because each ball can score 13 points, the winning (and highest possible) point total is 26 — unless the players have agreed upon a time limit, in which case the highest score wins after time expires.

Officials

A referee oversees the match and, when summoned by a player, judges hitting, ball movement, wicket points and strokes in question.

Fouls are committed if the striker:

- Plays out of turn
- Touches the mallet head
- Kicks the mallet into a ball
- Hits a ball two times on one shot
- Touches any ball with a body part

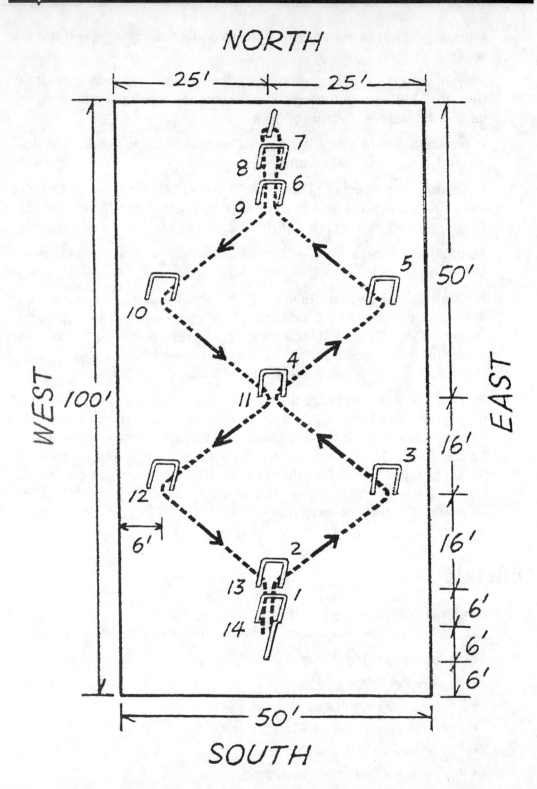

NORTH

SOUTH

WEST

EAST

25'   25'

50'

100'

16'

16'

6'

6'

6'

6'

6'

50'

Penalized players lose their turn and receive no points from their shot.

Players can act as referees; in a dispute, an opponent should defer to the opinion of the striker.

Standard American Nine-Wicket

Croquet also can be played in other ways. The object of the game, the basic rules of play and the equipment are similar to the six-wicket game, but there are differences.

The standard court size for American Nine-Wicket is 50 × 100 feet; smaller courts should be at least 30 × 60. (See illustration on previous page.)

Two stakes are used, one at each end of the court. The wickets are all white.

The first player to score 32 points wins. A player or side wins after both balls have gone through 14 wickets (seven wickets passed, each twice) and hit both stakes.

One point is scored for stroking the ball through a hoop and another point is scored for hitting the stake. Because each ball can score 16 points, the winning (and highest possible) point total is 32.

Note: After hitting (roqueting) a ball, the striker's ball may be placed one mallet head's length from the roqueted ball instead of in contact with it, or the player may hit it while holding it next to the other ball with one foot, moving the other ball away.

Golf Croquet

Six or more players compete on the six-wicket layout.

Each player starts one mallet's length from the center stake.

Each player has one shot per turn to try to score a wicket. The first ball played through the wicket wins that point. The stake is not used to get a point.

After a wicket has been scored, all players move on to the next; no player can play ahead.

In the game's short version, the first player to score seven points wins. The course is the first six wickets plus number 1 a second time for the seventh point.

In the long version, the first player to score 13 points wins. The course is the first 12 wickets plus number 3 for the 13th point.

History

The earliest recorded bicycle race was held inside a park in Paris less than 30 years after the invention of the first completely self-propelled bicycle by Kirkpatrick Macmillan, a Scotch blacksmith, in 1839. The winner of that first race — an Englishman, James Moore — also defeated more than 200 riders in the first road race, from Paris to Rouen, the next year on a 160-pound machine. Since that time, road races remain the most popular form of bicycle racing and the annual Tour de France, lasting 24 days and covering about 2,500 hundred miles in stages is world-famous. The first Olympic cycling events, road racing for men, were conducted in 1896; women's events began in 1980. The largest multi-day race in the U.S. is the Tour Du Pont, held annually through a changing series of cities.

Over the years, many technical advances and mechanical improvements have contributed to the growth and popularity of the sport. These include: the safety bicycle with both wheels the same size, coaster brakes, derailleur gears, steering devices and alloy frames with special narrow tires for racing.

The United States Cycling Federation is responsible for the development and administration of the sport within the United States. It establishes rules, conducts programs to assist riders in their skills and safety, coordinates competitions and oversees all bicycle racing matters.

Object of the Sport

Individuals or teams race bicycles on road courses or on tracks in events of various distances. The winner is the first to finish or has the best time or most points based on performance.

Equipment

The **bicycle** is pedal-driven and moved only by human force; no shield or device to reduce air resistance is permitted. The maximum size is 6 feet, 6 inches in length and 3 feet in width. The wheels may be different diameters.

Racing bicycles come in two varieties:

- A **road cycle** has one *free wheel* (multiple gears on the rear wheel) and a brake for each wheel.
- A **track cycle** has one *cog fixed wheel* (a single gear on the rear wheel) and no brakes.

Riders wear a molded protective helmet, a jersey that covers the shoulders and black pants to mid-thigh or a similar one-piece outfit; white socks are preferred. Goggles and mitts are optional.

Procedure

Cyclists begin a race in one of two ways: standing with one foot on the ground, with a holder (who cannot cross the starting line) or rolling in motion. A single signal (usually a gun or whistle) is sounded to start the race. A double signal is sounded to stop the race for a re-start, if necessary.

The race ends when the front tire of the first bicycle passes the finish line.

Following a crash or dismount, competitors may run and push their bicycles to the finish line.

Pacing is when a team member rides ahead, sets a speed and provides a windbreak for a racer.

Road Races

Road races are run over a route normally used for regular traffic, not on a special track. The course may be from one place to another, laps around a circuit, out to a point and back or a combination. The course should not cross itself so that riders do not have to intersect other competitors.

Interference with other road users is to be minimized. Riders should stay to the right of center but may pass another rider on either side. Control points, food and repair stops are to be located at appropriate and practical places.

Competitors may exchange refreshments and equipment or they may be received from someone on foot.

A marker is set one kilometer (.62 mile) from the finish; a white flag is placed 200 meters (219 yards) from the finish. The final lap may be signaled by a bell.

If two or more riders tie for first place, a sprint over the last 1000 meters (.62 mile) is held to determine the winner.

Road races come in several varieties, including the following:

Individual road race: The race begins in one of two ways: a *massed start* in which all riders begin at the same line, or a *handicap start* in which starting position is based on previous performance.

The race distance for men is approximately 75 miles; for women, approximately 50 miles. On a circuit course, each lap should be a minimum of .5 km (.31 mile). The winner is the first finisher.

Time trial: The riders start at intervals to cover a specific distance. There is no pacing in individual time trials. The individual or team with the fastest time wins.

Criterium: The race covers 25 to 60 miles on a closed circuit usually less than one mile long. The course is closed to traffic. The first finisher wins.

Stage race: Riders compete in a series of road events, including time trials and criteriums, with the distance divided into parts and covered over a number of days. The winner is the rider with the lowest cumulative time for all the stages. The *general classification* is the overall ranking of the competitors, including bonus time awards for high stage placing.

Cyclocross: Riders compete on a marked cross-country course (such as fields, woods and paths) with no more than 50 percent of it paved but approximately 75 percent of it suitable for cycling. Competitors may ride or carry their bicycles, depending on road conditions. The first rider to the finish wins.

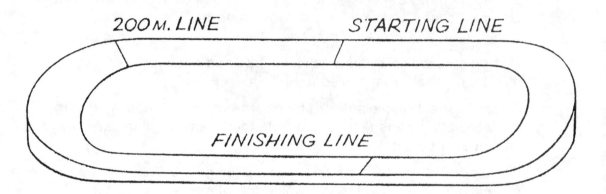

Track Races

In track races, riders compete on an oval circuit, one-tenth to one-third mile in length. The course is usually slightly *banked* (sloped in at an angle) on the straight sections and more at the corners. It can be indoors or outdoors on any suitable racing surface.

Track markings include distance labels, a red starting line and a black-on-white finish line, a line 200 meters from the finish, and sprint and pursuit lines. Movement is counter-clockwise.

Track races include the following:

Sprint: Two or more racers compete over short distances. A series of qualifying races are run to determine the participants in the final. Positions are chosen by lot. A match sprint is three laps (1000 meters).

The beginning stages of the race are devoted to maneuvering; only the last 200 meters are timed. If the lead bicycle is below the sprint line, passing must be done on the outside. If the leader is above the line, riders may pass on either side. The winner is the first to finish.

Handicap: Faster riders must cover a greater distance or start after the others, based on past performance. Holders may run with the cycle to push it off at the start. The first finisher wins.

Pursuit: In an individual pursuit race, two riders start directly opposite each other. Discs and flags are used to position competitors. The distance is four kilometers for men, three kilometers for women and junior men. The winner is the rider that overtakes the other or the rider that finishes the course first.

In a team pursuit race, four riders compete on each team. The time of the first three riders on each team determines winner.

Miss and out: The last rider over the finish line (judging by the back end of rear wheel) is eliminated on specific laps. The race is won by the last remaining rider or by a regular sprint from a group of survivors.

Time trials: Time trials on tracks are similar to those on road courses. In a kilometer time trial, riders race at full speed for 1000 meters.

Madison: Teams of two or three riders compete in a relay race, with only one rider racing at a time. The winner is the team that covers the most laps in the time allowed.

Points race: Riders earn points for sprints on specific laps. The winner is the rider with the highest score.

Officials

The races are officiated by a head referee, assistants, starters, timers and judges.

History

Darts originally were used to train archers during the Middle Ages. Warriors cut their arrows shorter and devised a competitive sport. The round ends (butts) of wine casks were used as targets. Darts was a favorite game of Henry VIII and his royal successors, but since the 19th century it has been a spirited activity in English pubs and inns. A sawed-off tree section was hung on the tavern wall. The webbed look of a modern dart board comes from the rings and splits in the wood that happened as the tree trunk targets dried out.

Darts came to America with the Pilgrims, who played the game on the Mayflower, and has been a recreational sport ever since. Darts had a great surge in popularity following World War II as many American servicemen began playing the game overseas and brought their interest home with them. The American Dart Association, the national "umbrella" organizing body for the sport, provides rules for play and equipment and organizes competitive activities through its affiliated local groups.

Darts has become a fast-growing American sport in the past five years for several reasons: the equipment is not expensive, the game requires only limited space, weather is not a factor, no uniforms are needed and age, sex, size or strength have no real effect on ability.

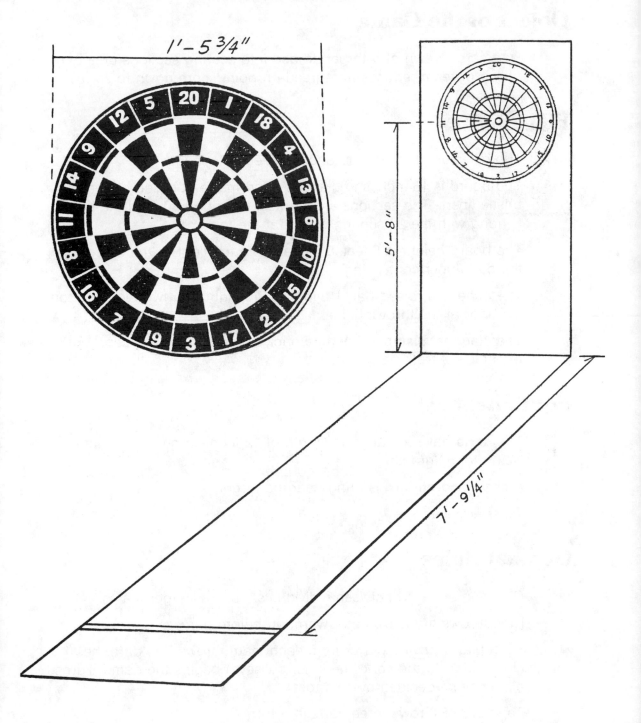

1' - 5 3/4"

5' - 8"

7' - 9 1/4"

Object of the Game

Darts are thrown at a target divided into scoring sections until one player or team reduces an agreed-on point score down to zero.

Playing Area

The minimum throwing distance is 7 feet, 9¼ inches.

The board is 18 inches in diameter, and made of coiled paper or bristle fibers. The sections are marked 1 through 20, and the board is hung with the 20 scoring wedge at the top.

The board height is 5 feet, 8 inches from the floor to the center of the *bull* (inner center ring).

The *oche* is a raised bar, 1½ inches in height and two feet long, on the floor at the throwing line.

The diagonal distance from the back of the oche to the center of the bull is 9 feet, 7½ inches.

Equipment

The **darts** have a maximum length of 12 inches and a maximum weight of 50 grams.

A chalk **scoreboard** is hung near the target.

Dress is casual.

General Rules

Games are played between individuals, pairs or larger teams.

Nine throws are allowed for warm-up before games.

Each player or one player from each team throws one dart; the closest dart to the *cork* (the inner bullseye) begins the game. Turns also may be decided by coin toss.

Each player throws three darts in a turn.

If a foot goes over the oche line, the throw counts but it does not score.

Darts must stay on the board for five seconds to score after each player throws the final dart. A dart does not score if it falls off or sticks in another dart. Rethrows are not permitted.

Darts score as follows:

- Doubles ring — two times the number hit
- Triples ring — three times the number hit
- Bullseye (outer bull) — 25 points
- Double bullseye (inner bull) — 50 points

Procedure

301

Each side begins with 301 points.

Each player must hit a double before any score counts. This rule may be waived so that all darts count from the beginning.

Each player's score is kept by subtracting the count of each dart from 301.

To win, players must throw a double or bullseye that reduces the score exactly to zero. For example, if 50 is needed to finish, a player can throw a single 18 and a double 16 ($18 + 16 \times 2 = 50$) or a double bull (50).

If more than the exact score needed is thrown, the whole turn of three darts does not count and the score remains as it was before the throws. For example, if 20 is required to win and 21 is scored, the score stays at 20. If 19 is scored, the turn does not count because a player cannot win without a double.

Each game is one *leg*. Two out of three legs wins the match.

501, 601, 1001

These games are played like 301, with the opening score based on team size.

A double is not required to begin, but the game must finish on a double.

Cricket

Cricket is played with numbers 15 through 20 plus the inner and outer bulls.

To start scoring, a player must score three of a number (three singles, a single and a double or a triple). The number is then *open* and all darts from the opening side count until the other side *closes* the number by also scoring three of the number.

A player can either try to increase a score or prevent the opponent from scoring.

The side that closes all the numbers first and has the most points wins.

History

Competitive diving evolved from purely acrobatic displays by European gymnasts in the 19th century into a challenging modern sport. As a program that emphasized body form precision, men's diving entered the Olympics in 1904 and the women's began in 1912. The rules are complex as the execution of each dive is measured to a precise formula based on its difficulty. The popularity of the sport grew as both participants and spectators learned how a combination of discipline, creativity, courage and individual skills could bring artistry into a highly competitive performance situation. United States Diving is the governing body that promotes and administers the sport.

Object of the Sport

Competitors dive into water from springboards or platforms by performing a prescribed number of dives in various body positions. The diver scoring the most points wins.

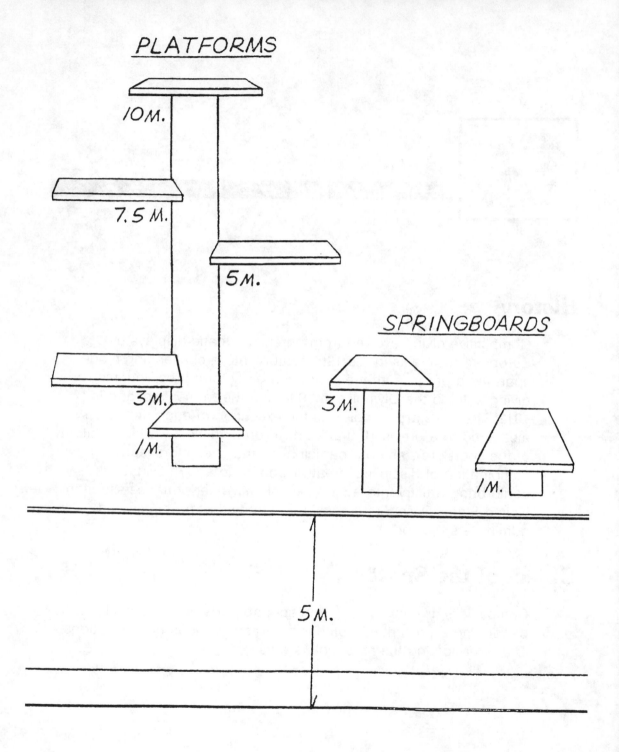

PLATFORMS

10M.

7.5 M.

5M.

3M.

1M.

SPRINGBOARDS

3M.

1M.

5M.

Pool

The *springboard* is flexible, with a non-skid surface. It has a *fulcrum* (movable support) for board adjustments. It is set at three meters (9 feet, 10 inches) or one meter (3 feet, 3 inches) from the water surface. It is 4.88 meters (16 feet) long.

The *platform* is rigid with a non-skid surface. The high platform is set at 10 meters (33 feet); the intermediate platforms are set at 7.5 meters (24 feet, 3 inches) and five meters (16 feet, 5 inches); the low platforms are set at three meters and one meter above the water. The platform is six meters (20 feet) long.

The *depth of water* varies for different heights.

General Rules

Men wear swim trunks; women wear one-piece swim suits. Caps are allowed.

The outdoor season lasts from June 1 to Sept. 30. The indoor season runs through the remaining months.

The classifications are as follows:

- Junior: under 19 years
- Senior: any age
- Master: over 21

The dives are grouped as follows:

- Forward: diver starts facing the water and enters the water forward
- Backward: diver starts facing the board and enters backward
- Reverse: diver starts facing the water, spins toward the board and enters backward
- Inward: diver starts facing the board, rotates and enters forward
- Twist: diver spins around a long axis during the dive
- Armstand: diver starts from a handstand position (platform only)

Competitors must list the dives they plan to execute prior to the event and only perform those listed.

Body positions are as follows:

- Straight: body not bent, legs straight, feet together with toes pointed
- Pike: body bent at hips, legs straight, feet together with toes pointed
- Tuck: body bent at knees and hips, hands pull knees up to chest; knees and feet together, toes pointed
- Free: combination of straight, pike or tuck during twisting dive

Scoring

Only the performance and technique of the dive between the starting position and entry into the water is to be judged, not any action before the start or under the surface.

Points are awarded on a scale of 0 through 10 by half points, as follows:

Very good — 8½ to 10

Good — 6½ to 8

Satisfactory — 5 to 6

Deficient — 2½ to 4½

Unsatisfactory — ½ to 2

Completely failed — 0

The highest and lowest awards are canceled and the remaining points added together when there are five judges.

The *degree of difficulty* is a figure that indicates the difficulty in performing a dive. There are 361 possible dives and each has an assigned difficulty. The lowest difficulty (1.2) is for the one-meter springboard and five-meter platform forward dive in the tuck position. The highest difficulty (3.5) is for a 10-meter platform inward 3½ somersault in the pike position or for a three-meter forward 4½ or reverse 3½ in the tuck position.

The sum of the awards is multiplied by the degree of difficulty value to give a total score for the dive.

The winner is the diver with the highest sum for all of the dives on the diver's list.

Senior Events

Each event has two parts: *voluntary* dives that have a total degree of difficulty maximum and *optional* dives that have no degree of difficulty limits. The same dive may not be performed in both sections.

Events include the following:

Men's platform, 10 meters: ten different dives, four each from different groups with a total degree of difficulty no greater than 7.6 and six without difficulty degree limits from different groups

Women's platform, 10 meters: eight different dives, four each from different groups with a total degree of difficulty no greater than 7.6 and four without degree limits from different groups

Men's springboard, three meters: eleven different dives, five from different groups with total degree limits of no more than 9.5 and six without limits (one dive from each group plus another from any group)

Women's springboard, three meters: ten different dives, five each from different groups with total degree limits not to exceed 9.5 and five without degree of difficulty limits (one from each group)

Juniors and masters have different combinations depending on age.

Procedure

The diving order is selected by lot for preliminary rounds. In the finals, competitors dive in reverse order of their earlier finish; the highest score goes last.

The name of the diver and a description of the dive is announced.

The diver has three minutes to perform or is out of the competition.

A junior diver may choose to take no score on any dive, but remains in the contest.

Events may be competed simultaneously.

Starting positions are as follows:

Standing dive: The diver stands at the end of the springboard or platform with the body straight, head raised, arms at the side or up or outstretched. The arms may move when the diver leaves the start. Bouncing is not permitted.

Running dive: The dive begins with the first forward step. The *approach* (first movements) must be smooth with at least three steps taken before the *hurdle* (the jump to the end of the springboard). The last step before the hurdle is with one foot only; then, both feet touch the end of the board just before *flight* (the time when the diver is in the air).

Armstand dive: The diver must be balanced and straight in a handstand before *takeoff* (leaving the platform).

The entry into the water is to be made vertically with the body straight and the toes pointed. If a head-first entry is required, the arms should be above the head; if the dive is feet-first, the arms should be straight at the sides. The dive is finished when the entire body is underwater.

Penalties

Judges can deduct points from the score of each diver for the following violations:

- Taking less than three steps before the hurdle (two points)
- Bouncing or rocking before the take-off (up to two points)
- Opening the knees in a tuck (one to two points)
- Also: diving out of a direct line, losing balance, having arms in an incorrect position upon entry, stopping and restarting, assuming an incorrect position during the dive

- A *balk* (error) is called if the diver starts an approach and then stops, or when a take-off is made from the hurdle and not from the end of the board.

- A referee can call a *failed dive* (no score) if the diver balks twice, gets help, takes off on one foot, does not dive or performs the wrong dive, or if the feet enter the water before the hands in a head-first dive.

Officials

The referee manages the competition and oversees the judges. Five to seven judges score the dives and signal their marks at the same time to a secretary to record and compute.

History

Field hockey dates back to ancient times; pictures of players hitting a ball with a curved stick can be seen in classic Greek art. The modern form of the sport is related to the British games of *hurly* and *bandy*. Played at Princeton in the late 1700s and at what became Duke in the early 19th century, the game was inactive until an English woman, Constance M. K. Applebee, re-introduced the sport while at Harvard summer school in 1901. She taught the game at many women's colleges, such as Smith, Vassar, Bryn Mawr and Mt. Holyoke. It was immediately popular as a competitive sport for girls and active women seeking a team activity. Soon after, men became interested in the sport and associations were formed to oversee the game for both sexes. Today, field hockey is widely played at high schools, colleges and universities, and by many clubs.

Object of the Game

Two teams compete to put a ball into their opponents' goal. The highest score wins.

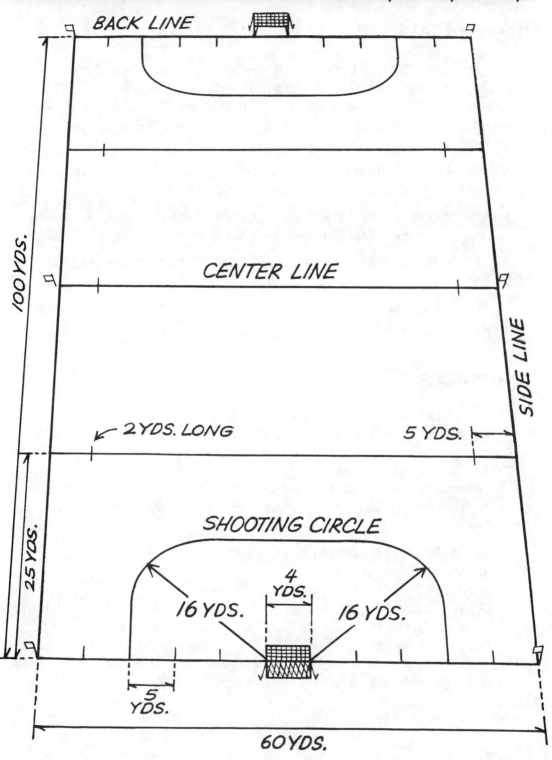

BACK LINE

CENTER LINE

SIDE LINE

100 YDS.

2 YDS. LONG

5 YDS.

SHOOTING CIRCLE

25 YDS.

16 YDS.

4 YDS.

16 YDS.

5 YDS.

60 YDS.

Playing Field

The field is 60 × 100 yards. A center line and two 25-yard lines divide the field, each with short (two-yard) lines marked five yards inside the field of play. There are 12-inch marks on each sideline, 16 yards from the back lines and five and 10 yards from the goal posts on the back lines.

The *shooting circles* are quarter circles with a 16-yard radius, from each goal post to a four-yard line parallel to the goal line.

The *goal* is a netted structure four yards wide between the posts and seven feet in height from the crossbar to the goal line.

The *goal line* is four yards long in front of the goal on the back line.

The *penalty spot* is seven yards from the center of the goal line.

Flags are positioned at each corner and the outside center line.

Equipment

The **stick** has a flat wood face on the left-hand side with a curved head. The diameter of the shaft is a maximum of two inches.

The **ball** used on grass surfaces is made of hard leather or composition and may be solid or hollow; white is the preferred color. It should be close to nine inches in circumference and weigh 5½ to 5¾ ounces.

The ball used on artificial turf is seamless and made of injection-molded plastic.

Dress is according to uniform. The players on each team wear the same design shirt, socks and shorts or skirt. Footwear consists of boots or artificial turf shoes. The goalkeepers wear different color shirts than their teammates and are allowed a face mask, head gear, gloves, pads and other protection.

General Rules

Eleven players from an overall squad of 16 are allowed on the field at any one time.

Field players can use only the flat side of the stick to advance the ball or score. The goalkeeper, while within the shooting circle, may use a body part to stop the ball and can kick it with the feet or pads. The keeper must always have a stick in hand when using other body parts.

Substitutions are unlimited.

Game length

Games consist of two periods, each 35 minutes long. A break of five minutes (a maximum of 10) is taken between periods.

The umpire can add time to replace time lost by injury or other reason.

Scoring

A goal (one point) is scored after a ball played from on or inside the shooting circle by a member of the attacking team fully crosses the goal line between the goal posts and under the crossbar.

A goal counts if the ball is touched by a defender before it crosses the goal line, but does not count if it is hit by an attacker from outside the circle.

The team that scores the most goals is the winner.

Procedure

The team winning the coin toss chooses between possession of the ball and end of the field.

All players must be in their own half of the field at the start of the game, at least five yards from the ball, except for the player making the *pass back* (a ball hit back from the center line to another member of the attacking team).

After a goal is scored, the game is restarted with a pass back by the team that did not score.

After halftime, teams change ends and the pass back is made by the team that did not have possession at the start of the game.

The game is restarted when the ball goes out of the field of play.

Out of bounds

If the ball crosses the side line, the opponent gets a *push-in* or *hit-in* and sends the ball back on the field from the place where it went out by pushing it along the ground. A player cannot play the ball again until others have touched it and they must be at least five yards away.

If the ball crosses a goal line or back line from an attacker's hit and no goal is scored, defenders are given a *free hit* in which the player strikes the ball from a point on the field opposite where the ball went out of play and 16 yards in from the goal line, even with the top end of the shooting circle.

Note: At a push-in or a free hit, all opposing players must be five yards away and the pusher or hitter cannot play the ball again until another player touches it.

If defenders accidentally hit or deflect the ball over their own goal line from less than 25 yards away, attackers get a *corner hit* from a point on the goal line five yards from the corner of the field.

Restarts

The *bully* is a way to restart the game after an interruption in play, such as from injury or off-setting fouls.

Two opponents face each other with the ball between them and with their own goal line to their right. Both players simultaneously tap the ground behind the ball with their sticks and then, using the face, tap each other's stick over the ball. After tapping sticks three times, the ball is in play and can be hit by either player.

The other players must be at least five yards away and may stand anywhere on the field permitted by the offside rule.

A bully is played where the stoppage happened. If inside the shooting circle, it must be set 16 yards from the goal line and even with the edge of the circle.

Offside

A player is in an offside position when:

- In the opponents' defensive 25 yard area, and
- Between the ball and the goal line, and
- Nearer the goal than two defenders or even with the second defender

An offside occurs at the time the ball is passed, not when the player receives the ball.

Fouls

Fouls include the following violations:

- Swinging or using the stick in a manner dangerous to another player
- Playing with the round side of the stick
- Kicking or moving the ball with any part of the body (does not apply to the goalkeeper)
- Tripping or pushing
- An obstruction, such as putting the body or stick between the ball and opponent
- Hitting the ball in a dangerous manner

Penalties

Fouls committed outside the shooting circles give the opposing team a *free hit* (a stroke at the ball) from where the offense occurred.

Fouls committed inside the circle by the attacking team give the defenders a free hit from any point in the circle or anywhere within 16 yards of the goal line.

Fouls committed inside the circle by the defending team give the attacking team a *penalty corner* or a *penalty stroke*, depending on the intent of the foul.

A penalty corner is a hit from a point on the goal line at least 10 yards from a goal post. It also is called if defenders purposely hit the ball over their goal line or foul intentionally within 25 yards of the goal line but outside the circle.

On a penalty corner:

> Attackers must stay outside the circle.
>
> Five defenders can be behind the goal line until the ball is hit.
>
> Other defenders stay behind the center line.
>
> A direct shot at the goal is not allowed until the ball is first stopped *dead* by the attacker before the shot can be taken.
>
> As soon as the ball is touched by a defender, the ball is *live* and a shot may be taken without a stop.

A penalty stroke is a push or *flick* shot from a spot seven yards in front of the goal. It also is called if defenders intentionally foul in the circle or unintentionally stop a probable goal. The shot is a one-on-one confrontation between the attacker and the goalkeeper.

On a penalty stroke:

> The attacker can take only one step before taking a shot and must wait until the official's whistle.
>
> The goalkeeper stands on the goal line and cannot move until the ball is played.
>
> All other players stay behind the 25-yard mark.
>
> If no goal is scored, the defenders take a free hit from a point 16 yards in front of the goal center.

Officials

Games are officiated by two umpires, each of whom control one half of the field without changing ends, and a timekeeper.

History

Skating on ice can be traced back to ancient times in Scandinavia. It was a recreational pastime since the Middle Ages in Northern Europe, but the first writing on figure skating appeared in *A Treatise of Skating* in 1772. In the mid-19th century, skating and dancing were popular American pastimes. Jackson Haines introduced free and expressive movements into a skating manner that had been very fixed and severe. Not well accepted at home, Haines went to Europe where his imaginative jumps and dance steps became known as the International Style. By the turn of the century, various groups in Canada and the U.S. established tests and competitions and the sport matured.

Men's and women's events were part of the 1908 Olympics and re-introduced at the first Winter Olympics in 1924. The United States Figure Skating Association was formed in 1921 to govern the sport and promote its growth on a national basis. Figure skating captured world attention during the 1930s with the skills of Sonja Henie in competition and in the movies. Local skating clubs, new facilities, available instruction and the impact of skating stars seen in ice shows and on television have combined to make figure skating popular with participants as a sport and to spectators as an entertainment.

FIGURE SKATING

Object of the Sport

Individuals and pairs compete on ice skates in various competitions and are judged on their performance.

Competition Area

A skating rink consists of a smooth ice surface, 85 × 185 feet minimum, with rounded corners on a low wall around the area, and a system to play recorded music.

Equipment

Skates have high tops to support the ankles. The blades are approximately ⅛-inch thick and rounded with inner and outer edges and *toe picks* or a *rake* (teeth) at the front.

The **costume** should be modest and appropriate, with no excessive ornamentation. Its design may be related to the performance music.

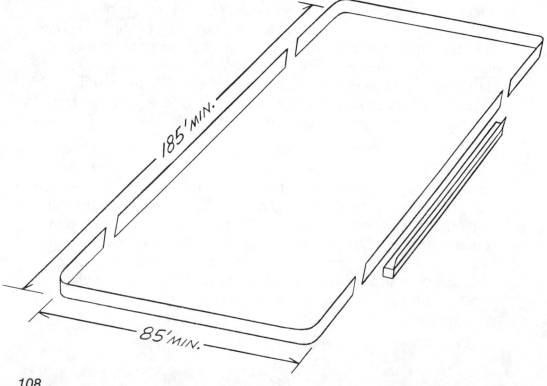

185' MIN.

85' MIN.

General Rules

Competitions include single skating, pair skating, ice dancing and precision.

Levels of competition include senior, junior, intermediate, novice and younger, based primarily on skill.

Classifications include club, regional, sectional and national.

Competitors provide their own music.

Judges award **marks** or grades. Each judge has a set of cards with black numbers 1 through 6 for whole numbers and another set with red numbers 1 through 10 for fractions. After a skater performs, each judge displays one card from each set as a score. The marking is now done electronically at major events.

The scoring scale is as follows:

    0 — did not skate
    1 — bad, very poor
    2 — poor
    3 — average
    4 — good
    5 — excellent
    6 — perfect

Decimal points are used for exact placements. High and low marks are not dropped and points are not added together.

Each judge's mark is converted into places — first, second and so on. The skater or pair who gets the highest mark from a judge, earns a first place from that judge. The skater with the most first places from the panel of judges wins the event.

If total marks are equal between skaters in the free skating competition, the skater with the highest mark in the artistic impression section is awarded first place.

After each event, the placements earned by the skaters are multiplied by a **factor** (a percentage value for the event) to get a **factored placement** number. The factored placements for each event are then added together. The skater with lowest total factored placement wins the contest.

FIGURE SKATING

Singles skating

Singles events are open to male and female skaters. Form, style, technique and concentration are the most important qualities.

In the original (short) program:

Eight *elements* (specific moves) are required, including jumps, spins, combinations and various connecting step sequences. No additional moves are permitted. Senior skaters perform the same elements in any order in 2 minutes, 40 seconds or less; other levels differ.

One mark is given for the accuracy of the required elements. A second mark is awarded for the presentation (harmony, speed, use of the ice, movement and relationship to the music, and so on).

The program accounts for 33.3% of the total score, with a 0.5 factor value.

In the free skating (long) program:

Competitors choose and arrange their own program of jumps, spins, spirals and steps, with a minimum of skating on two feet. The number of elements may vary but the program must be well-balanced. Men skate for 4 minutes, 30 seconds; senior ladies and junior men skate for four minutes; junior ladies skate for 3 minutes, 30 seconds.

Marks are given for *technical merit* (based on difficulty of the program and variety) and for *artistic impression* (choreography, originality, music interpretation, use of the rink, footwork skill, and so on).

The program accounts for 66.6% of the total score, with a 1.0 factor value.

Pair skating

A male and female skate as a couple in pair skating. They may separate, but their movements should be related and in harmony. Lifting is done only by the hands and with the lifting arm(s) fully extended.

In the original (short) program:

> Eight elements with connecting steps are required, including an overhead lift, a *twist lift* (the female is thrown in the air and rotates before being caught), a solo jump, a spin combination and so on, in any order. The program lasts no more than 2 minutes, 40 seconds for seniors and juniors.
>
> Marking is the same as the single skating original program. The program accounts for 33.3% of the total score, with a 0.5 factor value.

In the free style program:

> Partners create a well-balanced program using the full ice surface. Movements may include pair spins, three to five lifts, partner-assisted jumps, spirals and — while apart — *mirror skating* (facing each other) and *shadow skating* (parallel.) Seniors skate for 4 minutes, 30 seconds; juniors skate for four minutes.
>
> Marking is the same as for single skating free style, but with special attention to balance between the physical qualities of the partners. This program accounts for 66.6% of the total score, and has a 1.0 factor value.

Ice dancing

In ice dancing, a male and female dance as a couple, separating only briefly. It includes no lifts above waist height, and no dramatic poses.

In the compulsory dance:

> Each couple performs two selected patterns in time to specified music. Dances include waltz, polka, blues, tango, rhumba and so on. No time limit is set, but the skaters must skate a required number of times around the ice.
>
> Marking is based on how well the skaters perform in time to the music, the accuracy of their patterns and their body movements, positions, style, use of the ice, expression of the mood of the dance and so on.
>
> Each dance accounts for 10% of the total score, and has a 0.2 factor value.

In the original dance:

> Couples create a dance of their own to a prescribed rhythm. Their movement must be appropriate to ballroom dancing; clever footwork is required with at least one skate of each partner always on the ice. No time limit is set.

> One mark is given for *composition* (difficulty, variety, skating skill, use of ice) and one mark for *presentation* (movement to the rhythm and tempo of the music, choreography, expression and style).

> The program accounts for 30% of the total score, with a 0.6 factor value.

In free dancing:

> Couples create their own dance to express the essence of the music they selected; any type of music is allowed. The program should display the dancer's personal ideas in terms of concept and arrangement and include movements that feature the athletics of dancing as well as skating technique. No combinations may be repeated. The time limit for seniors is four minutes; for juniors, three minutes.

> One mark is awarded for technical merit, and one for composition.

> The program accounts for 50% of the total score, with a 1.0 factor value.

Precision

Precision skating consists of a team of eight or more skaters, male and female, performing various formations in unison. There are seven age divisions, from under nine years to adult. Vocal music is allowed except for junior and seniors.

In the technical program:

> Five maneuvers are required, including a revolving circle, a line across the ice, a block of skaters moving over the full rink, a spinning wheel and an intersecting move. The time limit for seniors and juniors is 2 minutes, 40 seconds.

One mark is given for accuracy in the required elements and one for the overall presentation.

In free skating:

An original routine is performed with emphasis on originality, synchronization of the group, match of the program to the music, use of the ink, speed and unity. The time limit is 2 minutes, 30 seconds to 4 minutes, 30 seconds, depending on the division.

One mark is awarded for composition and one for presentation.

Officials

Officials include a maximum of nine judges, a referee, an assistant, scorers and timekeepers.

History

Games based on kicking a ball were played in ancient civilizations and throughout all of recorded sport. By the 19th century in England, "futballe" had developed into soccer. At the Rugby School in 1823, a player named William Ellis picked up the ball during a soccer match and ran with it across the goal line. This was the beginning of rugby, a contact sport that included ballhandling and tackling. Soccer continued as the kicking-only game; rugby became independently popular, and evolved into American football.

In 1869, Rutgers beat Princeton 6-4 in a soccer-style game with 25 players on each side. A team from McGill University came to play Harvard in 1874 in a game that combined soccer and rugby; the ball could be kicked or carried or thrown. The players and the spectators liked the new elements of the game and, known as football, it quickly spread to other Eastern colleges. A major concept was introduced in 1880 — the *scrimmage* (one team had possession of the ball at the start of every offensive play).

In 1882, Walter Camp of Yale, the "father of modern football," created many new rules that shaped the game. These included *downs* (a team had three chances to gain five yards or it had to give its opponent the ball at the last place the ball carrier was brought down), the role of the quarterback and setting the number of players on each side at 11. By 1912, college rules committees had agreed on a scoring system, legalized the forward pass, changed the ball from round to elongated so that it was easier to hold and throw, allowed four downs to make 10 yards to earn a new first down and added regulations to reduce violence. By the 1920s, the game was firmly established as the principal sport of the fall season; college players and their coaches became well-known celebrities throughout the country.

Professional football was first played in 1895, and the first league was formed with 11 teams in 1920 with the great athlete, Jim Thorpe, as its president. Two years later, it became the National Football League. By 1922 there was play in two divisions with an annual championship. The American Football League began play in 1959. The two leagues merged in 1966 and the first Super Bowl was held the following January. Television has brought the pro game, with its 28 teams and its star players, to millions of new fans and is responsible for a better understanding of the rules.

The amateur game is played at all levels. The main governing bodies for the sport are the NCAA and the National Federation of State High School Associations. Many organizations at both the national and local level are dedicated to introducing young players to organized competition with supervision and with an emphasis on safety by establishing teams based on both the age and weight of the players.

Object of the Game

Two teams with 11 players on the field try to score points by running or passing a ball over their opponents' goal line or by kicking it through a goal post. The team with the most points wins.

Playing Field

The playing field is 53⅓ yards wide and 120 yards long.

The *end lines* are boundaries at each end of the field.

The *side lines* are boundaries on each side of the field.

The *goal lines* are 100 yards apart, 10 yards from the end lines.

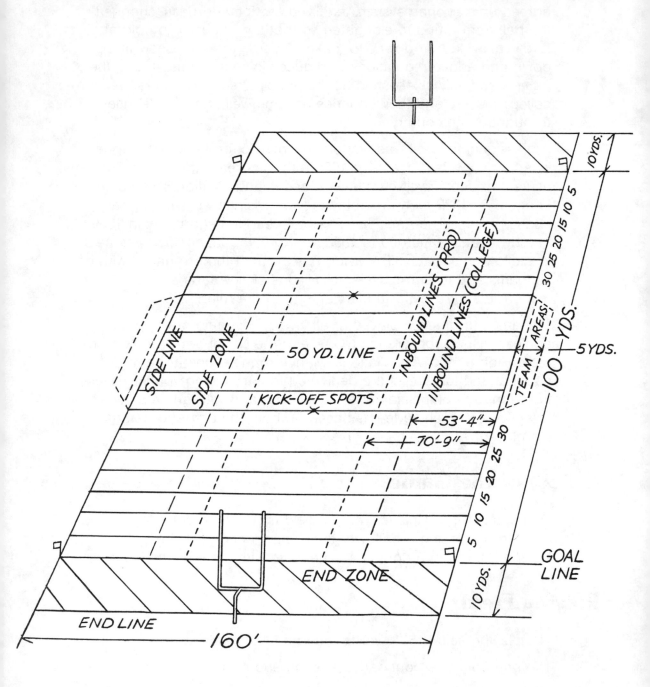

SIDE LINE

SIDE ZONE

50 YD. LINE

KICK-OFF SPOTS

INBOUND LINES (PRO)

INBOUND LINES (COLLEGE)

TEAM AREAS

100 — YDS.

10 YDS.

30 25 20 15 10 5

5 YDS.

53'-4"

70'-9"

5 10 15 20 25 30

GOAL LINE

10 YDS.

END ZONE

END LINE

160'

The *end zones* are 10 yards deep, bounded by end, side and goal lines.

Note: The end and side lines are out of bounds; the goal lines are inside the end zones.

The field is marked as follows:

With a white border, which is out-of-bounds

Every five yards across the width, between the side lines

Every one yard along the side lines

With numbers, every 10 yards by the side lines

With *hash marks*, two rows of broken inbound lines parallel to the side lines and marking the yards between the goal lines; in the NCAA, each row is 53 feet, four inches from a side line, in the NFL each is 70 feet, nine inches from a side line

With *side zones*, between the inbound lines and side lines

With a *point-after-touchdown line* (two yards from the goal line in the NFL and three yards in the NCAA)

The *goal posts* are gold or white metal structures on each end line. A horizontal crossbar is 10 feet above the ground. The vertical uprights are 18 feet, 6 inches apart with a minimum height of 30 feet. Padded posts may be *offset* (behind) the end line with the crossbar out over the plane of the line.

Pylons or *flags* on flexible poles are in each of the corners of the end zones.

A scoreboard, game clock and clocks that monitor the ready playing time are used.

Equipment

The **ball** is an inflated oval, made of natural tan pebble grain leather or composition. It is 11 to 11½ inches long and weighs 14 to 15 ounces.

The **yardage chain** is 10 yards long between two five-foot high sticks.

The **down marker** is a four-foot pole with four flip-over signs numbered 1, 2, 3 and 4. It marks the leading point of the ball at the start of every play and the number of the down.

Uniforms

Players on each team wear the same design jersey, pants, stockings and helmets with facemask and chin strap. Protective gear includes shoulder, chest, rib, hip, knee, thigh, shin, elbow, wrist and forearm pads. Approved footwear varies (barefoot kicking is permitted).

No colors are allowed similar to a football; slippery materials are not permitted.

Jerseys are numbered as follows:

NFL (required)

Quarterbacks, kickers: 1—19

Running and defensive backs: 20—49

Centers, linebackers: 50—59

Defensive and interior offensive linemen: 60—79

Wide receivers, tight ends: 80—89

Defensive linemen, linebackers: 90—99

NCAA (recommended)

Backs: 1—49

Centers: 50—59

Guards: 60—69

Tackles: 70—79

Ends: 80—99

A player can play any position, but in the NFL an official must be notified.

General Rules

Each team has 11 players on the playing field and all substitutes in a team area along the side lines between the 25-yard lines.

The team with *possession* (legal control of the ball) is the *offensive team*. Normally, five players are the interior linemen (a center, two guards, two tackles), two are ends (split or tight), one is a quarterback and three are backs (running backs or wide receivers).

The *defensive team* is usually made up of three or four *down* linemen (ends, tackles, guards), three or four *linebackers* (left, middle, right or inside and outside combinations) and the defensive backs, the *secondary* (cornerbacks, free and strong safeties).

Special team players include a *punter* (who drops the ball and kicks it before it touches the ground) and a *placekicker* (who kicks the ball off the ground for a kickoff, field goal or *extra point* after a touchdown) and a specialist in returning kickoffs or punts.

Only team captains are allowed to talk to the officials.

The team with possession of the ball must have at least seven players on or within a foot of the *line of scrimmage* (actually, two imaginary lines — offensive and defensive — running from the side lines through each end of the ball) and four players at least one yard behind the line.

The *neutral zone* is the space the length of the football between the two scrimmage lines. Only the center can have any body part in the neutral zone but cannot go beyond it.

Defensive players can line up anywhere behind their scrimmage line.

Any player can run with the ball; only the two ends and the backs are *eligible* receivers, permitted to catch a *pass* (a ball thrown by one player to another).

Substitutions are unlimited. Players can only enter the game when the ball is dead; players leaving the game must come off the field on their own team's side between the end lines before the next play begins.

Game length

Games in the NCAA and NFL last 60 minutes — four 15-minute quarters. A one-minute rest divides the periods of each half. The halftime intermission is 20 minutes in the NCAA and 13 minutes in the NFL.

High school teams play 12-minute quarters.

Ninth grade teams and below play eight-minute quarters.

Overtime (played only in NFL) is **sudden death**. A tied game continues into a 15-minute overtime period. The team scoring first wins. Playoff games cannot end in a tie, so 15-minute periods continue until there is a winner.

Each team is allowed three 90-second timeouts per half without penalty. The referee signals for play to start after 65 seconds, except in the last two minutes of a half (NFL only).

Automatic timeouts occur:

- After any score or field goal attempt
- During an extra-point attempt after a touchdown
- When the ball or ball carrier goes out-of-bounds
- At the end of the down after a foul
- On a change of possession
- When a receiver makes a **fair catch** (cannot advance the ball)
- At the **two-minute warning** , a signal that only two minutes remain to play in the half (NFL)
- At the end of a period when there is a one-minute pause while the teams change goals
- On measurements for first downs
- When the quarterback is tackled behind the line of scrimmage (NFL only)
- For an injury (two minutes)
- For equipment repair (three minutes, NFL only)

The **second clock** is used to count the time between plays. In the NFL, teams are allowed 45 seconds between the end of one play to when the ball is **snapped** (passed back through the legs of the center), 30 seconds after a timeout or injury. In the NCAA, teams are allowed 25 seconds from the time the ball is ready to play to the snap. Otherwise, a **delay of game** penalty is called.

A period does not end until play has been completed. If the defending team commits a foul in the last play of a half, the offense may run another play.

The clock starts when the ball is kicked off except in the last two minutes of the game. Then, the clock does not begin to run until the ball is touched by a receiver or a player on the kicking team if the ball has travelled 10 yards. In the NCAA, the clock starts when the ball is legally touched.

The clock also starts immediately after a penalty is called and the ball is ready to play.

Scoring

A *touchdown* (TD) worth six points is scored when the ball crosses the *plane* (an imaginary straight vertical line) of the opponents' goal line by a player running with it into the end zone or passing the ball to a teammate who catches it in the end zone or if a player recovers a ball in the opponents' end zone.

A *field goal* (FG) scores three points. The ball is place-kicked over the crossbar and between the uprights of the opponents' goal posts without touching the ground or a teammate. A *drop kick* (the ball is dropped to the ground and kicked as it touches the ground) is permitted but seldom used.

If a field goal is tried and missed from beyond the 20-yard line, the defense takes possession at line of scrimmage. If an attempt is tried and missed from inside the 20-yard line, the ball goes over to the defensive team at the 20-yard line.

A *safety* (S) scores two points when the ball is downed or becomes dead in the offensive team's end zone. For example, a runner is tackled there, or a snap from center or a blocked kick goes out of the end zone.

Play is restarted by a kickoff by the team that gave up the safety from its own 20-yard line.

A *point-after touchdown* (PAT) is one play following a TD. In the NFL, the ball is put on the two-yard line and scores one point if *converted* (successfully kicked through the opponents' uprights).

In amateur play, the ball is placed on the three-yard line. It may be kicked for a one-point conversion or run or passed over the goal line for two points.

The defensive team cannot score; if the kick is blocked or possession gained, the ball is dead. In the NCAA, the defensive team may score two points by returning a blocked kick, intercepted pass or recovered fumble to the opponents' end zone.

Procedure

The team captains meet at midfield for a coin toss and the visitors call. The winner may choose to kick off or receive or pick the goal to first defend.

At the start of the second half, the loser of the coin toss gets the choice.

Teams change goals after the first and third periods. Possession, ball location and down number remain the same; only the direction is changed.

The ball is put into play by a *free kick* (the defensive team cannot interfere with the kicker) to begin the game, the second half or after a score.

At the kickoff, the ball is in a fixed spot on the ground, on a tee or held by a teammate between the inbound lines from the team's own 35-yard line (40-yard line in high school).

All players on the kicking team must be behind the ball and all opposition players must be at least 10 yards away.

The ball must travel 10 yards or be touched by the receiving team. After it is touched, it is a *free ball* (live and in play). Receivers may recover and advance the ball. The kicking team may recover but not advance the ball, unless a receiver had possession and lost the ball.

If the kickoff goes out-of-bounds without being touched by a receiver, the ball must be rekicked after a five-yard penalty, or the receivers may take the ball 30 yards from where it was kicked. If the kickoff goes out-of-bounds and was last touched by a receiver, it is the receiving team's ball at the inbound mark nearest the spot where the ball went out.

An *onside kick* is a purposely short kickoff where the kicking team tries to keep possession by recovering the ball after it travels 10 yards and is touched — but not retained — by a receiver.

A kickoff that goes through the opponents' goal posts does not score; it is not a field goal.

A kickoff that goes beyond the opponents' goal line and is dead (a type of *touchback)* is put into play with a first down on the receiving team's 20-yard line.

The receiving team, now in possession of the ball and on the offensive, has four *downs* (units of play) to advance the ball 10 yards by running or passing or as awarded by a penalty. Each down begins when the ball is put into play and ends when the ball is dead.

The first try is called *first-and-10*, as 10 yards are needed. A team does not have to use all four downs to gain the necessary yardage. As soon as 10 yards (or more) have been gained, the team is given a new series of four downs. If not successful, possession is given to the opponent at the point the ball last became dead.

If the necessary yardage has not been made after the third down, the team in possession will usually punt so that the opponent begins its possession with the ball as far as possible away from the kicking team's goal line.

If a first down is inside the opponents' 10-yard line, the offense has four downs to go the remaining distance to the goal line. This is called "first and goal."

When necessary, the officials use the yardage chain to measure if the forward part of the ball has reached the 10 yards needed for the new first down.

A down ends and the ball is whistled dead under the following circumstances:

- The ballcarrier is tackled or forward progress halted
- The ball goes out-of-bounds
- A forward pass is *incomplete* (not caught before hitting the ground)
- A punt is not handled by the receiving team
- After a score or a *touchback* (the defender recovers the ball in his own end zone, often by intercepting a pass)

A player is out-of-bounds when he touches a boundary line, as is a loose ball or a ball in a player's possession who touches a boundary.

If the ball goes out of play over a side line, it is **spotted** (placed) on the hash mark at the nearest inbounds line.

The offensive team must line up at least seven players at the line of scrimmage.

Players on the line must have both hands and both feet or a hand and both feet on the ground.

Offensive backs, except for the quarterback, must be at least one yard behind the line.

Play begins when the center snaps the ball back to a player not on the line of scrimmage.

The center must keep the ball pointing toward the opponents' goal line, not slide his hands along the ball or move his feet until after the snap, and bring the ball back in a continuous motion.

All other linemen must be stationary until the ball is snapped; no move can be made into the neutral zone or toward an opponents' goal line.

One back may be in motion, but not toward the opponents' goal, when the ball is snapped.

On a punt from scrimmage, the team that receives the kick can advance the ball by running with it after the catch. If a receiving player **fumbles** (drops or mishandles a ball in play), it can be recovered by a player on either team. Both teams may advance a fumbled ball.

While a kick is in the air, a receiver can signal a fair catch by raising one arm over his head and waving from side to side more than once. The receiver gives up the opportunity to advance the ball in exchange for protection from being hit by an opponent. After a catch is made, only two steps can be taken and the ball is dead.

A **forward pass** is a ball thrown toward the opponents' goal line, intended for a teammate; one pass is allowed during each play.

The passer must be behind the line of scrimmage when the ball is thrown.

A **completion** is a pass legally caught. In the NFL, the receiver must touch the ground with both feet inbounds while in possession of the ball. In amateur play, the receiver only needs to have one foot

inbounds. In the NFL and in high school, if the receiver is pushed out-of-bounds but would have landed inbounds, the pass is complete.

Offensive interior linemen (guards, tackles and center) are *ineligible receivers* and cannot catch a pass. All defensive players are eligible receivers.

A receiver becomes ineligible if he goes out-of-bounds before a pass.

An *interception* is a pass caught by a defensive player who can then run with the ball.

If a pass is touched by one eligible offensive player and then caught by an eligible offensive player, the pass is legal. If a defensive player touches the ball in flight, all players on the offensive team become eligible.

A ball thrown in a forward pass is dead if it touches the ground, goes out-of-bounds or hits the goal post.

Pass interference is a deliberate movement that denies an eligible receiver the opportunity to catch a forward pass or make an interception. It is not illegal if simultaneous action is made by two or more players to catch or *bat* (strike with an arm or hand) the ball.

Pass interference restrictions begin for the defending team after the ball is thrown, but begin for the offensive team following the snap from center.

A *sack* is to throw the quarterback to the ground for a loss of yardage while he is trying to pass.

A forward pass may not be intentionally thrown to the ground or out of bounds to prevent loss of yardage from being sacked.

A team on defense gains possession of the ball when:

- The offense doesn't make a first down
- An offensive player *fumbles* (drops) the ball inbounds and a defensive player gets control
- It intercepts a pass
- It catches a punt or a kickoff

In the NFL, a running back or receiver carrying the ball may get up and continue running if he slips without being tackled. In amateur play, the runner may not continue if any part of his body except the hands or feet touch the ground.

A fumble may be picked up and advanced by any player on either team.

Tackling is a defensive move using the hands and arms to hold a ballcarrier and/or throw him down to the ground.

Blocking is an offensive or defensive move using the forearm, hands or body from above the knees to obstruct an opponent; most often, to protect a teammate with the ball.

A *lateral* is any pass that is not a forward pass. Any runner can make a backward pass at any time.

Pass interference is an illegal move that prevents a receiver or a defender from attempting to catch a pass by contact.

Officials

The referee (wearing a white cap) controls the game from behind the offensive backfield. His responsibilities include:

- Following the ball and spotting it after each play
- Determining if the ball is in play or dead
- Starting and ending the game by signaling to the official timer
- Keeping track of downs
- Signaling rule violations and stepping off yardage penalties
- Being the authority for scoring
- Explaining a team's options on a penalty
- Giving coaches the two-minute warning (NFL)

The umpire's duties include watching for illegal play from the middle of the defensive backfield, covering short passes, checking equipment and tracking timeouts.

The linesman is at the line of scrimmage and watches for *offsides* (when any body part of a player is over the line before the ball is moved) or *encroachment* (drawing an opponent offside or making contact), supervises the yardage chain and down indicator crew functions and counts downs.

Most used officials' signals

Offside

Illegal procedure

Timeout

Delay of game

Holding

Pass or kick interference

Incomplete forward pass
Penalty refused
FG or PAT missed

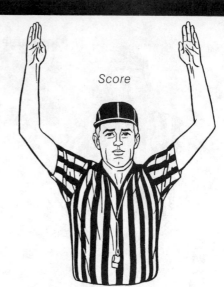

Score

First down

Personal foul

Illegal motion

Time is in

The field judge covers downfield play, including kicks and passes into the end zone and catching decisions, signals dead balls and timeouts, rules on field goals and extra points and has timing functions (NCAA only).

The side judge stands about 15 yards behind the defensive line and rules on plays at his side of the field, especially those involving pass receptions, running and out-of-bounds calls.

The back judge assists in various decisions involving pass receiving and defensive play and checks defensive actions.

The line judge times the game, signals the end of periods by shooting a pistol; watches for offside and encroachment and related scrimmage line play (such as holding and false starts), marks out-of-bounds spots and backs up the stadium clock (NFL only).

Fouls and Penalties

A foul is called when a rule of play is broken. When a team is charged with a foul, it loses yardage. Sometimes, it is to the advantage of a team that has been fouled to *decline* (refuse) a penalty; for example, on a third-down play when the offending team does not make a first down, declining the penalty by the defenders generally forces the offensive team to punt.

A penalty is measured from four starting places: (1) the exact spot of the foul, (2) where the ball was last put in play, (3) where an action related to the foul took place and (4) where the ball would be if there had not been a foul. A foul near the goal line cannot put the ball into the end zone. In that case, the penalty is *half the distance* from a designated spot.

The severity of penalties varies depending on the infraction.

Violations that are penalized five yards include the following:

- Crowd noise
- Defensive holding (NFL)
- Delay of game
- Encroachment
- Excessive celebration (NFL)
- False start
- Grasping the opponent's facemask

- Helping a runner (NCAA)
- Illegal formation, shift, motion
- Illegal substitution
- Ineligible kicking team member downfield before the kick (NFL)
- Ineligible receiver downfield on a forward pass
- Invalid fair catch signal (NFL)
- Less than seven players on the offensive line at the snap
- Offside
- Running into the kicker
- More than one man in motion at snap
- Taking too many timeouts

Violations that are penalized five yards and a loss of down include:

- Throwing a forward pass from beyond the line of scrimmage
- *Intentionally grounding* a forward pass by throwing it where it cannot be caught to avoid being sacked (NCAA)

Violations that are penalized 10 yards include the following:

- Batting, punching or kicking the ball (NFL)
- Helping a runner (NFL)
- Ineligible receiver downfield (NFL)
- Offensive and defensive holding
- Offensive pass interference (NFL)
- Tripping (NFL)

The intentional grounding of a forward pass is penalized 10 yards, with the loss of down in the NFL. It is a safety if the passer is in his own end zone.

Violations that are penalized 15 yards include the following:

- Fair catch interference
- Unsportsmanlike conduct

Violations that are penalized 15 yards plus a first down include the following:

- Chop block
- Clipping
- Crackback block

- Piling on
- Roughing the kicker
- Roughing the passer
- Spearing with the helmet
- Unnecessary roughness

An automatic first down is awarded to the offensive team on all defensive fouls, except the following:

- Offside
- Encroachment
- Delay of game
- Grabbing an opponent's facemask
- Illegal substitution
- Running into the kicker

The offense is penalized by a loss of down only when a forward pass:

- Goes out-of-bounds
- Hits the ground or a goal post
- Is touched by eligible receiver who first went out-of-bounds
- Is caught by an ineligible receiver
- Is thrown from behind the line of scrimmage after the ball had crossed the line

Flagrant fouls, such as hitting or kicking an opponent, may result in a penalty of 15 yards and disqualification from the game.

Versions of Play

Football can be played under other sets of rules, including the following:

Six-man: Teams consist of three linemen and three backs. The field is reduced to 120×240 feet. The ball can only be passed or kicked; running plays are not permitted.

Eight-man: Teams consist of five linemen and three backs. A regulation field is used.

Touch: There is no limit to the number of players. The field can be any size. Tackling is not permitted; the play is over when the ballcarrier is touched by one or two hands (local rules decide) of an opponent.

Canadian: Rules are similar to the standard game played in the United States, with the following major differences.

The playing field is larger (65 × 165 yards) and the goal lines are 110 yards apart

The goal posts are on the goal line; the *dead line* (end line) is 25 yards behind the goal line

Each team has 12 men (the additional player is a back)

Teams have three downs to gain 10 yards

A punt that goes into the end zone must be run out or the kicking team scores one point

Fair catches are not permitted on punt returns

Teams are issued three-minute warnings instead of two-minute warnings; timeouts are not permitted except one in the last three minutes of each half

Overtime consists of two five-minute halves; no sudden death

Extra-point conversions are taken from the five-yard line; two points are awarded for running or passing the ball into the end zone and one point for a kick.

History

Golf generally is believed to have been first played in 15th century Scotland on sandy, hilly ground near the seacoast. There are traces of a stick and ball street game of the Romans, who occupied part of the British Isles in ancient times. The Scots used a leather ball stuffed with feathers — as had the Romans — and played on grounds that had been rabbit runs. There was also a sport played in Holland called *kolf* (Dutch for club) that suggests an early golf-like game.

Documentation includes a decree of the English Parliament that "golfe" interfered with archery, which was important to the defense of the Kingdom of James II, and a record of payment for "clubbis and ballis" for royalty in the 1500s. Mary, Queen of Scots, is thought to have been the first woman golfer. The Royal and Ancient Golf Club of St. Andrews, Scotland (known as the R and A) was established in 1754 and was greatly responsible for the development of the rules over the years (such as 18 holes on a standard course).

Golf was first played in the United States in the late 1700s, and by the 1880s several clubs had been organized, including St. Andrews in Yonkers, N.Y. A national association was established in 1894 to oversee the amateur game and its rules. Three U.S. championships began the next year: the Amateur, the Women's Amateur and the Open. By the end of the 19th century, more than 1000 courses had

133

been built in North America and golf was being played around the world — in Europe, throughout the British Empire and beyond to Siam and China.

The early years of the 20th century introduced professional golfers into what had been an amateur game; the PGA was formed in 1916. The 1920s and 1930s were a time of growth for the sport, fueled by the popularity of celebrated men and women golfers. Tours and tournaments became a part of top international sport competition. There were major advances in equipment; steel replaced hickory shafts on clubs, the rubber core ball made the game easier to play and attracted many new players. In the past 30 years, the game has been greatly stimulated by extensive television coverage of events.

Today, golf is a major participant and spectator sport for many reasons — the impact of the professionals, the growing number of female players and young entrants, the ability for seniors to continue active in a competitive sport, the availability of quality instruction, new facilities (public and private) and the handicap system that allows golfers of varying skills to play against each other.

The United States Golf Association is the sports' governing body. It works with the R and A on rules and interpretations, runs national events, rates courses and handles national handicaps, sets equipment standards and has a museum, library and research facilities.

Object of the Game

Players try to hit small balls with a variety of clubs into a series of holes set into the ground of a *course* (the entire area where play is allowed) without interference by an opponent. The winner is the player or team that uses the least number of *strokes* (attempts) to finish or the side that wins a majority of the holes.

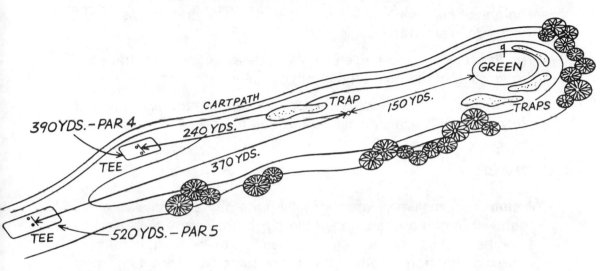

390 YDS. – PAR 4
CARTPATH
240 YDS.
TRAP
150 YDS.
GREEN
TRAPS
TEE
370 YDS.
520 YDS. – PAR 5
TEE

Playing Field

The design and playing characteristics of each course vary,
therefore local rules — usually stated on the back of a scorecard —
should be read.

A *hole* is each part of the course between a teeing ground and its
putting green. A standard course contains 18 holes that are
approximately 100 to 600 yards long.

The *teeing ground* (also called the *tee*) is a flat, rectangular area
that is the starting place for each hole.

Tee markers define the forward limits and the ball must be played
within two club lengths behind the markers. Red markers are for
women's golf, white for men's and blue for championship golf.

The *fairway* is an expanse of lawn-like cut grass between the teeing
ground and the putting green at the far end of the hole.

The *rough* is longer, courser grass and non-landscaped terrain on
either side of the fairway.

A *bunker* is a *hazard* (a sand-filled hollow, also called a *trap*)

A *water hazard* is a stream, pond, lake, ditch or other area whether
or not it is covered with water. A *lateral water hazard* generally
runs parallel to the line of play.

The *putting green* is a closely-groomed grass area at the end of the
fairway. The *apron* (short collar) around the green is not part of it.

135

The actual *hole* is a cup 4¼ inches in diameter and at least four inches deep set in the putting green.

The *flagstick* is a moveable pole at least seven feet long that shows the position of the hole on the putting green. It is also called a *pin*.

The entire area of the course except the teeing ground, the putting green and any hazards is called *through the green*.

Equipment

A **club** is an implement used for hitting the ball and consists of a shaft with a grip and a clubhead. A player may carry a maximum of 14 clubs, and can replace any that become damaged but cannot borrow a club from another player. The three types are as follows:

A **wood** has a clubhead of wood, lightweight metal or plastic that is shaped and thick from front to back. Used for longer shots, the woods are numbered 1 to 10, but the most often used are 1, 3 and 5.

An **iron** has a narrow steel clubhead and a shorter shaft than a wood. Used for shorter shots, irons are numbered 1 to 10.

A **putter** is usually all metal with many styles of clubheads, and is used to play on the putting green.

The length of the shaft and the slant of the *face* (front of the clubhead) is different on each club to give varying trajectories to a well-hit ball. The *loft* (angle) goes from flat (on a putter) to more than 50 degrees (on high numbered iron). In general, the lower numbered clubs provide the most distance with the least height and the higher numbers give, progressively, less distance and more height.

The **ball** is plastic or rubber coated over a core material and dimpled to improve its flight. The American ball is 1.68 inches in diameter and the British ball is 1.62 inches, but both weigh a minimum of 1.62 ounces.

A **tee** is a small peg, about two inches long, on which a golf ball is placed before hitting it from the teeing ground.

Players dress in active sportswear, with golf shoes.

Other equipment includes anything worn, carried or used, including electric or hand carts, as permitted locally.

Match Play

The game is decided by the most holes won. The winner of a hole is the side that *holes out* (hits the ball into the hole) in the fewest number of strokes.

The score is kept by *holes up* (ahead) or *to play*. For example, if player A has won three holes and player B has won two holes and five holes have been played, player A is one-up. A hole is halved if each side holes out in the same number of strokes.

The match is won when one side is leading by a number of holes greater than the number of holes left to be played. As such, the game may end before 18 holes are completed.

If the sides are tied at the end of the match, it is halved and play may continue until one side wins a hole, which wins the match.

Stroke Play

The game is decided by the total number of strokes taken by each side. Also known as *medal play*, the winner is the side with the lowest score — the fewest strokes used — in a *stipulated round* (a set number of holes, usually 18, played in their correct order.)

Ties are decided by a playoff; the competitors play until one side has a lower score on a hole. In tournaments, ties are sometimes broken by an 18-hole playoff.

Sides and matches

Two, three or four players compete as individuals or in teams. A *side* is a player, or two or more players who are partners.

Games can be played as follows:

Single: one plays against another; usually referred to as a *match*

Threesome: one plays against two and each side plays one ball; teammates alternate shots, including teeing off at each new hole

Foursome: two play against two and each side plays one ball; teammates alternate shots

Three-Ball: three play against each other, each with their own ball, in match play

Best-Ball: one plays against the better ball of two, or the best ball of three players in match play

Four-Ball: two play their better ball against the better ball of two others in match play

Four-Ball Stroke Play: two competitors play as partners, each playing their own ball; the lower score of the partner become the score for the hole

Par

The concept of par is basic to stroke play. It is the number of strokes that an expert is expected to take on each hole based on the length of the hole and allowing two *putts* (strokes on the green). The yardage guidance is as follows:

Par	Men	Women
3	up to 250	up to 210
4	251 to 470	211 to 400
5	471 and over	401 to 575
6		576 and over

A *birdie* is one stroke under par; an *eagle* is two strokes under. A *bogey* is one stroke over par; a *double bogey* is two strokes over.

Scoring

A *stroke* is the forward movement of the club with intent to hit the ball; if the downward swing is stopped before the clubhead reaches the ball, it is not a stroke. Each player must record the number of strokes taken on each hole on a scorecard. In match play, the margin between players is not important; winning the hole is what matters. In stroke play, every stroke counts as the lowest total score wins the game.

Handicaps

In order to allow players of different ability to play on equal terms, a designated number of points (the *handicap*) may be subtracted from the *gross* (actual number of strokes) score. Handicaps are determined on the basis of a competitor's recent play; such as, the lowest 10 rounds of the last 20. The best players are *scratch* and have a handicap of zero. As example, in stroke play, a player with a 15 handicap who completes the course in 100 strokes would have a *net* score of 85. In match play, strokes are taken at specific holes.

Terminology

The following are terms common to golf.

Addressing the ball: a player has taken a stance and placed the club on the ground (except in a hazard) before swinging

Approach shot: a stroke made to hit the ball onto the green

Away: the ball that is the farthest from the hole when two or more are in play

Caddie: person who carries or handles the players clubs and generally advises on distance and how to play specific holes

Casual water: a temporary accumulation of water, not a planned part of the course

Chip: a low approach shot to the hole from close to the green

Divot: a piece of turf lifted out of the ground by the clubhead

Drive: to hit the ball from the teeing ground

Drop: a player's right to replace a lost ball with a new one or to move the ball from an unplayable position and put it down where it can be playled

"Fore": called out to warn players of a ball coming in their direction

Honor: the right to play first off the tee

Hook: a shot that curves to the left (or right for a left-handed player)

Lie: the ball's position on the ground

Line of play: the direction that the player wants the ball to travel after it is hit

Links: a seaside course

Loose impediments: natural objects on the course (such as stones and leaves) that are not growing or firmly attached to the ground

Lost ball: one that cannot be found within five minutes

Moved: when a ball leaves its place and rolls to another position

Obstruction: an artificial object on the course, but not boundary markers or anything deemed to be a part of the course

Out: the first nine holes; *in* is the second or *back* nine played

Out-of-bounds: the area beyond the boundaries that mark the playing parts of the course; no play allowed

Penalty stroke: one or two strokes added to a player's score for a rule violation

Pitch: a high shot near the green that does not continue far after landing; a *pitch and run* does roll

Playing through: when one group that has been slowed down allows another group to pass them

Provisional ball: played for a ball that may be lost (except in a water hazard) or out-of-bounds

Rub of the green: a ball in motion is deflected or stopped by an *outside agency*, something or someone other than the player, the player's partner or caddie or an official

Shank: a mis-hit to the right (left for a left-hander)

Short game: pitching, chipping, putting

Slice: a shot that curves to the right (left for a left-hander)

Unplayable lie: a ball that, in the player's opinion, cannot be played

Winter rules: allow improving a lie on the fairway; check local rules

Wrong ball: a ball other than the ball being played or a provisional ball

Etiquette

Rules that make the game safer and more pleasing include the following:

- No moving or talking when a player is making a stroke
- Do not stand directly behind a ball or a hole being played
- Do not tee the ball until the opponent's ball has come to rest
- In a mixed game, men tee off before women
- Never play a shot when the players in the group in front are still in range
- Play in turn and without delay
- Let faster players play through
- If looking for a lost ball, signal players behind to play through
- Replace divots and smooth footprints in bunkers
- No golf bags or carts on the putting green; repair ball and spike marks
- Hold flagstick for other players at arm's length
- Stay on greens until all have putted, then leave promptly
- Put an identification mark on all balls

General Rules

The following rules include the penalties for some of the most common violations. The general penalty for breaking a rule in stroke play is two strokes; in match play it is the loss of the hole. These are marked PEN. One-stroke penalties are shown next to the violations that cause them.

Players are responsible for playing the right ball and not a wrong ball (PEN).

The ball must be struck with the clubhead and not pushed or scooped (PEN).

No practice shots on the course; practice swings are allowed (PEN).

If a ball is struck twice on a single stroke, the stroke is counted plus one penalty stroke.

A player may lift the ball for identification, except in a hazard, and it must be replaced in the exact spot.

If a player (only in stroke play) is in doubt about procedure, the hole may be completed with the ball in play and also with a second ball.

A ball that interferes with play may be lifted and replaced after the blocked player's stroke is made.

All strokes count, whether or not the ball is hit. Penalty strokes are added to the total for the hole where they are incurred.

If the ball is played from outside the teeing area in match play, it must be replayed (no PEN); in stroke play, PEN.

Players may only ask advice from, or give advice to, partners or their caddies. A player may have the line of play pointed out by anyone except on the putting green.

If a ball is damaged (such as, cut or cracked) and unfit for play, it may be replaced where it lay. Players must first declare intention.

The position of a lifted ball must be marked by a coin or small object (one-stroke penalty in match or stroke play).

When it is necessary to drop a ball, a player must stand erect, hold the ball at shoulder height and arm's length and drop it.

A ball shall be re-dropped, without penalty, if the ball touches the player, a partner or caddie; if it rolls into or out of a hazard, onto the green, out-of-bounds or more than two club lengths from where it had landed on the course.

A ball cannot be moved by a player after addressing it (except if knocked off the tee by accident) or by a caddie (one-stroke penalty in match or stroke play).

Any penalties incurred in match play must be disclosed unless the penalty has been observed by an opponent. A player must give correct information before the opponent plays the next stroke (PEN).

No devices to measure distance may be used (disqualification).

A player is allowed only one caddie to carry clubs and note the position of the ball (disqualification).

Procedure

A draw determines which side plays first and partners decide their own playing order. After the start, the side that wins each hole plays first at the next teeing ground. If the hole was halved, the honor is kept by the side that had it.

The ball must be teed from behind the markers. If the ball falls off the tee or is knocked off while being addressed, it may be teed-up again.

If a provisional ball is played from the teeing ground, it is done after the other players have taken their first stroke.

Procedure through the green

The ball must be played where it lies. It must not be moved or touched, except as otherwise permitted. The playing area around the ball cannot be changed (such as, by pressing down grass in the rough, moving or breaking anything fixed or growing). Loose impediments may be removed.

A player cannot improve the position of a ball, the area of the swing or the line of play. Loose impediments on the teeing ground and the putting green may be picked up.

The player farthest away from the hole plays first. If a competitor plays out of turn in stroke play, the game continues; in match play, the stroke may be canceled at the opponent's option.

If a ball is lost or out-of-bounds (except in a water hazard), the player takes the next stroke from as close as possible to the place from where the ball had originally been played. A ball played from the tee must be re-played from there. If the ball was played from anywhere through the green or from a hazard, the new ball is dropped from where it had been played; if from the putting green, it is placed down. In all cases, one penalty stroke is added.

If a ball is unplayable (except if in a water hazard), the player may play again from the point of the previous shot or drop the ball within two club lengths of where the ball now lies (but not nearer to the hole) and add one penalty stroke.

If a ball is in a water hazard and no play is possible, a player may play again from the point of the previous shot or drop a new ball at any distance behind the water hazard in line with where the original shot crossed into the water. At a lateral water hazard, the player also has the option of dropping a ball outside the hazard within two club lengths of either side. One penalty stroke is added for any of the above.

If a ball seems to have gone out-of-bounds or become lost, a provisional ball may be played before any search is made. If found, the original ball must be played, even if it is in an unplayable lie or in a water hazard. After the second ball has been played beyond the point where the original ball went out, it becomes the ball in play. The first ball is considered lost and one penalty stroke is taken.

A moving ball touched by an outside agency is played where it lies. If touched by its owner (or partner, caddie or equipment) there is a penalty. If touched by the opposing side in match play, the owner may replay or play the ball where it lies; in stroke play, the ball is played from where it lies. A player may not hit a moving ball unless it is in water.

A ball moved by another ball shall be set back in place.

A ball deflected or stopped by a ball *at rest* (not in play) shall be played as it lies; no penalty.

A ball that becomes embedded in the ground through the green may be lifted, cleaned and dropped or placed (no closer to the hole) without penalty. A ball that lands in an immovable obstruction, in casual water, in ground under repair and so on, may also be dropped in a new location.

Procedure on the green

The ball may be marked and cleaned while on the green.

The line of play is not to be touched, but may be indicated by a partner or caddie. Before putting, the player may place the club in front of the ball without pressing down.

A player cannot take a stroke standing astride the line of putt or with either foot touching it.

Practice shots or rolling the ball to test the green are not permitted.

When a ball is in motion, only the next player in turn can putt (PEN).

When a ball is lifted, its position must be marked; otherwise, a one-stroke penalty is incurred.

If a ball played from off the green hits a ball on the green, there is no penalty. The moved ball is placed back in its original position. If both balls are on the green in stroke play, the player receives a two-stroke penalty; there is no penalty in match play.

The flagstick may be left in the hole or *attended* (removed or held up in the air to show position). It cannot be moved once a ball is in motion.

A ball may not hit the flagstick with a putt or an attended flagstick or the person attending it (PEN).

When a ball hangs over the lip of the hole for at least 10 seconds after the player comes to the hole, it is considered at rest. If it falls in later, it is scored as being holed out on the last stroke and one penalty stroke is added.

If a ball resting against the flagstick falls into the hole when the stick is removed, the ball is considered holed on the previous stroke.

Recording Scores

Players are responsible for the correctness of their own scores for each hole. At the end of the round, players should check all their scores before signing and turning in their scorecard.

History

The ancient Greeks believed that perfecting the human body was important in the development and education of young people; their word for gymnasium meant "a place to exercise naked." Several of the exercises became sport events in the classic Olympic games. Modern gymnastics were largely the creation of a German, Friedrich Ludwig Jahn, in the early part of the 19th century. Jahn invented many of the *apparatus* (pieces of equipment) that are still used today: the parallel and horizontal bars, the rings, the horse and the balance beam. His first gymnastic club in 1811 became the model for other associations in central Europe.

Immigrants brought these groups to the U.S. and the followers of Jahn — often called *turners* after the German word for gymnastics — were greatly responsible for the growth of the sport in this country after the Civil War. International competitions were organized in the 1880s and gymnastics (for men) were included in the first of the modern Olympic Games of 1896. Competition for women began 40 years later and has become one of the most popular of all events.

The United States Gymnastic Federation is the sole national governing body for the sport in the U.S. Through its 20 member associations, the USGF produces events and tours, runs competitions, clinics and training camps, publishes rule books and conducts other activities that support gymnastics.

Object of the Games

Male and female gymnasts compete as individuals and on teams to earn points based on their performances on various pieces of apparatus. The highest score wins each event.

Competition Area

An indoor arena with appropriate space and a safe environment for simultaneous gymnastic events on equipment and for floor exercises.

Apparatus

Women's artistic events

The *vault* is a leather or vinyl covered wood vaulting *horse* on a metal frame. It is five feet long, four feet high and 14 inches wide.

The *springboard* is made of a non-slip material on a shaped plywood form. It is four feet long. The *runway* is 82 feet long and three feet wide.

The *uneven bars* are made of flexible steel-reinforced wood or fiberglass and have a metal support. The upper bar is 7 feet, 9 inches high, and the lower bar is 5 feet, 2 inches high. The bars are 11 feet, 5 inches long and 17 inches apart.

The *balance beam* is made of vinyl or leather over foam rubber padding on wood; the frame is made of metal. It is 15 feet long, four feet high and four inches wide.

The *floor exercise* is performed on a 40-foot square mat that is made of padded foam rubber over spring-mounted plywood.

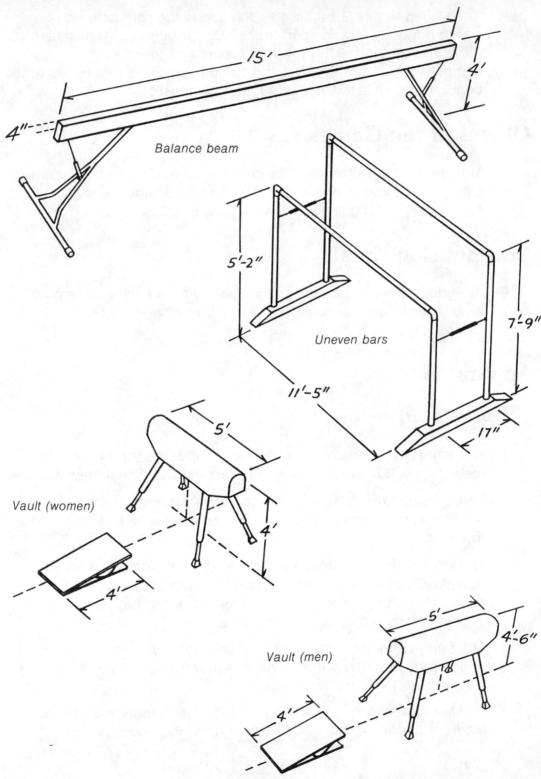

Balance beam

15'

4'

4"

Uneven bars

5'-2"

7'-9"

11'-5"

17"

Vault (women)

5'

4'

4'

Vault (men)

5'

4'-6"

4'

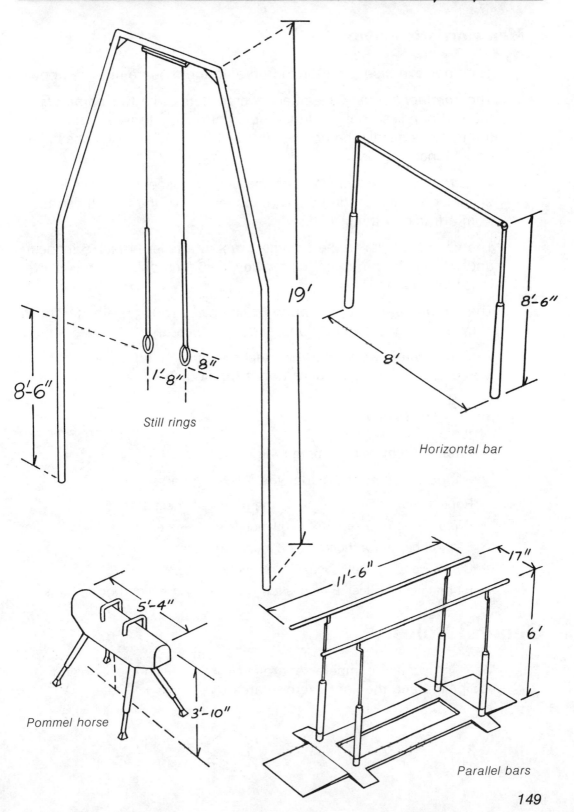

19'

8'-6"

1'-8"   8"

Still rings

Horizontal bar

8'-6"

8'

5'-4"

3'-10"

Pommel horse

11'-6"

17"

6'

Parallel bars

149

Men's artistic events

The *floor exercise* is performed on a 40-foot square mat, as above.

The *pommel horse* is a leather covered horse with two *pommels* (curved handles) that divide the upper surface into three sections; the frame is metal. The horse is five feet long, 3 feet, 10 inches high and 14 inches wide.

The *still rings* are two wood or fiberglass rings, eight inches in diameter and suspended 8 feet, 6 inches above the floor by straps from a frame or the ceiling.

The *vault* is similar to the pommel horse but taller (4 feet, 6 inches) and without the handles. The runway is 80 feet long and has a four-foot springboard.

The *parallel bars* are two wood or fiberglass rods on a metal frame. They are 11 feet, 6 inches long and 17 inches apart.

The *horizontal bar* is a flexible steel rod on a metal frame. It is eight feet long and 8 feet, 6 inches above the floor.

Women's rhythmic events

The *field of play* is a carpeted 40-foot square.

The *hand equipment* includes the following items:

- Rope: hemp or synthetic, twice the gymnast's height
- Hoop: wood or plastic, 32 to 39 inches in diameter
- Ball: rubber or synthetic, 7 to 8 inches in diameter
- Clubs: wood or synthetic, 20 to 24 inches long
- Ribbon: satin, 6 feet, 6 inches long, attached to a wood or plastic stick

General Rules

Men and women compete separately in the artistic events using equipment and the floor exercise area.

Two sets of *routines* (a combination of movements) are performed on each apparatus, as follows:

Compulsories: predesigned routines that include specific moves that all gymnasts must perform

Optionals: personal routines, individually created to best demonstrate each gymnast's style and skills

Judging

A score of 10.0 is perfect; men begin with 9.0 points and women with 9.4.

Judges may award bonus points — up to 1.0 for men and .6 for women — for innovation, risk, *virtuosity* (artistry, rhythm, harmony), flowing execution and so on.

Judges may make deductions for *faults* (errors in performance) or missing required elements.

Skills are classified into five levels of difficulty, from A (easiest) to E (hardest). Each routine must have elements that are determined by the level of competition.

The highest and lowest scores are averaged to a middle mark. Marks are adjusted mathematically to determine a final score.

Scoring

Competitions have three segments, as follows:

Team: Each of six members performs a compulsory and an optional routine on each apparatus. The five highest scores on each apparatus are added together for a team total. The team with the most points wins.

All-around: The best gymnasts from each team do an optional routine on each apparatus. Individual scores are totaled and the gymnast with the most points wins.

Individual: The gymnasts with the highest scores on each apparatus compete again on optionals. The best individual performance (most points) on each piece of equipment wins.

Women's Events

Vault

The vault is divided into four categories for judging, with various body positions and movements defining each section after the run, as follows:

- First flight (springboard to the horse)
- Support phase (push off the horse)
- Second flight (horse to dismount)
- Landing

The leap is made over the horse crosswise, not lengthwise.

An optional vault may not be the same as a compulsory.

Compulsory and optional vaults are both done twice; the best score in each routine counts.

Uneven bars

The gymnast must use both the high and low bars.

Only four elements in a row may be used on the same bar.

At least 10 moves must be made without stopping. Pauses and extra swings are not allowed.

Balance beam

The routine must last 70 to 90 seconds.

The optional series should include non-stop acrobatic, tumbling and dance movements.

The entire length of the beam must be used.

Floor exercise

Acrobatic and gymnastic elements are performed to taped music and last 70 to 90 seconds.

Gymnasts are to use the full floor area but not step beyond the boundary.

At least one *salto* (somersault) must be included in each of three tumbling passes that convey grace, strength, flexibility and balance.

Men's Events

Floor exercise

The entire floor area must be used. Routines must last 50 to 70 seconds, with no music.

Tumbling must occur in at least two directions.

Gymnasts cannot take more than three steps or cross out-of-bounds.

Pommel horse

All three sections of the horse must be worked.

Motions must be continuous and circular.

Only the hands may touch the apparatus.

Routines must include a *scissors* (open legged) vertical swing.

Still rings

The routine must have two handstands; one by strength, one through the swing.

The rings must remain still; no swaying.

Holds (stationery positions) must be maintained for a minimum of two seconds.

Vault

The exercise is done over the length of the horse.

Minimum height and distance requirements must be observed, such as how far the gymnast's body is to rise above the horse and travel in the second flight.

Gymnasts perform two optional vaults in the finals.

Parallel bars

Gymnasts must *release* (let go of a bar to perform a move) and regrasp the bars with both hands.

Holds must be maintained for two seconds.

Horizontal bar

Routines must be performed with non-stop swinging.

Routines must include one move with a release and regrasp of the bar and one *giant* swing (360-degree rotation) of the body around the bar.

Women's Rhythmic Events

Body and dance movements — such as jumps, leaps, turns, skips and hops — are performed while handling small pieces of equipment.

Events are performed to music.

A time limit of one minute to 1 minute, 30 seconds is imposed for individuals; for groups, the time limit is two minutes to 2 minutes, 30 seconds.

Gymnasts must cover the full floor area.

Equipment handling may include the following:

- Ball: rolled, bounced, thrown, caught
- Rope: thrown, caught, swung, twirled

- Hoop: swung, thrown, caught, passed through
- Clubs: thrown, caught, swung
- Ribbon: thrown in spirals, loops and circles

One of the ball, rope or ribbon routines must be done with the left hand.

Judging/scoring

Judging and scoring is the same as for the women's artistic events. The base score is 9.4 with bonus points and deductions.

Uniforms

Women wear long-sleeved leotards, with bare legs. Slippers are optional.

Men wear sleeveless shirts with long pants (leotard style), soft footwear.

Officials

Four to six judges at each apparatus score the routines.

History

Handball dates back to ancient Rome, and was later played in France and Spain. It is considered the origin of jai alai. The game appeared in Ireland during the Middle Ages and was played on a hard mud floor against a stone wall. It had become popular by the middle of the 19th century, and local championships were held throughout the country. Irish immigrants brought the game to America; the first court was built in Brooklyn, N.Y. in 1886.

The rules have changed little in the past 100 years, although the soft tennis ball was replaced by a smaller, harder ball and court size was reduced to its current dimensions. The one-wall game, once thought of as a New York beach and playground sport, has become familiar in schoolyards, parks, YMCAs, public facilities and private clubs across the country. The U.S. Handball Association administers the sport, conducts various programs and competitions and has been responsible for introducing the game to thousands of young players.

Object of the Game

Two players or teams use gloved hands to try to hit a ball to a wall by serving or returning it in a way that the other side cannot keep the ball in play. The first person or team to score 21 points wins the game; matches are best two-out-of-three games.

Playing Field

Four-wall court

The court is 20 × 40 feet. The front and side walls should be 20 feet high. The back wall should be at least 14 feet high.

The lines marking the floor are two inches wide.

The *service line* is 15 feet from the front wall.

The *short line* is 20 feet from the wall, midway between the front and back walls.

The *service zone* is a five-foot area between the service and short lines.

The *service boxes* in the service zone are 18 inches from each side wall and parallel to the wall.

The *receiving lines* are five feet behind the short line and extend six inches from the side walls.

One-wall court

The one-wall court is 20 × 34 feet. The wall is 20 feet wide and 16 feet high. The *short line* is 16 feet from the wall.

The *long line* is 18 feet behind the short line, which defines the back court

The *service markers* (short lines) are midway between the short and long lines, which extend six inches from the side lines.

The *side lines* extend 37 feet from the front wall.

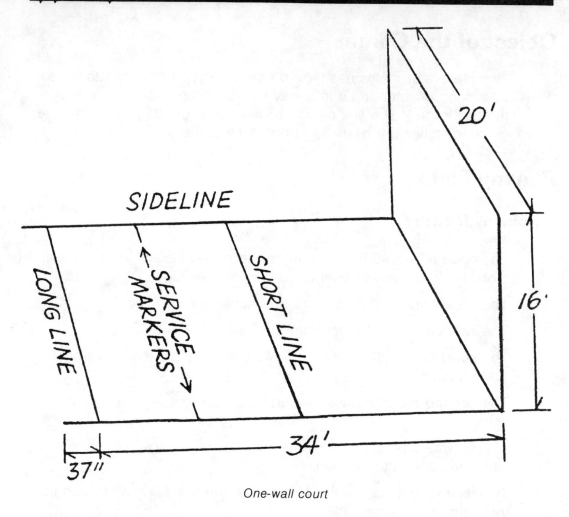

One-wall court

Three-wall court

The size and markings for a three-wall court are the same as for a four-wall court, but the two side walls extend from the top of the front wall to a point four feet beyond the long line, which is 40 feet from the front wall.

Equipment

Gloves are made of leather or other soft material. They should fit snugly, be of a light color so they contrast with the ball and have no webbing. Gauze wrap under the gloves is permitted.

The **ball** is made of rubber or synthetic material and is uniform in color. It is round, 1⅞ inches in diameter and weighs 2.3 ounces, although a lighter ball may be used in various levels of play.

Dress is informal; active sports attire is appropriate.

General Rules

Singles matches are played by two players. Doubles matches are played by four players. *Cut throat* matches are played by three players; the server plays against the other pair. On the loss of serve, players rotate clockwise.

Scoring

Points can only be made by the serving side. One point is scored when an *ace* is served (the ball cannot be properly returned) or when the serving side wins a *rally* (the exchange of shots that decides a point). If the side that did not serve wins a rally, it gets to serve but earns no points.

The first side to score 21 points wins the game.

The first person or team to win two games, plus a tiebreaker if needed, wins the match. The first side to score 11 points wins the tiebreaker.

Opposing sides must take turns hitting the ball during a rally, but players on the same team need not alternate hits.

A player may only hit the ball with the front or back of one hand; using both hands is not allowed. No other part of the body can be used, including the wrist.

Each side can swing and miss until the ball bounces on the floor twice, but only one player can hit it.

Timeouts last for one minute. Three per side are permitted in each game (two in a tiebreaker). An injured player is given 15 minutes to return or retire.

Rest periods between games are five minutes in length.

The ball or gloves can be changed if wet. Two minutes are allowed to do so.

Procedure

The winner of a coin toss chooses whether to serve or receive. In a tiebreaker, the side with the most points in the first two games chooses.

The referee calls "play ball."

Serving

The server stands within the service zone, bounces the ball one time on the floor and then hits it with one hand on the *fly* (in the air) to the front wall.

To be a good serve, the ball must rebound off the front wall and land behind the short line. In a four-wall game, the ball may also touch a side wall before crossing the short line. If there is a **service fault** (illegal serve), the referee calls "second serve" and the player serves again. Faults occur when:

- The server and/or partner steps out of the serving zone before the rebounding ball passes the short line
- The ball rebounds off the front wall and hits the floor in front of the short line (**short serve**) or hits the back wall without touching the floor (**long serve**) or hits any two other walls before touching the floor (**three-wall serve**) or hits the ceiling with or without touching a side wall (**ceiling serve**) or goes off the court without touching the floor (**out-of-court-serve**)
- In a one-wall game, the ball lands beyond the long line or outside the side lines

Two faults in a row loses the serve. Otherwise, a player continues to serve as long as points are scored.

Out serves are errors that mean an immediate loss of serve. They occur when:

- The server swings at the ball and misses
- The ball touches the wall or ceiling before hitting the front wall
- A served ball hits the *crotch* (where the floor meets the front wall)
- A team serves out of order in doubles

In a *dead ball* serve, the player gets another serve, without a penalty, if any of the following occur:

- The server's partner is hit by the rebounding ball before it touches the ground
- One of the serving side players blocks the view of an opponent
- The rebounding ball goes through the server's legs

Two consecutive *screens* (the ball rebounds so close to a defensive player that it interferes with offensive player's view) result in a fault.

In doubles, the team partners serve one after the other; that is, both players on a side must lose their service before the serve passes over to the opposing team. An exception: on first serve in a game, the serve goes to the other side after the initial server fails to score.

Service return and play

In four-wall, the receiver must be at least five feet behind the short line until the server strikes the ball; in one-wall, the receiver is to stay behind the service line until the rebound crosses the short line.

A served ball may be returned to the front wall on the fly (a *volley*) before it bounces on the floor or after one bounce. The return may touch the side walls but must hit the front wall.

A returned ball may not touch the floor before it reaches the front wall but may first hit other walls or the ceiling.

The rally continues, each side hitting the ball until one side cannot return the ball to the front wall. If a receiver misses, the server gets a point. If the server does not score, the receiving side wins the right to serve but does not score a point.

A side loses a rally if:

- A player hits the ball twice consecutively
- Touches the ball
- Purposely interferes (an *avoidable hinder*) with an opponent by pushing or blocking or moving into the way of a ball just hit

A point is replayed for *dead ball hinders,* such as unavoidable interference or body contact or a ball that breaks or goes out of play because of the court condition.

Officials

The referee controls the match and decides all controversies. A linesman and a scorer assist whenever possible.

History

Roman officers played a target game similar to quoits and were imitated by their troops who used discarded horseshoes in their place. Horseshoe pitching may have been brought to England by the Romans or by the Normans when they invaded. It was well established and popular there in the 18th century, played by men, women and children. The sport came to America in Colonial times and was a major competitive game. The Duke of Wellington said, "the war of Liberation was won on the village greens by pitchers of horse hardware."

The first club was formed in 1899 but there were no set rules or standards for equipment until 1914, when a group that later became the National Horseshoe Pitchers Association of America assembled to define them. Today, the NHPA is the governing body for the sport and holds annual national and world championships.

Object of the Game

Players pitch (throw underhand) horseshoes at stakes in the ground, trying to land the shoes around or close to the stakes until one player or team wins the contest.

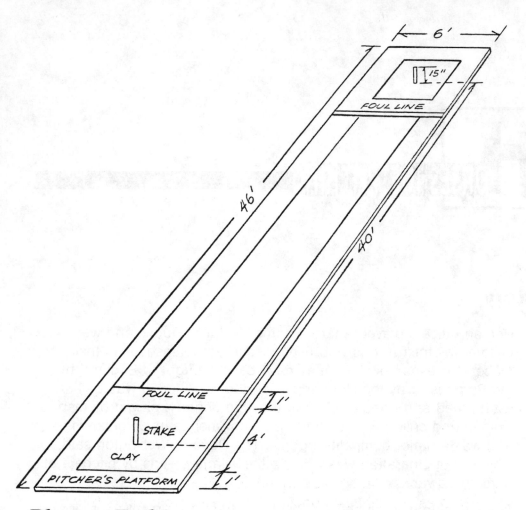

Playing Field

The standard court is 6 × 46 feet, with a *pit* at each end.

Two *stakes* are set 40 feet apart. They are 15 inches in height and one inch in diameter, centered in the target area and slightly inclined (12 degrees) toward each other.

A *foul line* is three feet in front of each stake. For 40-foot pitchers, the line is 37 feet from the target stake.

The *target area* is a 3 × 4 foot pit set one foot back from the foul line and the end of the court and 18 inches from each side. It should be sand, dirt, moist clay or other substance so that the shoes do not bounce, skip or roll upon landing.

The *pitcher's platform* is 18 inches wide on each side of the target area and six feet in length from the foul line to the back end of the court.

Women and junior players (17 and under) may pitch from 30 feet. The foul line is 27 feet from the target stake; all other measurements are the same.

Equipment

Tournament **horseshoes** have curved edges, called *heel calks*, at each open end and a raised *toe calk* at the center. The dimensions are as follows:

- Maximum size: $7\frac{1}{4} \times 7\frac{5}{8}$ inches
- Maximum weight: 2 pounds, 10 ounces
- Minimum weight: 2 pounds, four ounces (non-official, common)
- Opening between heel calks: $3\frac{1}{2}$ inches

Dress is informal.

Procedure

The game is divided into innings, with four shoes pitched — two by each player — in each inning. Games may consist of 25 innings (50 shoes), 20 innings (40 shoes), 15 innings (30 shoes), or until a player scores 50 points, 40 points or a score agreed upon by opponents before the start of a game. Ties are broken by pitching two innings (four shoes by each player) until a winner is decided and the tie is broken.

The first player to throw is determined in one of the following ways:

- A coin toss
- A shoe throw (closest to the stake wins)
- A shoe flip (each player flips the shoe, with one player calling out whether they will land in a like or opposite direction)

The winner has the choice of pitching first or second.

The pitcher's feet must be on the pitching platform and behind the foul line until the horseshoe is released.

The opponent stays on the other side of the stake and behind the pitcher's box. The pitchers may throw from either side, as preferred, but both shoes must be pitched from the same side.

The players stay in the pitcher's box until an inning is finished.

Singles play

Both players stand in the pitcher's box at the same end of the court.

Each player pitches two shoes to the target area. One player pitches both shoes and then the opponent pitches.

The players walk to the target stake and record the scores of the inning.

The player who is to pitch first steps to the platform while the opponent marks the score.

The players pitch back to the original stake. The player who scored earns the first pitch back to the original stake.

The players repeat the cycle until the game ends.

Doubles play

One partner stands in the pitcher's box at each end of the court.

Two shoes are pitched in alternate throws by each player from one end.

The scores of the first two players are recorded, ending the inning.

The shoes are pitched back, in turn, by the partners. (Players do not change ends during the game.)

The partner's scores are added, ending the next inning.

The cycle is repeated until the game ends.

The loser of the preceding game has the choice of whether to pitch first in the next game.

Scoring

Cancellation method

Only one player scores in an inning. Ringers cancel each other and the closest shoe scores.

Only shoes that land within six inches of the stake are eligible for scoring points.

A *ringer* is a thrown shoe that lands far enough around a stake that a straight line run between the heel calks will pass by the stake.

The shoe closest to the stake scores one point.

Two shoes closer than both of the opponent's shoes score two points.

One ringer scores three points; two ringers score six points.

One ringer plus the closest shoe by the same player scores four points.

Only the difference between the scores of an inning count; if scores are the same, no points are earned. Ringers are recorded on a scoresheet so each player's ringer averages are correct.

Equal scores are ties and no points count. For example: each player has a ringer (canceling each other) but the next closest shoe scores one point in the inning (called *ringer alike one*).

A standard game consists of 50 shoes (25 innings) or 40 shoes (20 innings).

Tournaments are set up by classes based on the players' skill level and age. Classes may be for 50, 40 or even 30 shoe games for junior pitchers.

The player winning the most games in a class wins.

Notes: A shoe leaning against a stake scores one point, the same as a shoe flat on the ground or other close shoe. At the same time, if the opponent has a shoe on the ground that is touching the stake, it is a tie.

If a shoe breaks, it is removed and a replacement shoe is pitched.

The highest score pitches first in the following inning; players alternate when there is a tie or no score.

Alternate method

Ringers score three points. All shoes within six inches of the stake score one point.

Games last 25 innings, with 50 shoes pitched by each player or team.

The team with the most points wins.

Ties are resolved by pitching at least two extra innings until the tie is broken.

Players alternate pitches throughout the game. One player pitches first to start the game and then pitches first in all odd-numbered innings; the opponent pitches first in the even innings.

Each player scores the points they pitch in an inning.

Fouls

Fouls include the following violations:

- Distracting the pitcher
- Touching the pitched shoes before the scores are noted

Note: Telling a player his shoe positions before the inning is over means loss of score in that inning by the offender.

A shoe does not score if it:

- Is pitched from an improper position
- Hits the ground and then enters the target area
- Strikes the pitcher's box

Officials

Major contests have a referee to resolve scoring matters and enforce rules. plus an official court scorer.

History

Ice hockey appears to have been derived from a game played by the Micmac native Americans in early 19th century Nova Scotia. As an outdoor sport, it was then spread through Canada by settlers and the army. The first recorded indoor game was played in 1875 between two teams from McGill University in Montreal. Following that, rules were established (with seven players on a side) and a league and a national organization created. In 1892, the Governor General of Canada, Lord Stanley, donated a trophy for the best Canadian team; today, it goes to the winner of the National Hockey League championship.

Organized intercollegiate hockey was being played in the U.S. by 1898. Professional hockey began in Michigan in 1903. As interest in the sport grew, artificial-ice arenas were built across the country. Various rule changes were introduced that made the game more exciting. The National Hockey League was formed in 1917 and the first U.S. team (the Boston Bruins) joined in 1924. Hockey has been an Olympic sport since 1924.

USA Hockey is the national governing body and regulates play, establishes age classifications, runs competitions and promotes the sport in the U.S. Affiliate groups in each state administer amateur hockey regionally to a fast-growing number of participants and fans. Other official organizations are the NCAA and the National Federation of State High School Associations.

National Hockey League (NHL) rule differences are noted.

Object of the Game

Two teams of six players wearing skates and using curved sticks compete on ice and try to move a hard rubber disc into their opponents' goal. The side that scores the most goals wins.

Field of Play

The *rink* has an ice surface and is 85 × 200 feet.

The *boards* are a white wood or fiberglass fence around the ice, measuring 40-48 inches high.

Safety glass or a protective screen, 40 to 48 inches high, is placed atop the boards.

The *goal lines* are red, 10 feet from each end of the rink and across the width of the ice.

The goal *crease* is a red line, 4 × 8 feet, centered on each goal line. It includes a red semi-circle, with a radius of six feet.

The *blue lines* are 60 feet from each goal line and divide the area into three equal spaces, as follows:

- The *defending zone* (the section of ice where the goal is defended)
- The *neutral zone* (center portion)
- The *attacking zone* (section farthest from the defended goal)

The *center line* is red and divides the rink in half.

The *center ice spot* is blue and 12 inches in diameter at the center of the rink.

The *center circle* is blue and has a radius of 15 feet around the center spot.

The *face-off spots* are two red spots, 24 inches in diameter, five feet from each blue line and 44 feet apart in the neutral zone.

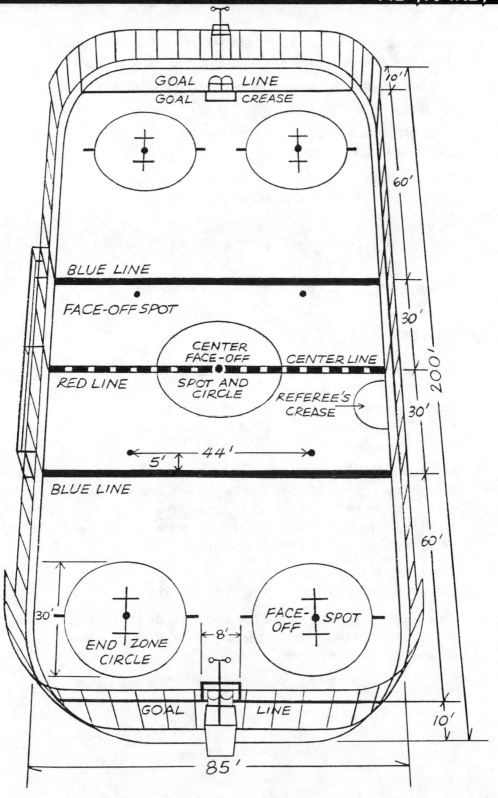

GOAL LINE

GOAL CREASE

10'

60'

BLUE LINE

FACE-OFF SPOT

30'

CENTER
FACE-OFF
SPOT AND
CIRCLE

CENTER LINE

RED LINE

REFEREE'S
CREASE

30'

200'

5' 44'

BLUE LINE

60'

30'

END ZONE
CIRCLE

FACE-
OFF SPOT

8'

GOAL LINE

10'

85'

171

The *end zone face-off spots* are two red spots, 24 inches in diameter, 20 feet from each goal line and 44 feet apart.

The *end zone face-off circles* are red with a 15-foot radius around the end zone spots.

The *referee's crease* is a red semi-circle with a 10-foot radius at the center of one side.

The *goal cage* is six feet long and four feet high and is centered on the goal line. It has red posts and a crossbar, with a white nylon net.

The *players' benches* are placed behind the sideboards with doors into the neutral zone.

The *penalty box* is opposite the players' bench.

Equipment

The **stick** is made of wood or other approved material. Tape wrap is allowed for reinforcement or control. It has a maximum length of 60 inches from the heel to the end of the shaft, and 12½ inches to the end of the blade. It has a minimum width of two inches and a maximum width of three inches.

The **goalkeeper's stick** is the same as above, except the blade has a maximum length of 15½ inches. The maximum width is 3½ inches except at the heel, which has a maximum width of 4½ inches. The shaft is 3½ inches wide to a point 26 inches up from the heel. A white tape knob at the top is permitted.

The **puck** is made of black vulcanized rubber. It is three inches in diameter, one inch thick and weighs 5½ to 6 ounces.

The **skates** are made of leather and steel and include safety heels for all players (except goalkeepers) and on-ice officials. Speed skates are not permitted.

Signals include a siren, clock and red and green lights.

Uniforms

Players wear a shirt or sweater, knee-length pants, stockings and a helmet with a chin strap. The team captain's sweater has a "C" on the front.

Protective equipment (such as shin, shoulder, elbow and hip pads, padded pants and cup) other than gloves, headgear and goalkeeper's leg guards must be worn underneath the uniform.

The goalkeeper also wears a chest protector and face mask. One glove, the *blocker*, hits puck shots away; the other glove is used to catch pucks and to throw them away from the goal.

Male players under 18 years old and all female players must wear a face mask and protective equipment, including a mouthpiece. Dangerous equipment is not allowed.

General Rules

Each team includes 20 players. The six on the ice are a goalkeeper, two defenders (left and right) and three forwards (center, left and right wings). An alternate goalkeeper and 13 other players are in reserve.

Players can be changed while the game is in progress, but the departing player must be at the bench and out of play before the replacement player enters the game.

Play is not stopped for an injured player unless that player's team is in possession of the puck. If so, play stops at once (unless the team is in scoring position). Play stops immediately for serious injury.

The puck must be kept in motion at all times.

An attacking player cannot enter the defender's goal crease unless the player is trying to reach the puck.

A goal does not count if an attacking player is in the goal crease when the puck crossed the goal line.

Face-offs

A referee or linesman drops the puck to the ice between the sticks of two opposing players. Players face their opponents' goal with the blade of the stick on the ice surface and try to hit the puck to a teammate.

No other players are allowed inside the face-off circle or within 15 feet of the puck. Players must stand onside in all face-offs.

Face-offs are not permitted within 15 feet of the goal or side boards.

Substitutions are not permitted until the face-off is complete.

Players must not touch the puck until it is on the ice.

The location of the face-off is as follows:

> At the start of the game or period: the center ice spot
>
> If the game is stopped by action of the attacker in the attacker's team's attacking zone: the nearest face-off spot in the neutral zone
>
> If the game is stopped by action of the defender in the defender's team's defense zone, or any stoppage in the neutral zone: the point of stoppage
>
> If the game is stopped between the end face-off spots and the end of the rink: at the nearest end face-off spot

A puck that goes out of bounds or becomes unplayable is put back in play by a face-off.

A puck on top of the boards is in play and can be moved by a hand or a stick.

Game length

Games last three 20-minute periods (may be less in amateur games). A 15-minute intermission is taken between periods. The game clock stops when play stops.

Scoring

A goal (one point) is scored when the puck completely crosses the goal line between the goal posts and under the crossbar.

A score counts if the puck is sent into the goal by a defending player. The last player on the attacking team to touch the puck gets credit for the goal.

If the puck is deflected into the goal from the stick of an attacking player's teammate, the goal counts and the last player to touch the puck gets credit.

Any puck sent into a goal by an official does not count.

A player who scores a goal earns one point on personal scoring records. A player who *assists* (takes part in the play immediately before a goal) earns one point in the records. No more than two assists may be given for any one goal.

A *slap shot* occurs when the stick is lifted in a backswing before hitting the puck.

A *wrist shot* occurs when a stick blade stays on the ice during a scoring attempt.

A *hat trick* is when a player scores three goals in a game.

Winning

The team scoring the most points after three periods wins. In league competition, a win is worth two points in the standings.

If the score is tied, players are given a five-minute rest period (two in the NHL) and then play a 10-minute overtime period (five in the NHL). The first team to score wins.

If neither team scores in the overtime period, the game is a tie; both teams earn one point.

Note: If an NHL playoff game ends in a tie, teams play 20-minute *sudden-death* overtime periods until one team scores.

Timeouts

Each team is permitted one 30-second timeout during a game. It must be taken after play has stopped.

Classifications

Players are classified according to age, as follows:

	Male	Female
Seniors	20-up	any age
Juniors	17-19	
Midgets	16-17	16-19
Bantams	14-15	
PeeWees	12-13	13-15
Squirts	10-11	8-12
Mites	under 9	

Procedure

The home team has its choice of the goal to defend; teams change ends at the start of every period.

A game starts with a face-off at the center face-off spot and at the beginning of every period.

A face-off also starts the game again after it has been stopped for penalties or any other reasons.

The team with possession in its own defensive zone may take the puck behind its own goal one time; otherwise, the puck must always be moved forward towards the opponent's goal.

After leaving the defending zone, a player cannot pass the puck back into that zone, unless the team is below the on-ice numerical strength of the opponent.

Passes (moving the puck between players) can be executed in the following ways:

Flat pass: the puck moves along the ice surface

Flip pass: the puck travels through the air

Drop pass: the puck is left behind for a teammate

The puck may be passed by a player to a teammate within one of the three zones (attacking, neutral, defending) but it may not be passed forward from a player in one zone to a teammate in another zone. (This applies to upper age levels only.)

A defending player can make or receive forward passes from the defending zone to the center line. The puck must cross the center line before the pass receiver. (This applies to upper age levels only.)

If an attacker passes the puck backward from the attacking zone, an opponent may play the puck anywhere as long as the puck precedes the player into the attacking zone.

It is the position of the puck, not the skater, that determines from which zone the pass was made.

The pass is complete if it touches the body, skates or stick of an *onside* (legally positioned) teammate.

The player last touched by the puck is in possession of the puck; rebounds off the goalkeeper are not a change of possession.

In classifications up to and including the Junior level, the following rules apply:

- The puck may be passed to any teammate within any of the zones and may be passed from the defending zone to the neutral zone.
- If the puck precedes attacking players into their attacking zone, any player can play the puck.

Kicking the puck is allowed in all zones, but a goal cannot be scored on a direct kick from an attacking player.

A player may *bat* (stop) a puck in the air or push it on the ice with an open hand.

A player keeps playing with a broken stick if the broken part is dropped on the ice; the player must get a new stick from the bench. The goalkeeper may play with a broken stick until receiving a new one from a teammate.

Rule Violations

Icing

Icing the puck occurs when a defending player shoots or deflects the puck from the player's own side of the center line past the opponents' goal line. Play is stopped and a face-off held at the offending team's end face-off spot.

If the puck enters the goal, the score counts.

Icing is over when a puck crosses the goal line; in the NHL, icing is over when a defensive player (other than the goalkeeper) touches the puck after it has crossed the goal line.

It is not icing if the shooting player's team has fewer members on the ice than the defenders; play continues, with no face-off.

It is not icing if the puck was hit from a face-off or if, in the referee's opinion, a defender other than the goalkeeper could have played the puck before it crossed the goal line. Play continues.

Offside

An attacking player cannot precede the puck into the attacking zone; that is, a player cannot cross the blue line into the opposing team's defending zone ahead of the puck.

In Junior B and older leagues, along with the NHL, a player cannot pass the puck from that player's team's defending zone to a teammate beyond the center line.

A player is offside if both skates are past the blue line when the puck enters the same zone.

Offside does not occur and play continues if:

- The attacking player is offside but a defender reaches the puck and passes or skates with it into the neutral zone
- A player skates with or passes the puck into that player's own defending zone while an opponent is in that area
- A player crosses the line before the puck but is in control and moving the puck forward.

When an offside penalty is called, play is stopped and a face-off is held.

If the puck was carried over the blue line, a face-off is conducted at the nearest neutral zone face-off spot.

If the puck was passed over the blue line, a face-off is conducted at the place the shot was taken.

If a linesman decides that the offside play was intentional, a face-off is conducted at the end face-off spot in the defending zone of the offending team.

If the puck is out of the referee's sight, play is stopped and a face-off is held. Play does not stop if a puck touches an official.

Fouls and penalties

A penalty shot is awarded for certain fouls. The referee sets the puck on the center face-off spot.

A player taking the shot may skate with the puck in the neutral zone but, after the puck has crossed the blue line into the attacking zone, it must stay in motion to the goal line.

After the shot at goal is taken, the play is over; no goal can be scored on a rebound.

Fouls are called by the officials; players are usually penalized by spending time in the penalty box.

If a player in possession of the puck makes a foul, play is stopped by the referee and a penalty is given. If the foul is made by a player not in possession of the puck, a penalty is called but not given until the play is over.

The actual penalty depends on the foul and, sometimes, where it took place on the ice.

Penalties are categorized as follows:

Minor penalty: A two-minute suspension for the player; no substitute. The goalkeeper's penalty may be taken by a teammate.

Bench minor: Two minutes off the ice for any player (except the goalkeeper) designated to serve out the penalty time for the team.

Note: When a team is *short-handed* (fewer players on the ice than the opponent) and the opposing team scores a goal, the first of any minor penalties is canceled.

Major penalty: The offender, except a goalkeeper, goes off the ice for five minutes; no substitute allowed. A major penalty is served before a minor.

Misconduct penalty: A 10-minute suspension for any offenders, except goalkeepers. A substitute is allowed.

Note: If a player receives a minor and a misconduct penalty, a substitute serves the minor penalty.

Game misconduct penalty: A player is suspended for the game, but a substitute is allowed.

Match penalty: A player is suspended for the game and sent to the dressing room. A substitute serves the penalty time.

Goalkeeper's penalty: The penalty is served by a teammate who was on the ice when the offense occurred.

Note: After two major penalties (three in the NHL), a goalkeeper is out of the game and replaced by a substitute.

Delayed penalty: If a third player is penalized while two teammates are serving penalties, penalty time shall not start until one of the other players' time is finished. The third player goes to the penalty bench and can be replaced by a substitute.

The referee calls penalties by blowing a whistle. A face-off occurs where play was stopped, unless in the attacking zone of the offending player; then, the face-off occurs at the nearest spot in the neutral zone.

If a penalty is committed by a player on the defensive team (not in possession of the puck), the referee stops play and gives the penalty after the team with the puck completes the play.

The following violations are minor penalties:

- Unsportsmanlike conduct
- Excessive violence
- *Cross-checking* (holding the stick in both hands off the ice and blocking an opponent's movement)

- *Slashing* (hitting or trying to hit an opponent with the stick)
- Obstruction
- *Body-checking* (use of the body to block an opponent's progress)
- Delay of game
- *Freezing* (holding the puck to stop play)
- Falling on the puck, except for the goalkeeper
- Catching and holding the puck, except for the goalkeeper
- Holding an opponent with the hands or stick
- Shooting a puck after the whistle has blown
- Attacking a player other than the goalkeeper inside the goal crease area without the puck; if the puck enters the goal there is no score and a face-off in the neutral zone
- Interference with an opponent who is not in possession of the puck
- *Hooking* (using the blade end to interfere with an opponent's progress)
- Tripping

The following violations can be minor or major penalties, depending on the degree of the infraction:

- Vicious *board checking* (forcing an opponent against the boards)
- *Charging* (skates more than two steps or jumps into an opponent)
- Offensive use of the elbow or knee
- *Slashing* (swinging the stick at an opponent)
- *High sticks* (carrying or using the stick from above shoulder height)

The following violation is a minor or double minor penalty, depending on the degree of the infraction:

- Unnecessary roughness

The following violations are major penalties:

- Grabbing an opponent's face mask
- Hooking, if injury results
- *Butt-ending* (pushing the top of the stick into an opponent)

The following violations are misconduct or game misconduct penalties, depending on the degree of the infraction:

- Fighting after being ordered to stop
- Abuse of officials

The following violations are match penalties:

- Kicking another player
- Injuring or attempting to injure an opponent
- Deliberate head-butting

If an attacker has the puck beyond the center line with no defender ahead except the goalkeeper and is tripped from behind, a penalty shot is awarded after possession is lost. If the goalkeeper has been removed from the game and the attacker has no opponent and is tripped, play is stopped and a goal is given to the attacking team.

If a stick is thrown by the defending side in the defending zone, a penalty shot is awarded to the attacker if no goal was scored. If the goal is unattended and a stick is thrown by the defender, a goal is awarded. Otherwise, the player who threw the stick is assessed a minor penalty.

The penalty for *spearing* (stabbing an opponent with the point of the stick blade) is a major and game misconduct.

The penalty for *fisticuffs* (fighting) depends on the player's role. The player who starts the fight is given a major and a minor, or a major and/or game misconduct. A player who fights back is given a minor or double minor or game misconduct. Any other player involved is given a major. The first player to leave the bench is given a double minor and all others who leave the bench are given game misconducts.

The penalty for striking an official is a gross misconduct plus suspension.

An equal number of major and/or minor penalties given to opposing players at the same stoppage are *offset* (no reduction in the on-ice number of players).

Holding

Cross-checking

Tripping

Charging

Hooking

Boarding

Icing

Misconduct

Interference

183

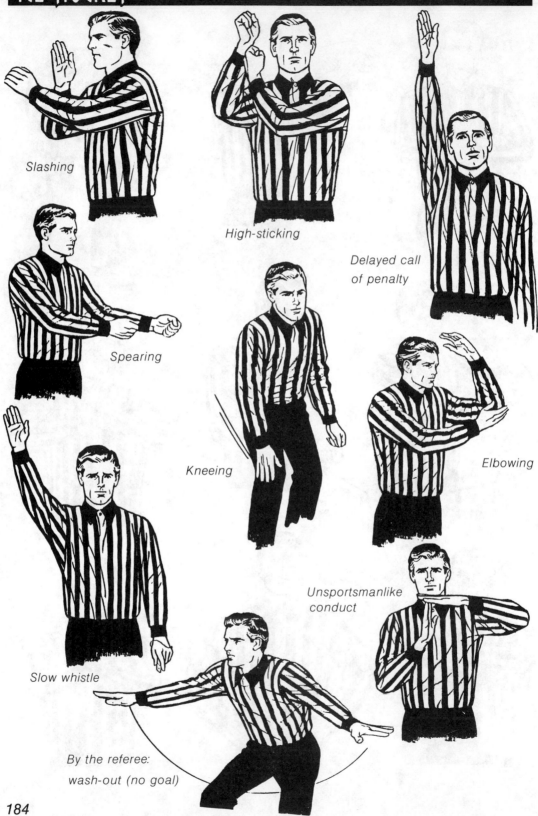

Slashing

High-sticking

Delayed call
of penalty

Spearing

Kneeing

Elbowing

Unsportsmanlike
conduct

Slow whistle

By the referee:
wash-out (no goal)

184

Officials

A referee is in charge of the game and controls players and officials.

Two linesmen watch for rule violations.

Goal judges sit above and behind each goal and flash a red goal light if a score has been made.

Other officials include the penalty timekeeper (keeps time of the players in the penalty box), the game timekeeper (tracks actual playing time) and scorer (records all game data).

Note: Only the team captains can speak to the referee on rule matters.

History

Lacrosse is the oldest sport in North America. It was originally played by Native Americans in what is now northern New York and Canada. Called **baggataway** (little brother of war), the tribal game was on a much larger scale. It was played by hundreds of players, games often lasted several days and goals were placed up to 15 miles apart. French missionaries thought the shaped stick resembled a bishop's crozier (**la crosse**) and that became the popular name for the game.

The first lacrosse club was founded in Montreal in 1842 and by 1860, standard rules for play and equipment were established that are the basis of today's sport.

Enthusiasm for the game extended to most English-speaking countries and lacrosse was often an Olympic event. Organized lacrosse is played by high school, college and club teams, in camps and in youth league (ages 5 to 16) programs. There has been particular growth of the sport among girls and women. The Lacrosse Foundation was chartered in 1959 to develop, promote and coordinate all aspects of the game.

Object of the Game

Two teams of players using long-handled *sticks* (racquets) try to throw a ball into their opponents' goal. The highest score wins.

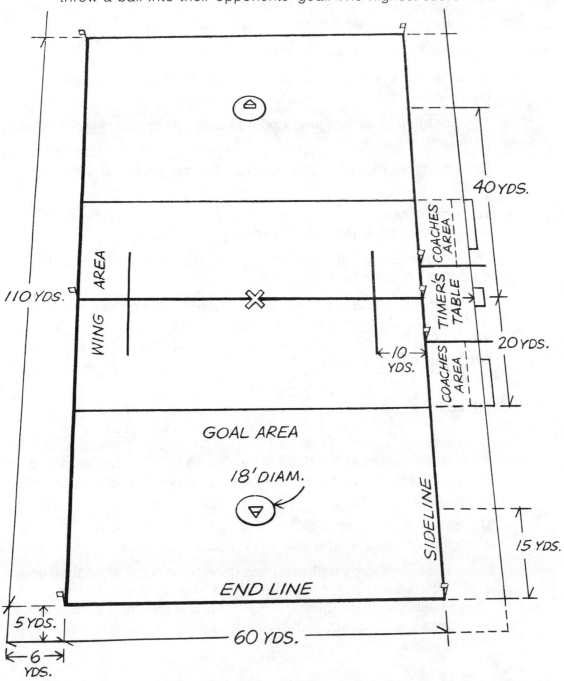

Men

Playing Field

The playing field measures 60 × 110 yards.

A *center line* runs across midfield.

A *center point* is marked with a cross at the middle of the center line.

The *goal line* is six feet long and centered 15 yards from and parallel to the end lines

The *goal area line* runs 20 yards from the center line and parallel to it.

The *goal crease* is a circle, 18 feet in diameter with a nine-foot radius, centered at the goal line midpoint.

The *wing area* runs 10 yards in from the side line and parallel to it. It extends 10 yards from each side of the center line.

The *goal* is a netted structure, six feet wide between the posts and six feet in height from the crossbar to the goal line (inside measurements). The net extends seven feet behind the crossbar. The goals are 80 yards apart.

Equipment

The **crosse** is a stick of laminated wood or synthetic material with a shaped net pocket at the head. It can be 40 to 72 inches long and 6½ to 10 inches wide, except for the goalkeeper's, which may be 12 inches wide.

The **ball** is made of solid rubber and is 7¾ to 8 inches in circumference and weighs 5 to 5¼ ounces.

Dress is according by uniform. Players on each team wear the same design shirts with numbers, shorts, socks, low-cut cleated shoes, plastic helmet with faceguard, gloves and shoulder and arm pads. Goalkeepers wear chest and throat protectors. All players wear mouthguards.

General Rules

Each team has 10 players: a goalkeeper and three defensemen, midfielders and attackers.

Each team must keep at least four players (including the goalkeeper) in its defending half of the field and three in the offensive half.

Unlimited substitutions are permitted, and may be made at any time in the game.

Games last four quarters, each 15 minutes long. Some levels might play shorter games.

Teams change ends between periods. A 10-minute break is allowed at halftime, and two-minute breaks between the first and second and third and fourth quarters.

Each team is permitted two timeouts, not to exceed two minutes, in each half. They may be called only when the ball is out of play or by the team in possession of the ball.

If the score is tied at the end of four quarters, there is a two-minute rest before a four-minute sudden death period. Each sudden death period is divided by a two-minute break. One timeout is permitted per sudden death period.

Scoring

A goal (one point) is scored after a ball has been thrown from a crosse completely over the goal line between the posts and under the crossbar.

The goal does not count if:

- The attacking player is inside the goal crease
- One or both teams is *offside* (too few players in the offensive or defensive halves of the field)
- A whistle has sounded
- The period has ended
- More than 10 attackers are in the game

The team that scores the most goals is the winner.

Procedure

The team winning the coin toss chooses which end of the field to attack.

At the start of play, four players are positioned behind their own goal area line, one at the center, two in the wing areas and three beyond the opponents' goal area line.

The ball is put into play with a *face-off*. Two opposing players crouch facing each other across the center line, with their crosses on the ground and their backs to their own goals. The referee puts the ball on the ground. The players place their sticks parallel to the center line with the ball centered on the crosse heads and their sticks not touching. Each player's head, hands and feet must be behind and to the left of the crosses' heads.

Play begins at the sound of a whistle. Each player tries to get control of the ball. The players in the wing areas can move; the others must wait until one player has the ball or the ball has crossed a goal area line.

Game play

A player may run with the ball in the crosse, and pass or catch it, but — except for the goalkeeper — may not touch the ball with a hand.

Defending players may jab or slap the stick and gloved hands of the player or hit the cross with their sticks to try to knock the ball out.

Body checking is permitted if the opponent has the ball or is within five yards of it; it must be done from the front or sides, above the waist and below the shoulder. The opponents' crosse may also be struck at if it is within five yards of a loose ball or the ball is in the air.

If a ball or player with the ball goes out of bounds, the other team gets a *free play* (possession to restart game) and the opposing players must stay five yards away. If the ball goes out of play after an unsuccessful shot at a goal, the player nearest the ball where and when it goes out is given a free play.

An attacking player cannot enter the goal crease but may reach in with the stick to catch a ball or get a loose ball.

Center faceoffs are used after a goal and at the start of each period.

Faceoffs also are held if the game is stopped, but must be at least 20 yards from a goal and 20 feet from a boundary. The player closest to the goal has his back to it; other players must be 10 yards away from the faceoff.

Fouls

Personal fouls include the following violations:

- Spearing and cross-checking
- Body checks beyond five yards of the ball
- Body checks after the ball has been thrown
- Body checks from the rear, below the waist or above the shoulders
- Reckless or dangerous use of the stick (*slashing*)
- Tripping or violent play
- Unsportsmanlike conduct

The penalty for a personal foul is a one- to three-minute suspension and a free play for the team fouled. A player with five fouls is out of game.

Technical fouls include the following violations:

- Offsides
- Touching the ball with the hands (except for the goalkeeper)
- Pushing or holding an opponent, or limiting his movement

The penalty for a technical foul is a 30-second suspension if the team fouled is in possession of the ball; otherwise, a free play is awarded to the fouled team.

Officials

A referee, an umpire and a field judge supervise field play; a chief bench official, timekeepers and scorers assist.

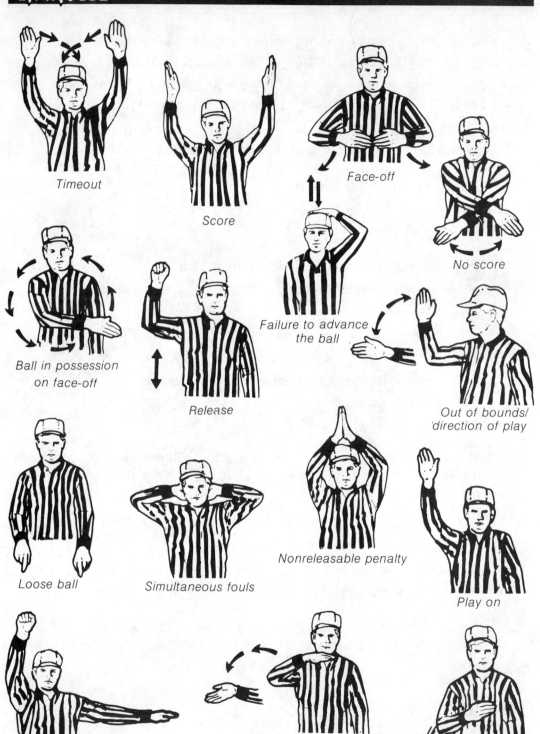

Timeout

Score

Face-off

No score

Ball in possession
on face-off

Release

Failure to advance
the ball

Out of bounds/
direction of play

Loose ball

Simultaneous fouls

Nonreleasable penalty

Play on

Stalling warning

Reentry of the crease

Counts

Personal foul

Illegal bodycheck

Slashing

Crosse checking

Tripping

Unnecessary roughness

Unsportsmanlike conduct

Illegal crosse

Illegal procedure

Expulsion foul

Technical foul

Interference

Illegal screening

Holding

Warding off

Pushing

Withholding ball from play

Stalling

Offside

Crease violations

Illegal team personnel action

Women

Playing Field

There is no official measured playing area. The boundaries are agreed on by the team captains and game officials. An area of 70 × 120 yards is desirable. There must be 10 yards behind each goal.

The *goal lines* are 6 feet, 6 inches long, with a minimum of 90 feet between each goal line.

The *goal crease* is 17 feet in diameter and is centered at the goal line midpoint.

The *goal* is the same as the men's, except the net extends six feet.

The *center line* is one foot long, midway between the goals.

The *center circle* is 20 feet in diameter from the midpoint of the center line.

Equipment

The **crosse** measures 36-44 inches in length and 7-9 inches in width. The goalkeeper's crosse is 36-48 inches long and 7-12 inches wide.

The **ball** is made of solid rubber, measures eight inches in circumference and weighs five ounces.

Dress is according to uniform. Players should wear shirts with numbers and kilts or shorts. Shoes should have leather or rubber cleats. The goalkeeper must wear a facemask and/or helmet and a throat and chest protector. Mouthguards are mandatory for all players. Gloves, nose and eye guards are permitted.

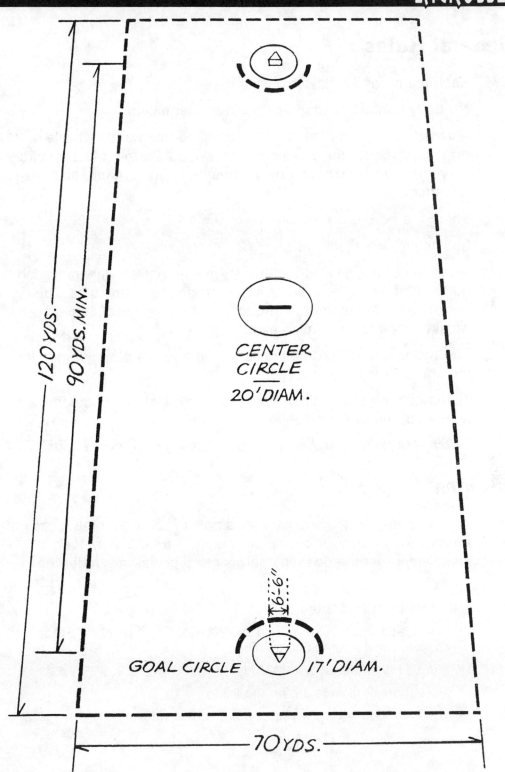

120 YDS.

90 YDS. MIN.

CENTER
CIRCLE
20' DIAM.

6'-6"

GOAL CIRCLE 17' DIAM.

70 YDS.

General Rules

Each team has 12 players.

No body contact or rough stick play is permitted.

A *stand* occurs on a dead ball. The umpire blows the whistle and no player, except the goalkeeper or a deputy within the goal circle, may move unless directed by the umpire until the game has been restarted.

There are no offside penalties.

Substitutions are unlimited.

Most games are divided into two 25-minute halves, depending on the level of play. The maximum playing time is 60 minutes. The clock is stopped after each goal throughout the game and at every whistle in the last two minutes of play.

The halftime break is 10 minutes, and the teams change ends for the start of the second half.

Timeouts are not permitted in college play; high school teams are permitted one two-minute timeout per half.

Ties are broken by six-minute sudden death overtime periods.

Scoring

A goal (one point) is scored after a ball, propelled by the crosse of an attacking player or crosse or person of a defender, goes completely over the goal line between the posts and under the crossbar.

The goal does not count if:

- The attacking player or her crosse is inside the goal circle or the crosses circle after taking the shot
- The ball is off the attacker's body
- More than 12 players are on the field
- The team that scores the most points is the winner.

Procedure

The team winning the coin toss chooses the end of the field.

The game starts with a *draw*. Two opposing players stand across the center line, each with one foot touching the line. The sticks are held back-to-back, waist high and parallel to the center line. The referee puts the ball between the crosses and calls, "Ready, draw." Players pull their sticks up and away, lifting the ball into the air. All other players must be outside the center circle.

Game play

Players may run with ball in the crosse or pass, catch or roll it, but — except for the goalkeeper — may not touch the ball with the hand. The ball may not be kicked to a team's advantage.

If the ball goes *out of bounds* (over the agreed-on boundaries), play stops and the ball is given to the nearest player. If two players from opposite teams are the same distance from the out of bounds line, the game restarts with a *throw*. The players stand side-by-side, one yard apart; the umpire, with his back to the center of the field, throws the ball high in the air for them to catch on the run. All other players stand away. No throws closer than five yards from the designated boundaries or 10 yards from a goal are permitted.

Only the goalkeeper is allowed inside the goal circle; no other player is to be inside it or reach in with her crosse. The goalkeeper can stop the ball by hand, body part, or with a crosse. If caught, the ball is to be thrown back into play with the stick.

Players may block the movement of an opponent by *body checking* (the defender shadows an opponent without body contact occurring, following each movement of the opponent's body and crosse with her body and causing her to slow down, change direction or pass off).

Fouls

Fouls include the following violations:

- Body contact
- Blocking
- Kicking or holding the ball with a foot
- Touching ball with a hand (except for the goalkeeper)
- Moving into the goal circle, charging, tripping or any dangerous play.

Fouls are penalized with a *free position*. The player who has been fouled or another team member gets the ball in her crosse at the place of the foul and may run or throw at the sound of the whistle. All other players must be at least five yards away.

Officials

An umpire and a referee officiate the game.

History

Although hitting a ball with a hand or club is one of the oldest of
sports, the origins of paddleball appear to be from the beginning of
the 20th century. Handball was quite popular at that time, but the
hard ball often caused sore hands. Dr. Frank Beale of Brooklyn,
N.Y. created a *paddle stick* to use to hit a ball against a wall. In the
1930s, Earl Riskey, Director of Intramural Sports at the University of
Michigan, invented four-wall paddleball as a game that tennis
players could use for practice indoors on handball courts. He
soaked a tennis ball in gasoline and stripped off its fuzzy cover to
get one that would be light and have more bounce. Wooden
paddles replaced racquets. The game was first called "paddle tennis
on the court." During World War II, Army recruits training at
Michigan learned the sport and it eventually spread to other parts of
the country.

The one-wall game is the version most often played, especially in
the eastern states. As with racquetball, the sport has greatly
expanded because it is simple, yet highly competitive, and requires
little equipment. The American Paddleball Association issues rules
and promotes the sport to both active and casual participants.

Object of the Game

Two players or teams using short-handled paddles try to hit a ball to a wall by serving or returning the ball in a way that the other side cannot return it to the wall before it bounces twice on the floor. The first player or team to score 21 points wins the game.

Playing Field

The court is the same as in racquetball. (See racquetball chapter.)

Equipment

The **paddle** is made of wood, with a maximum length of 17½ inches and a maximum width of nine inches. A wrist thong is optional.

The **ball** is made of rubber. It is 1⅞ inches in diameter and weighs 2³⁄₁₀ ounces. A racquetball may be used.

Dress is informal; white or light clothing is preferred. Doubles team members must wear similar clothing. Safety equipment is allowed.

General Rules

Singles matches are played by two players. Doubles matches are played by four players.

Cut throat matches are played by three players, with the server playing against the other pair. On loss of serve, the players rotate clockwise.

Points can only be scored by the serving side. One point is scored when an *ace* is served (the ball bounces twice before the receiver can return it) or when the serving side wins a *rally* (the exchange of shots that decides a point).

The first side to score 21 points (or another pre-determined score, such as 15, 25 or 30) wins the game. All games must be won by two points.

The first side to win two games out of three wins the match.

If each side wins one game, the third game is won by the first side to score 11 points (or 15 points if agreed upon.)

Opposing sides must take turns hitting the ball during a rally but players on the same side in doubles play need not alternate hits.

A player may only hit the ball with the paddle, which cannot be switched between hands except in a one-wall game.

Each side can swing and miss until the ball bounces twice.

Each side is allowed three timeouts of one-minute during each game. Injured players are given 15 minutes to return or retire.

A rest period of five minutes is allowed between the first two games; 10 minutes is permitted after the second game.

Substitutions are not allowed.

Procedure

The winner of the coin toss chooses to serve or receive. Whoever serves first in the first game serves first in the third game.

Serving

The server stands in the service zone with both feet inside or on the lines. The paddle may extend over the lines.

Before each serve, the server calls out the score.

The server bounces the ball one time inside the zone and then hits it to the front wall. The serve can be sent to any part of the court and need not be alternated between opponents.

In a one-wall or three-wall game, the server's partner stands off the court between the short line and the service line. In a four-wall game, the server's partner stands in the service box, back to the side wall.

The server and his partner stay in the serving zone until the ball rebounds back over the short line. The partner cannot come on to the court until the ball has passed the line. In three-wall and four-wall games, the ball may first touch a side wall.

In singles play, the opponent must be shown which side of the server the ball will return. The court is divided into three imaginary sections (1) the *automatic fault area* — the lane that passes through the outside right and left foot positions of the server, (2) the *major service area* — the larger of the two remaining sections, either at left or right and (3) the *minor service area* — the smaller section.

When the automatic fault area is centered on the court, both the other service areas are minor. If the automatic area is along a sideline, the rest of the court is called major. A player can serve to either major or minor service areas but must point to the minor area if that is where the serve will be directed.

In singles, a player continues to serve as long as points are scored. In doubles, the team partners serve one after the other; that is, both players on a side must lose their service before the serve passes over to the opposing team. Exception: on the first serve in a game, the serve goes to the other side after the initial server fails to score.

A serve is lost if a player makes two consecutive illegal serves. Illegal serves include the following violations:

- The ball rebounds off the front wall and hits the floor before crossing the short line (*short serve*)
- The ball goes over the end line and hits the back wall (*long serve*)
- The ball hits the ceiling or hits two walls before it hits the floor
- The ball goes out of the court before bouncing twice on the floor
- The server or partner leaves the service zone before the ball passes the short line

Certain service errors, called *serve outs*, mean an immediate loss of service. They include the following violations:

- Bouncing the ball three times before serving
- Hitting the ball before it bounces
- Swinging at the ball and missing
- Serving out of turn
- Hitting the ball out of the court
- Hitting the ball twice while serving
- Serving the ball and hitting the partner who is out of the service box, unless the ball is short

And, except for one-wall:

- The ball touching the body or side wall when it is bounced
- The ball hitting the front wall and another surface at the same time
- The ball hitting another surface before it hits the front wall
- Obstructing the opponent's view and/or stroke on the rebound

Service returns

The receiver must stay nine feet behind the service line and return the ball before crossing the service line with the body or paddle.

A served ball may be returned to the front wall before it bounces on the floor or after one bounce. If the rebound is played on the fly, no part of the receiver's body may cross the short line.

Except in a one-wall game, a served ball may be returned directly to the front wall or after touching one or both side walls, the back wall or the ceiling — but it cannot touch the floor.

A return is good even if both partners hit the ball at the same time.

Failure to return a served ball before it touches the floor twice scores a point for the server.

After a serve is returned, players can be anywhere on the court.

Play continues with each side hitting alternately until one player cannot return the ball to the front wall.

A side loses a rally if a player:

- Hits the ball twice consecutively
- Touches the ball
- Hits a partner with the ball
- *Intentionally hinders* (purposely interferes with) opponents by pushing or blocking or moving into the way of a ball just hit
- A point is replayed for *unintentional hinders* (unavoidable obstruction or body contact) if a player moves illegally and is hit by the opponent's ball or if the ball breaks or goes out of play because of the court condition.
- If the serving side fails to score, the receivers get to serve and another rally begins.

Blocks

A block occurs if a player interferes with an opponent's play. A player must call out "block" and not swing the racquet if there is a danger of hitting an opponent. A referee decides between a replay or loss of point or service.

An opponent may call "block" if interfered with but continue to play. The referee will confirm or deny.

The referee also can call "block" for safety reasons or deliberate obstruction incidents.

Penalties

A point is awarded or service is lost for the following violations:

- A ball struck out-of-bounds
- A returned ball that hits the floor before it hits the front wall
- An improper return
- Serving out of turn

Officials

The referee controls the match. A scorer and linesperson are optional.

History

Paddle tennis was invented in 1898 in Albion, MI by the Reverend Frank P. Beals for children not yet old enough for lawn tennis. His original court was 18 × 39 feet (about half the size of a tennis court) and he replaced the strung racquet with a wooden paddle. A hard rubber ball was used instead of a tennis ball. He brought the concept to New York City when his ministry was transferred to Greenwich Village, where the sport became popular. The U.S. Paddle Tennis Association was formed in 1926. A larger court was specified in 1937 but youths under 15 still play in the smaller area.

Object of the Game

Two or four players using short paddles try to hit a *deadened* (punctured) tennis ball over a net so that it cannot be successfully returned.

Playing Field

The playing court is 50 feet long at the side line and 20 feet wide at the base line.

The *service line* is three feet in front of the base line.

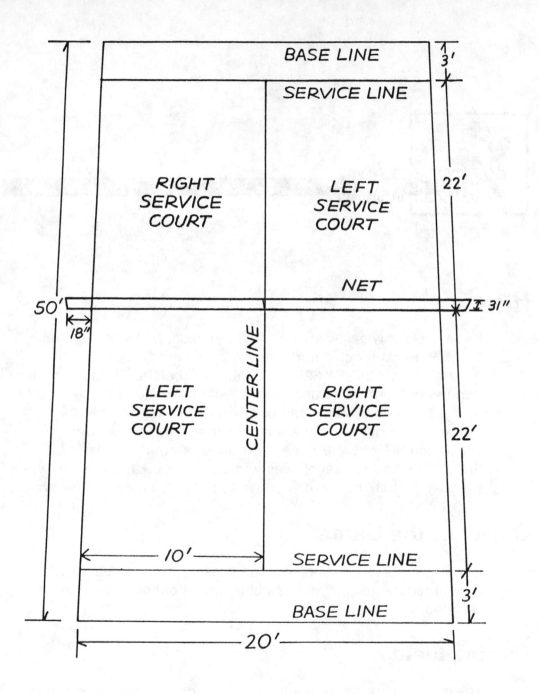

The court is divided into four *service courts*, each 22 feet long and 10 feet wide. The *center line* is 44 feet long and connects the service lines.

The *net* is 23 feet long and 31 inches high. It is connected to posts that extend 18 inches beyond the side lines.

Equipment

The **paddle** is made of a solid surface or perforated with small holes; it is not strung. It has a maximum length of 17½ inches and a maximum width of 8½ inches.

The **ball** is a tennis ball that is punctured to reduce the internal pressure. If dropped from a height of six feet, the ball should bounce from 31 to 33 inches.

Dress is informal, similar to tennis. Court footwear is required.

General Rules

Play is the same as tennis in procedure, scoring and all rules of play, with some exceptions.

Serving:

> One underhand serve is permitted. If the serve is a *fault*, the server loses the point.

> The server is to stand with both feet behind the baseline and lined up with a service court. Only two steps may be taken during the serve. Neither foot can move into or over any area in front of the baseline until the racket hits the ball.

> The server may bounce the ball off the court surface behind the base line and hit it before it reaches net height, 31 inches. Or, the server may throw the ball into the air and hit it with the paddle at a point not higher than 31 inches. Whichever serving method is used at the start must be continued for the entire set of games. Players can switch service methods at the beginning of a new set.

Returning:

> In singles play, the serve must be played by the receiver after one bounce. After that, it can be returned as a *volley* (on the fly).

History

Platform tennis was invented in the winter of 1928-29 by two Scarsdale, NY men — F. S. Blanchard and James K. Cogswell. They had originally built an elevated platform for badminton that was easy to clear of snow. Winter winds made play difficult so they created a new game that used paddle tennis paddles and sponge rubber balls. They called it "mini-tennis." Fencing was added around the former badminton court when the men tired of getting off and on the platform to chase balls.

An organization was formed in 1934 to support the sport, and in 1950 it became the American Platform Tennis Association. The game became nationally popular in the 1970s when tournaments were televised and gran prix tours established for men and women.

Object of the Game

Four players in a screened-in court use short paddles to score points by hitting a ball over a net and in a way that it cannot be successfully returned.

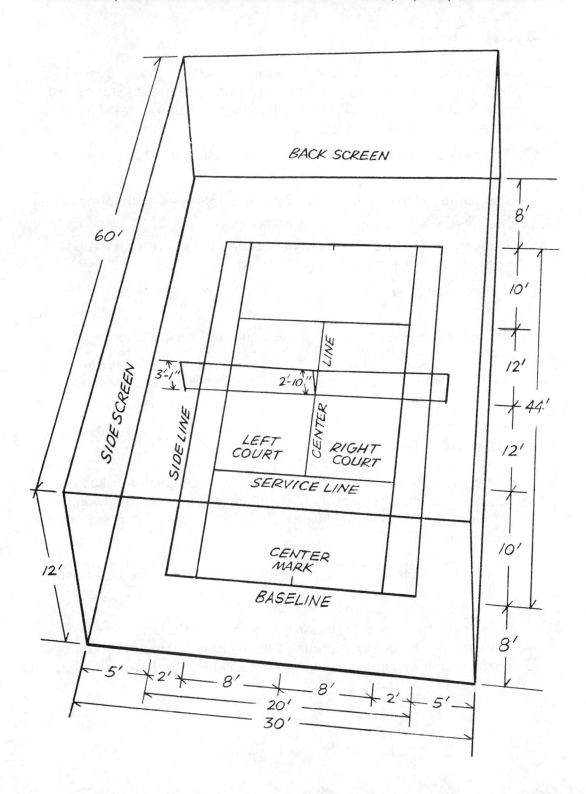

BACK SCREEN

8'

10'

12'

44'

12'

10'

8'

60'

SIDE SCREEN

SIDE LINE

3'-1"

2'-10"

CENTER LINE

LEFT COURT

RIGHT COURT

SERVICE LINE

CENTER MARK

BASELINE

12'

5' | 2' | 8' | 8' | 2' | 5'

20'

30'

Playing Field

The *court* is a wood surface on a raised platform that is 30 × 60 feet. It is surrounded by a 12-foot high wire screen that stands five feet from the side lines and eight feet from the base lines. The playing area is 20 × 44 feet.

The *service lines* are 10 feet inside the base line, 12 feet from the net.

The *center service line* is parallel to the side lines and connects the service lines.

The *center line* is a four-inch mark inside the court from the base lines, midway between the singles side lines.

The *service area* is between the service lines and net and is 12 × 8 feet.

The *back court* is between the base line and service line.

The *net* is made of cord, across the midpoint of the court parallel to the base lines. It is 34 inches high in the center, 37 inches high at the supporting side posts.

Equipment

The **paddle** for platform tennis is made of wood, metal or fiberglass. It has a maximum length of 18 1/16 inches and a maximum width of 9 5/16 inches. It is perforated with 3/8-inch holes, of which there are a maximum of 87.

The **ball** is made of solid sponge rubber, is fuzzy-coated and usually is yellow. It is 2½ inches in diameter and weighs 70 to 75 grams.

Dress is casual; court footwear is required. Platform tennis is primarily played outdoors during the winter months; appropriate cold weather clothing, including gloves, is permitted.

General Rules

The game is similar to tennis, but played with a paddle. The ball may be hit off the wire walls around the court after first landing within the playing area defined by the side lines and the base line. The only other difference is that just one serve is permitted.

Doubles play, with two players per team, is most common. Singles play usually is limited to recreational play, but there are national singles championships.

The ball may be played off one or more screens.

Scoring and winning are the same as tennis, except for a 12-point tiebreaker.

Procedure

The player winning the coin toss has the choice of service or side, as in tennis.

Serving

Serving is similar to tennis, with the following exceptions:
- Only one serve is allowed
- The server loses a point for a service fault or foot fault
- A let service is repeated

Receiving and play

The game is the same as tennis after the service except that the wire screens may be used to keep the ball in play.

Points are won and lost as in tennis.

Officials

The APTA appoints officials for national championships.

History

Quoits is recorded as one of the five events in the ancient Greek pentathlon. It may have been adapted from discus throwing as a sport for more casual participants. It was popular with soldiers of the Roman army, who spread it throughout their empire. Similar to horseshoe pitching, it became a peasant's pastime. Eventually, quoits was adopted by landowners and the general population as an outdoor competition that required little space, equipment or experience.

Today, it is played by all age groups and is considered an excellent entry into the target sport games.

Object of the Game

Players throw rings at stakes in the ground, trying to encircle them or land as close as possible. The first player to score 21 points wins the contest.

Playing Field

The court has no standard size. It should be approximately 6 × 60 feet, but it may be shorter.

The *mott* is a stake or peg, also called a *hob*. There is no regulation height; they are set 54 feet apart in tournament play.

The *target* is a white circle, four to five inches in diameter around the mott.

Equipment

A **quoit** is a metal ring, approximately eight inches in diameter, and weighs about three pounds. It may also be made of hard rubber or rope for use in shorter distances.

Dress is casual.

General Rules

The game is played by two (singles) or four (doubles) contestants.

A quoit that lands over the mott scores two points.

A quoit that lands closer to the mott than the opponent's scores one point.

Note: A quoit leaning against a mott has the same value (one point) as a quoit flat on the ground or other close quoit.

Games are played to 21 points. If the score is tied at 20, play continues until one side wins by two points.

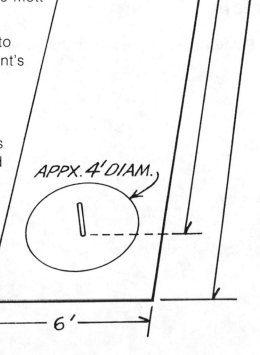

54'

60'

APPX. 4' DIAM.

6'

Procedure

A coin toss or quoit throw (closest to the mott) determines the start. The winner has a choice of throwing first in the game.

In singles play:

> Both players stand behind a mott at the same end of the court. One player throws two quoits at the mott at the other end; the opponent then throws. The players walk to the target area and record their scores. The player with the highest score throws the first quoit back to the original mott. If the score is tied, the player who did not throw first in the previous toss begins. The cycle is repeated until the game ends.

In doubles play:

> One partner stands behind the mott at each end of the court. Two quoits are thrown in alternate tosses by each player from one end. The scores are recorded. The quoits are thrown back, in turn, by the partners. (No walking is necessary between motts.) Partners scores are added. The cycle is repeated until the game ends.

Officials

Referees are not required; the players resolve any disputes.

History

Racquetball, the newest of the racquet games, has had great growth in the past 50 years. It was developed in the 1940s by a Connecticut squash and tennis pro who realized that paddleball could be a totally different kind of game if played with a strung racquet instead of a solid one. A racquet was designed and a ball selected that made the game fast and physically demanding.

Following its introduction at a YMCA as *paddle-rackets*, the game spread across the country. The rules, somewhat like handball and paddleball, were standardized and the first championships were held in 1969. The American Amateur Racquetball Association, representing over 10 million players, is recognized by the United States Olympic Committee as the national governing body for the sport. Amateur racquetball is played on many levels of skill at schools, clubs, and private and public courts.

Object of the Game

Two players or teams take turns hitting a ball with short-handled racquets to a wall by serving or returning the ball in a manner that the other side cannot keep the ball in play. The first player or team to score 15 points wins.

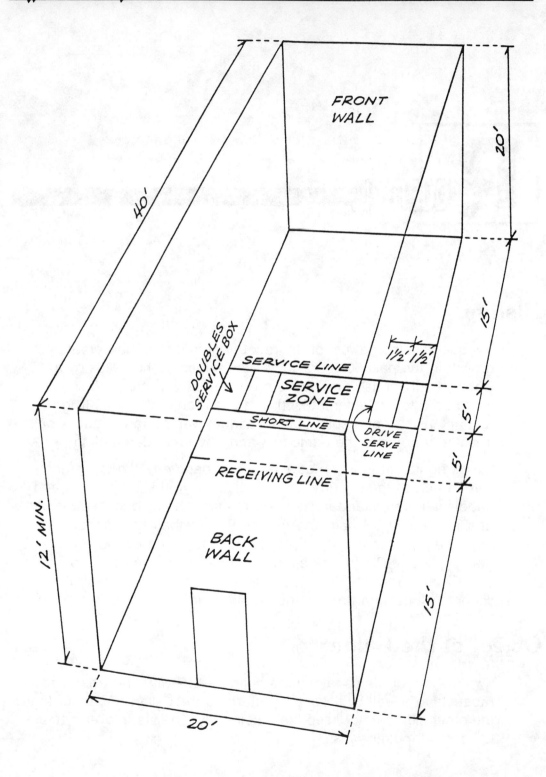

Playing Field

Four-wall court

The court is 20 × 40 feet, with a ceiling.

The *front and side walls* are 20 feet high and the **back wall** is a minimum of 12 feet high.

The *service line* is 15 feet from the front wall.

The *short line* is 20 feet from the front wall, midway between the front and back walls.

The *receiving line* is 25 feet from the front wall.

The *service zone* is a five-foot area between the service and short lines.

The *services boxes* in the service zone are 18 inches from each side wall.

One-wall court

The court is 20 × 34 feet, with no ceiling.

The *wall* is 16 feet high.

The *short line* is 16 feet from the wall, and defines the front court.

The *long line* is 18 feet behind the short line, and defines the back court.

The *service markers* are six inches long, midway between the short and long lines.

The *service zone* is the area between the short line and service lines.

Three-wall court

The court has the same size and markings as the one-wall court, and has two side walls from the top of the front wall to a point 12 feet above each side line at the short line.

RACQUETBALL

Equipment

The **racquet** is made of various materials, is stringed, has a maximum length of 21 inches and has a wrist thong.

The **ball** is made of rubber, is 2¼ inches in diameter and weighs 1.4 ounces.

Dress is informal; white or light clothing is preferred; protective eyegear is required.

General Rules

Matches can be played between two players (singles) or four players (doubles). *Cut throat* is played between three players; the server plays against the other two. On loss of serve, one of the receivers becomes the server.

Points can only be made by the serving side. One point is scored when an *ace* is served (the ball bounces twice before the receiver can return it) or when the serving side wins a *rally* (the exchange of shots that decides a point.)

The first side to score 15 points wins a game. The first side to win two games wins a match. Ties are broken by playing to 11.

Opposing players or teams must take turns hitting ball during a rally, but players on the same team need not alternate hits.

A player may only hit the ball with the racquet, which must remain firmly attached with the wrist thong.

A player can swing and miss until the ball bounces twice.

Timeouts last 30 seconds. Each side is awarded three per game (two in a tiebreaker). The injured player is given 15 minutes to return or retire.

A rest period of two minutes is permitted between the first two games; 5 minutes after the second game.

Substitutions are not allowed.

Procedure

The winner of a coin toss has the option of serving first or receiving. The first server in a tiebreaker is the player scoring the most points in the first two games.

The server stands in the service zone with both feet inside or on the lines. The racquet may extend over the lines.

Before each serve, the server calls out the score (when there is no referee).

The server bounces the ball one time and then hits it to the front wall. The serve can be sent to any part of the court and need not be alternated between opponents.

In a four-wall game, the server's doubles partner stands in the service box with his/her back to the wall. In a one-wall or three-wall game, the partner stands off the court between the short line and the service line.

The server and partner must stay in the zone until the ball rebounds back over the short line. In three-wall and four-wall games, the ball may first touch a side wall.

In singles, a player continues to serve as long as points are scored. In doubles, team partners serve one after the other; that is, both players on a side must lose their service before the serve passes over to the opposing team. Exception: On the first serve in a game, the serve goes to the other side after the initial server fails to score.

Serving

A *fault serve* is a service error that allows a second attempt. If two consecutive faults occur, serve is lost to the opponent.

A fault occurs when:

- The ball rebounds off the front wall and hits the floor in front of the short line (*short serve*)
- The ball goes over the end line or hits the back wall before touching the floor (*long serve*)
- The ball hits the ceiling (*ceiling serve*) or both side walls (*three-wall serve*) before hitting the floor

- The ball goes out of the court (*out-of-court serve*) before bouncing twice on the floor
- The receiver's view of the ball is blocked by the server's body
- The server or partner leave the service zone before the ball passes the short line on the rebound
- The server commits a *foot fault* (leaves the service zone before the ball comes back across the short line)

An *out serve* is an illegal serve that results in the immediate loss of service to the opponent. It occurs when:

- The server bounces the ball three times before serving
- The server hits the ball before it bounces
- The server swings at the ball and misses
- The server touches the ball with a body part during the serve or on the rebound
- The server hits the ball out of the court
- The ball hits the front wall and another surface at the same time
- The ball hits another surface before it hits the front wall

A *dead ball serve* is replayed with no penalty. It occurs when the ball rebounds and hits the server's partner standing in the box before it touches the floor.

Returning

The receiver must stay behind the receiving line until the ball either crosses the receiving line or else touches the floor. A violation results in a point for the server.

The served ball must be returned before it bounces on the floor a second time.

After being struck, the ball must travel on the fly to the front wall without touching the floor. The ball may touch any combination of walls and the ceiling, but not the floor.

Failure to return a served ball before it touches the floor twice or hitting the ball to the floor before it receives the front wall scores a point for the server.

Rallies

After a serve is returned, the players can be anywhere on the court. Play continues with both sides hitting alternately until one player cannot return the ball to the front wall without touching the floor first.

Play is stopped when an interference seriously limits a player.

A *deadball hinder* is one in which no one is at fault and results in a replay with no penalty.

An *avoidable hinder*is one in which one player could have done something to prevent the interference. The affected player is declared the winner of the rally.

Penalties

A point is awarded or service is lost for the following violations:

- The ball is struck out-of-bounds without first touching the front wall
- A returned ball hits the floor before hitting the front wall
- An improper return
- Switching the racquet between hands
- Serving out of turn
- A technical foul is unsportsmanlike conduct that may result in a warning, or, if the conduct is severe, the deduction of a point. Extremely offensive behavior may cause forfeit of the match.

Officials

A referee controls the match. Two line judges are optional.

History

The modern roller skate, whose design provided great freedom of movement, was invented in the 1860s by an American, James Plympton. The first ball bearing skate was introduced in 1884. Roller hockey — a non-contact sport that combines skating ability with ball control — was born and developed in England near the end of the 19th century. Beginning around 1900, the game, then called *rink hockey*, was organized into local leagues and an association was formed. A 1912 photograph shows Charlie Chaplin as a playing member of a celebrity team of that era.

The sport soon spread to other countries, including the United States, about the same time. The first European championship was in 1926 and the first world championship was held 10 years later in Germany. The American program did not have an officially-recognized national championship until 1966, when it joined the world federation, FIRS. Roller Hockey became a full medal sport in the U.S. Olympic Festival and appeared in the Pan American Games in 1979, was one of the charter sports in the World Games and had demonstration status at the 1992 Olympics in Barcelona.

The U. S. Amateur Confederation of Roller Skating is the national governing body that promotes the sport, issues rules, hosts competitions and offers development opportunities for male and female players. It also manages a special program that uses a softer ball and a smaller rink that is especially popular with younger boys and girls.

The following rules are for the sport as played in the USA; the international game has some different regulations.

Standard Ball Roller Hockey

Object of the Game

Two teams of five players wearing roller skates and using curved sticks compete on a non-slippery surface and try to move a ball into their opponent's goal. The side that scores the most points wins.

Field of Play

The *rink* is a flat and level surface of wood, asphalt, concrete or other material; it can be indoors or outside. It measures 62 × 112 feet minimum, and 66 × 132 feet maximum. It is surrounded by a retaining barrier with a preferred height of three feet. The size of the rink may vary but the ratio of length to width must be 2:1.

A *center line* divides the rink in half

A *center spot* is at the center of the rink

A *center circle* with a radius of 9 feet, 10 inches is around the center spot

Penalty spots are 17 feet, 9 inches in front of each goal

Four *base spots* are at each end of the rink. Two are 39 feet, 11 inches apart, even with the goal, and two are 39 feet, 11 inches apart, even with the penalty spot

The *penalty area* is a rectangle between the base spots, 39 feet, 11 inches wide by 17 feet, 9 inches long

Optional *base spot circles* with a radius of 9 feet, 10 inches are around the base spots

An *anti-play line* is 72 feet from each end

The *goalkeeper's penalty line* is 61 inches long, 20 inches in front of the goal

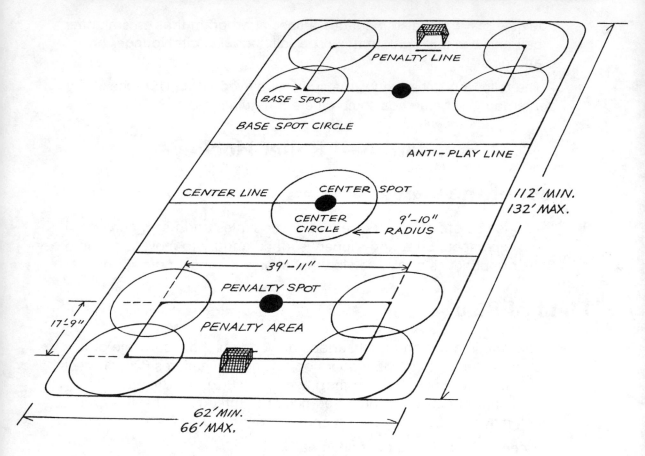

The *goal line* is between the vertical posts at the front of the goal cage

The *goal cage* is a rectangular metal or wood frame with a white wood front and a string net; the inside measurements are 3 feet, 5½ inches tall, 5 feet, 1 inch wide, 1 foot, 2 inches deep at the top and 3 feet, 1 inch deep at the bottom, and the rear of the goal should be 1 foot, 8 inches from the end of the rink

Equipment

The **sticks** can be made of wood or plastic, with no metal parts. They have a minimum length of three feet and a maximum length of 3 feet, 9 inches. The maximum diameter is two inches and the maximum weight is 10 ounces. A binding on the shaft is permitted.

The **ball** is made of hard, black rubber and has a cork center. It has a circumference of nine inches and weighs 5.5 ounces.

The **roller skates** are attached to boots. The wheels have a minimum diameter of 1⅜ inches. There are toe stops at the front of each skate.

Players wear uniforms consisting of a shirt/jersey, shorts and stockings; headbands are allowed. Protective equipment includes shin pads, knee pads and a helmet with a chin strap.

The goalkeepers wear helmets with face masks, shoulder and arm guards, leg pads and gloves with fingers.

General Rules

A team consists of four players and one goalkeeper, plus any number of substitutes. The team captain is the only player allowed contact with the officials.

Players can be changed while the game is in progress, but the departing player must be off the rink before the replacement player enters the game. Goalkeepers can change only when game play is stopped.

Players are divided into age groups as follows:

Midgets: under 12
Freshmen: 11 and not yet 15
Sophomore: 14 and not yet 18
Women: 14 and older
Bronze: men and women, 25 and older
Silver: men, 16 and older (based on experience)
Gold: 16 and older (based on experience)

The length of the games varies according to the age group, as follows:

Gold: two 20-minute halves
Silver: two 15-minute halves
Bronze, Women, Sophomores: two 12-minute halves
Freshmen, Midgets: two 10-minute halves

All levels include a 10-minute rest period between halves.

Each team is permitted one one-minute timeout during a game. Either the captain or coach can request the timeout, but the team must have possession of the ball.

In the last two minutes of the game, if the score is tied or only one point separates the teams, the clock is stopped each time the referee's whistle sounds and is restarted when play resumes.

If the game ends in a tie, a rest of three minutes is followed by two overtime periods of five minutes each. Goals are changed between periods. No timeouts or additional rest intervals are permitted. The first team to score wins the game.

If the score remains tied, each team takes 10 direct penalty shots. Shots are taken in alternate turns by five players on each team. A coin toss determines which team starts first. The team scoring the most points wins.

If the score is still tied, the outcome is determined by players from each team taking alternate penalty shots until one team scores and the other fails to score. A single player may take one, some or all of the shots for the team.

Any team which takes a lead of eight points during the game is declared the winner at that point.

Procedure

The team captains meet for a coin toss. The winner chooses the rink end or possession of the ball.

The ball is placed on the center spot to start each period.

The team that starts the first half does not start the second half; overtime periods use the same sequence as the regulation game.

After every goal, play is started at the center spot by the team that did not score.

At center spot starts, all players must be on their own team's side of the center line. Only one player from each team is allowed inside the center circle. The player who is to start must remain still. At the whistle, a player may hit the ball in any direction; if the player hesitates, the opposing player may play the ball first.

Whenever play is stopped, it is restarted by a *face-off*. The referee indicates the point where play begins. If a stoppage occurs inside the penalty area or behind the goal, a face-off is held from the corner spot nearest to the place where the play ended.

Two opposing players stand facing each other with their backs to their own goal and their sticks resting on the rink surface eight inches from where the referee placed the ball.

At the whistle, players can hit the ball; a penalty is given for playing the ball before the whistle.

The ball may only be played with the stick, which cannot be raised above the height of the shoulders. A player can raise the stick over the shoulders (to wind up before hitting or in follow-through) when it does not endanger another player.

Inside either penalty area, the ball can only be played with the stick and may be stopped with the skate or any part of the body, but not with the hand.

When shooting or passing, a player cannot *chop* (hit the ball with the sharp edge of the stick's blade). The ball may only be hit with the flat parts of the edge.

The ball must not rise above 4 feet, 8 inches, except when deflected by a goalkeeper or from a ricochet off two sticks outside the penalty area. The ball's height limit for Midgets and Juniors is 3 feet, 7 inches.

A player cannot kick, pick up, carry, push or pull the ball with any body part or skate.

The goalkeeper may play the ball within the penalty area with any part of the body, including the hands, even if down on the surface. The goalkeeper cannot kneel, sit or crawl around the front of the goal, except when actually stopping a shot, and must get back up on skates without delay.

If the ball gets caught in a goalkeeper's pad or in the outside of the netting, the ball is *dead* (out of play); a face-off is taken from the nearest base spot.

A player cannot play the ball:

- If a skate is damaged
- Without a stick
- With any part of the body touching the rink (does not apply to the goalkeeper)
- While holding the barrier or goal cage
- While standing still behind the goal cage

If the ball goes out of the rink, the opposing team is given an indirect free hit 2 feet, 6 inches from the point at the barrier where it went out.

The referee awards a face-off if the ball has ricocheted off two sticks or if there is uncertainty as to which team sent the ball out of play.

Anti-play is not trying to win or score. The anti-play line defines the attacking zones of the teams. No team may keep the ball in its own anti-play area (not in the attacking zone) for more than 10 seconds. The rule does not apply when one or more opponents are in the anti-play zone of the opposing team within the count. The violation allows a free hit from the front corner of the penalty area nearest to where the ball was when the 10 seconds expired.

Scoring

A goal (one point) is scored when the ball has completely crossed the goal line.

A score counts if the ball is sent by a player into the player's own team's goal, either off a stick or body part or equipment.

Fouls and Penalties

Players are not allowed to charge, fight, trip, kick, tackle, obstruct, push or grab an opponent with the arms.

Hitting or hooking a player with a stick is an act of violence and is forbidden.

The game is to be stopped for any rule violation and the offending team penalized. If the stoppage is to the advantage of the offending team (the *advantage rule*), the referee allows play to continue.

Fouls will be penalized according to the circumstances.

Indirect free hit

An indirect free hit (usually called a *free hit*) is awarded by the referee to a player when a member of the opposing team has committed an infraction.

The ball is to be stationary.

Opposing players must be 10 feet away; teammates may be anywhere on the rink.

The player making the hit may not play the ball again until it has been touched by another player of either side.

A goal cannot be scored directly from a free hit; it must be first touched by any other player.

Free hits from outside the penalty area are taken from the place where the foul was committed.

Free hits awarded inside the penalty area or behind the goal are taken from the nearest corner spot; opposing players must be outside the base spot circle.

Direct free hit

A direct free hit is awarded for serious fouls (such as rough play, punching, violent or dangerous tackling) or after a player has been expelled from the game.

All players except the one taking the hit and the defending goalkeeper must be 16 feet in back of the ball.

The goalkeeper must be behind the penalty line but the stick may be in front of it.

Only the player taking the hit can move before the referee's whistle.

A goal scored from a direct free hit is good without any other player touching the ball.

A player taking the hit does not have to shoot directly at the goal; the ball can be *dribbled* (moved forward using the stick) in an attempt to beat the goalkeeper.

A penalty shot is awarded to the opposing team if any member of the defending team commits a serious foul inside the penalty area.

The shot is taken from the penalty spot.

All players except the one taking the hit and the defending goalkeeper must be in back of the center line.

The player taking the hit and the goalkeeper's positions are as in a direct free hit, except that all other players must be behind the center line and cannot move until the whistle.

A player may take a direct shot or dribble to the goal.

After a shot, the player cannot play again unless the ball hits the goalkeeper, the outside of the goal cage or another player.

A ball rebounded off the barrier cannot be replayed until touched by another player.

If the player decides to dribble, instead of shooting directly, the ball can be passed to a teammate and/or replayed from a barrier without being touched by another player or the goal.

Officials

The referee is in total control of the game. Three cards are used, as follows:

- Yellow: first warning
- Blue: the player is sent off the rink for two to five minutes and can be replaced
- Red: the player is out of the game and the next game and cannot be replaced

Two goal judges signal scores to the referee by raising a flag or arms.

Two timekeepers clock the game and penalties.

Standard Softball and Junior Olympic Roller Hockey

This version is a non-contact game played between two teams with equipment specially designed for safety. Each team tries to shoot the ball into the opponents' cage to score a goal. The team with the most points after two periods wins.

Field of Play

The *rink* is a rectangular, flat, level, non-slippery playing surface. It measures 70 × 140 feet maximum and has a retaining barrier. The rink can be smaller, but the ratio of length to width should be 2:1.

Markings include a *center spot* that is an equal distance from the side and end barriers, and two *imaginary lines* parallel to and three feet inside the side barriers for free hits and face-offs. The *penalty spot* is 12 feet from the mouth of the goal.

The *goal cage* is a tubular frame with a mesh netting that is 60 inches wide and 44 inches high. It is set three to six feet from each end.

Equipment

The **sticks** are tubular plastic, 44.8 inches in length and weighing less than one pound. The stick may be shortened, if necessary.

The **ball** is soft, flexible plastic with a circumference of 9.75 inches. It should have little bounce.

The **skates** are the in-line or conventional *quad* style with four wheels and a toe-stop.

Dress is by uniform. Players wear short-sleeved shirts, shorts and high socks.

Protective equipment includes a sports cup for boys and an optional molded plastic helmet, shin guards, knee pads and gloves.

Goalkeepers must wear a face mask.

General Rules

Teams consist of five players, including the goalkeeper. A maximum of five substitutions are permitted.

Teams may be all-boy, all-girl or co-ed; games can be played between any combination of teams (such as co-ed vs. all-boy).

Teams are categorized by age, as follows:

Standard Softball
Freshmen — under 12
Junior — 12 to 15
Senior — 16 and older

Junior Olympic
Division A — under 10
Division B — 9 but not 14
Division C — 13 but not yet 18
Division D — 17 and older

The Game

Rules and procedures generally follow Standard Roller Hockey, with the following differences:

- Games consist of two eight-minute periods with a three-minute rest and change of ends between periods.
- Face-offs are held within three feet of the side barrier, closest to where the play stopped.
- Free hits are taken either three feet from the side barrier or at the center spot, whichever is closer to where the violation took place.

Officials

One referee controls the game.

History

The word *yacht* comes from a Dutch term meaning a ship for chasing. In the 1600s, Holland was the scene of early pleasure sailing and racing was a natural extension of that pastime. Yachting also was a recreation of the English court and the upper class. The first clubs were started in the 18th century, but racing was more of a pursuit sport than a direct contest between competitors. Modern racing took form in the early 1800s under royal sponsorship and races were staged as betting events. By the 1880s, rules for *regattas* (sailing races) were in effect in England and in most European countries.

The New York Yacht Club was founded in 1813 and many clubs were established over the years on and between the east and west coasts for inshore (mostly, small boats) and offshore (larger yachts) racing and for boats of a particular design.

The availability of many types of yachts — especially, the dinghy classes — has allowed a sport that was once only a pastime of the wealthy to be enjoyed by a broad following of adults and young sailors.

The U.S. Sailing Association governs, promotes and represents sailboat racing through the efforts of its volunteers and member organizations.

Object of the Sport

Competitors race *yachts* (sailboats) of various types over specified courses and attempt to finish in the shortest time.

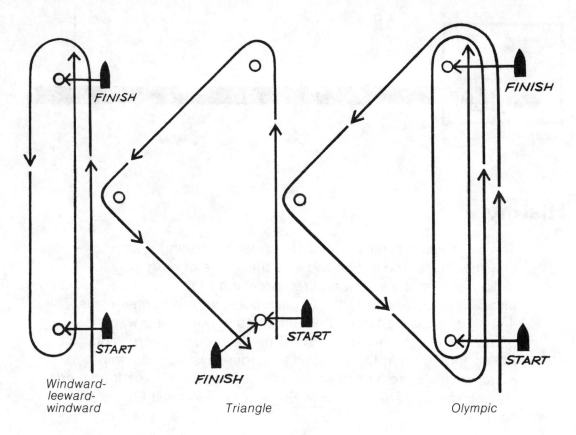

Windward-
leeward-
windward

Triangle

Olympic

Layout

A race committee sets the length and direction of a course based on weather, tide and wind conditions, the *class* (yacht type of design) and number of boats in the event. See diagram.

Marks are floating objects (*buoys*) or any object that defines the course and that the yachts must pass around.

The *starting line* is an imaginary line between two marks at the beginning of the course.

The *finishing line* is the same as the starting line, but at the end of the course.

Yacht Types

A *dinghy* is an open craft without a *ballast* (added weight).

A *keel boat* is a boat with a lead ballast under the *hull* (boat body).

A *catamaran* is a boat with two hulls connected by a deck or beams or a trampoline.

Classes

All yachts race in one of four types of classes, as follows:

One design: all boats have the same measurements and specifications

Development: boats have similar specifications, but design differences are allowed

Formula: various measurements (length, sail area and so on) are calculated as limits; keel boats only

Handicap: yachts of different designs race together, but their elapsed times are "corrected" (based on handicaps) and the winner is the yacht with the lowest corrected time

Equipment

Anchors, sails, flags and so on vary by class and event.

Competitors dress as appropriate; total weight is sometimes regulated.

Terminology

The following are terms common to sailing:

Sailing: Using only wind and the forces of the water to propel a boat

Racing: A boat is racing from five minutes before her start until she has crossed the finish line or dropped out of the race

Port: The lefthand side of a boat when facing the *bow* (forward end)

Starboard: Righthand side

Port tack: When the **boom** (pole that holds the bottom of the sail) is over the starboard (right) side of boat

Starboard tack: When the boom is over the port (left) side

Tacking: Changing tacks by turning the bow into the wind

Gybing: Changing tacks by turning the **stern** (rear end of the boat) into the wind

Leeward: The side of the yacht on which the boom is being carried

Windward: The side of the yacht opposite the leeward side

Beat: To sail into the wind by sailing alternately on one tack and then the other

Reach: Sailing with the wind blowing from the **beam** (side)

Run: Sailing **downwind** (with the wind from behind)

Luffing: Changing direction by turning toward the wind

General Rules

The boats are powered only by the wind.

Right of way is determined as follows:

- A port tack boat must keep **clear** (move out of the way) of a starboard tack boat.
- When boats are overlapped on the same tack, a windward boat clears.
- When boats are on same tack and one is overtaking the other, the boat coming from behind keeps clear.
- A boat changing tacks keeps clear.
- A boat should always keep clear of another that is anchored, capsized or aground.

A boat without the right of way must get clear, but both yachts must try to prevent an accident.

Procedure

The yachts maneuver near the starting line. Flag signals are displayed to indicate the class racing and a five-minute warning.

Both flags are dropped to start the race. A sound signal also is given.

A yacht officially starts when any part of the boat crosses the starting line toward the first mark on the course after the starting signal.

The yachts proceed to the first mark.

Rounding marks

Marks must be passed in order and on the correct side.

If a mark is rounded on the wrong side, the yacht must turn around, pass it again on the wrong side, and then pass it on the correct side.

If a yacht touches a mark, she may correct herself by sailing clear of other yachts and turning a complete 360-degree circle.

Usually, when yachts overlap two boat lengths or more from a mark, the one on the outside must give room to the inside yacht to round the mark.

Overtaking

The yacht in front may luff a yacht overtaking her on her windward side.

The yacht in front may not sail below the proper course to the next mark to block a yacht overtaking her on the leeward side.

Winning and scoring

Yachts race on the course, tacking and reaching, beating and running, rounding marks.

A yacht finishes when any part crosses the finishing line from the direction of the last mark.

The first yacht to cross is the winner.

Points are awarded as follows:

	Olympic	Low Point (most common)
First place	0	0.75
Second	3	2.0
Third	5.7	3.0
Fourth	8	4.0
Fifth	10	5.0
Sixth	11.7	6.0

Seventh and over - finish place plus 6

A series of races may be run for each class. The lowest total point score over all races wins.

Officials

The race is controlled by a committee, but competitors are to recognize their own violations and may also protest the action of another yacht.

Penalties include having a boat make penalty turns, receive penalty points and disqualification.

History

Games in which coins were slid along a table are mentioned as far back as Shakespeare, who refers to both *shovel board* and *shove groat* in his plays. A similar contest was held in colonial taverns before the American Revolution.

Shuffleboard, as we know it today, was introduced as a shipboard sport in the 1870s and was popular during the era of ocean liner travel. The first club was founded in St. Petersburg, FL in 1924. Rules were standardized in 1929 when the National Shuffleboard Association was organized. National tournaments began in 1931. The sport, once associated with older players, has been discovered by several generations of younger participants as a game that requires skill and accuracy to create both offensive and defensive moves.

Object of the Game

Two players or teams push discs with a *cue* (long stick) to a scoring area marked at the opposite end of a court to score points or interfere with the opponent's scoring. The first player or team to score 75 points wins the game.

Playing Field

The court is 52 feet long at the side line and six feet wide at the base line. The playing area is 39 feet long.

The scoring *diagram* is a triangle, nine feet long, set 18 inches in from the baseline with the point centered three feet from each side line.

Markings include one 10-point, two 8-point, two 7-point and one 10-off area.

The *dead line* runs across the court, six feet back of the center and 13 feet, 6 inches from the base line.

Equipment

The **cue** has a maximum length of 75 inches.

The **discs** are made of a composition material and measure six inches in diameter with a maximum height of one inch and weigh 11½ to 15 ounces. There are four black and four red (or white or yellow) discs.

Dress is casual.

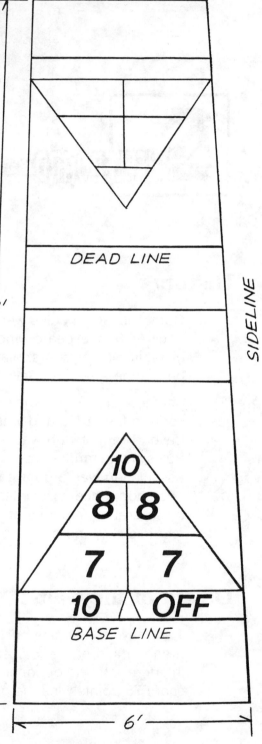

General Rules

The game is played by two (singles) or four (doubles) players.

Each player may shoot two discs to determine the court surface speed.

All discs are lined up and shot from within the 10-off area. Each player must shoot from only one half of the 10-off area. A player cannot step on or over the base line while shooting.

In a match, players (teams) play one color in the first game and switch in the second. If there is a third game, one player from each side shoots four discs at the dead line beyond the center of the court. The discs are shot alternately — red, black, red, black and so on. The first three discs are considered practice and are removed; the final disc stays in place. The player whose disc is closest to the dead line gets to choose which color to play. If the last black disc moves the red disc, the red player wins.

A frame is a shooting turn from one end of the court, including all eight discs.

The first player or team to score 75 points wins. If the game is tied, play continues (two frames for singles, four for doubles) and the side with the higher score wins.

The first side to win two games out of three wins the match.

Procedure

The red disc starts the game and play alternates between the colors. The red is always shot from the righthand side of the *head* (beginning) end and back from the right side of the *foot* (opposite) end.

In singles play:

> Both players start at the head end. After all discs have been shot, players proceed to the foot of the court and play again; then, black goes first. The sequence continues until the game is won.

In doubles play:

> One partner starts at each end. After all discs have been shot from the head end, play is made by each player from the foot. Red shoots at head and foot, then black shoots first at head and foot. The same rotation is followed until one team wins.

The game is to be played with friendliness and courtesy.

When an opponent is shooting, the other player steps back and raises the cue to avoid distracting the shooter.

Players do not talk when opponents are shooting.

Scoring

A disc must be completely within a numbered area to score and not touching any line, except the triangle in the 10-off area.

After eight discs from one end have been shot, scores are recorded: 7, 8, 10 or minus-10 (from the 10-off zone).

All scores are counted; that is, scores do not cancel, as in horseshoes.

If one disc is *mounted* (on top of another disc), both score.

Any disc that stops short of the far dead line is *dead* (out of play). If a disc is touching the far dead line or past the far dead line, it is in play.

Players may try to prevent opponents from scoring by knocking their discs out of the scoring areas.

Penalties

Players are penalized varying point totals for violations, as follows:

- A disc throw not started from the 10-off area — 5 points
- Stepping over the base line when shooting — 10 points
- Interfering with opponent's play — 5 points
- Touching discs in play — 10 points

- Shooting while an opponent's disc is moving — 10 points
- Shooting in a hesitating (not smooth and continuous) motion — 10 points
- Shooting a *hook shot* (the cue and disc not moving in a straight line) — 10 points
- Playing two shots in a row — 10 points

Officials

Referees are not required in informal games; players resolve their own disputes. Tournaments have a Tournament Director in charge with Divisional Referees for assistance, Court Referees for play and scoring matters and a Scorer.

History

Games resembling soccer can be traced to many places and cultures. About 2,500 years ago, the Chinese played *tsu-ch'iu*. The ancient Greeks played *hapraston* which was adopted by the Romans and, eventually, spread through their Empire. Great Britain is recognized as the home of the modern sport. Evolving from a street pastime of the Middle Ages, the London Football Association established the rules for a team kicking game in 1863. The sport became known as Association Football then as Association, which was shortened to A-soc and, finally, soccer. It has been an Olympic event since 1908.

A version was played in the United States by the Indians before English settlers arrived, and during Colonial days, but the immigrants of the late 19th century provided the foundation of the sport in this country. The time of greatest growth began in the 1970s when many young boys and girls became involved in organized games. The United States Soccer Federation governs the development and competitive activities and oversees the sport at all levels. The United States will be the host country for the 1994 World Cup.

Today, soccer — known as *football* everywhere in the world except in North America — is the most frequently played and most popular of all team sports. Combining simplicity with creativity and individual skills, soccer is the most universal of sports.

Object of the Game

Two teams of 11 players, including the goalkeeper, compete to put a ball into their opponents' goal. The highest score wins.

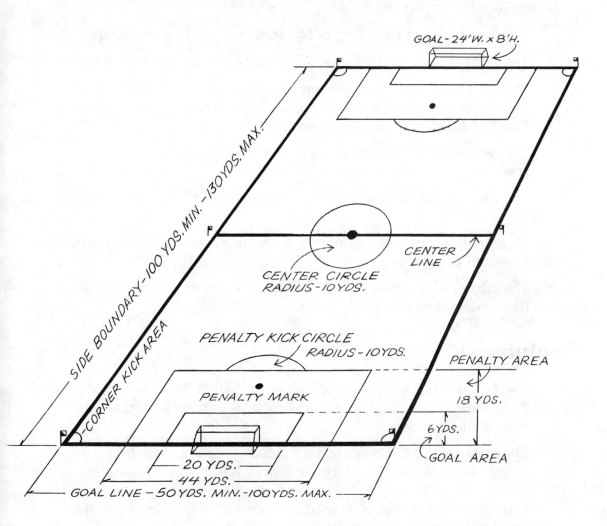

Playing Field

The playing field for major competition must be 100-130 yards long and 50-100 yards wide.

The *touch lines* (side boundaries) and *goal lines* (end boundaries) are part of the playing area.

A *halfway line* (center) runs across midfield.

The *center circle* is a 10-yard radius around a spot (field mark) at the exact center of the field.

A *penalty area* at each end is 44 yards wide by 18 yards deep.

The *goal area* at each end is 20 × 6 yards in front of each goal.

The *goal* is 24 feet wide between two goal posts and eight feet in height from the crossbar to the goal line. The posts and crossbar may be square, rectangular or round.

The *penalty kick mark* is 12 yards from the midpoint of the goal line.

The *penalty kick arc* is 10 yards from the kick mark and outside of the penalty area.

Flags with a minimum height of five feet are placed at each corner (optional at midfield).

The *corner kick areas* (quarter circles at each corner of the field) have a radius of one yard.

Equipment

The **ball** must be made with a leather or leather-like cover, measure 27-28 inches in circumference, weigh 14-16 ounces and have 14 pounds of air pressure.

Shoes may have studs or bars, rounded or flat, not less than ½ inch in diameter and no more than ¾ inch in height. Metal plates are not permitted. Molded studs must number at least 10 and be at least ⅜ inch in diameter. Any equipment that might cause harm to another player is not permitted.

Dress is by uniform. Players on each team must wear the same design shirt, shorts and socks. Goalkeepers wear different colors than the other members of their team, and referees traditionally wear black.

General Rules

Each team has 11 players. One must be the goalkeeper. The others, known in general terms as field players, are defenders, midfielders and forwards *(strikers)*. The number of players at each position depends on the playing style favored by the coach. A common breakdown would be to have four defenders, two or three midfielders and four or three forwards.

Ball play

Players must kick the ball or use their head or chest to play it. They may not play, move, carry or hit it with a hand or any part of an arm, with the following exceptions:

- At a *throw-in* (a two-handed, over-the-head throw to put the ball in play after it has crossed a touch line).
- The goalkeeper can use his hands and arms to catch, punch, roll or throw the ball when it is inside his own penalty area.

The ball is out of play:

- After it completely crosses a goal line or touch line on the ground or in the air
- If the referee stops the game

The ball is in play:

- After a throw-in
- After any free kick, including a goal kick
- If it bounces back onto the field after hitting a goal post, crossbar or corner post
- If it rebounds off an official who is on the field

Substitutions

Players can be replaced only when the game is stopped and only with the referee's permission.

After a player leaves, the substitute enters the game at midfield.

Any player may exchange positions with the goalkeeper after receiving permission from the referee.

In major competition, only two substitutes are allowed each team during a game. In most other games, the number of substitutions permitted is determined by the local authorities.

Injured players may not be replaced after the substitution limit has been reached.

Game length

In major competition, games last two halves, each 45 minutes. The clock does not stop except at the discretion of the referee.

A minimum of five minutes is allowed between halves.

The referee can add playing time to replace time lost by injury or another reason.

Either period can be extended for a penalty kick.

Scoring

A goal (one point) is scored after the entire ball crosses the goal line between the goal posts and under the crossbar. The attacking team cannot throw, carry or hit the ball by a hand or arm to score.

The team that scores the most goals is the winner.

If no goals are scored or the teams are tied at the end of regulation play, the game can be decided by a kick from the penalty spot or extra playing time.

Modification of Rules

Providing that the basic principles of the laws of soccer are maintained, modifications are permitted for players under 16 years and over 35 years, and for women. Acceptable modifications include the following:

- Size of the field of play
- Size, weight and material of the ball
- Width between goal posts and height of crossbar from the ground
- Length of each period
- Number of substitutions

Procedure

The team winning the coin toss chooses to kick off or defend the goal of its choice.

All players must be in their own half of the field.

Defensive players must stay outside the center circle until the ball is kicked and travels the distance of its own circumference.

After the referee's whistle, the kickoff is made (to a teammate) from the center spot into the opponents' half of the field.

The kicker cannot play the ball again until it has been touched by another player.

A goal cannot be scored directly from a player's kickoff.

If the ball goes out of play, the game restarts by a throw-in (if the ball crossed the touch line) or by a goal kick or corner kick (if the ball crossed the goal line.)

If the game is stopped by the referee for any reason where there is no *infraction* (rule violation) when the ball is in play, the game restarts when the referee drops the ball where it was when play was halted. The ball must touch the ground before players can play it.

After a goal is scored, the game is restarted with a kickoff at the center of the field by a member of the team that did not score.

After halftime, the teams change ends and the kickoff is made by the team that did not kick off to start the game.

Throw-in

A throw-in is made at the touch line where the ball went out of play.

The throw is made by a player from the team that did not touch the ball last.

The thrower must face the field and keep part of each foot behind or on the touch line.

The ball is thrown with both hands from behind and over the head.

A goal cannot be scored on a direct throw.

The thrower cannot play the ball again until it has been played by another player.

If the ball is not thrown correctly, the throw-in should be made by a player from the other team.

Offside

A player is in an offside position when in the opponents' half of the field, and closer to the opponents' goal then the ball, and nearer the goal than two defenders. If even with the second-to-last defender, a player is not offside.

The referee may call an infraction at the time the ball is played by a teammate if the offside player is interfering with the play of an opponent (such as goalkeeper distraction).

An offside occurs at the time the ball leaves the foot of the teammate, not when the player receives the ball.

A player is not called offside just for being in an offside position, or if the ball is played by an opponent, or if the ball is received directly from a goal kick, corner kick or a throw in.

An offside may be declared if the player receives the ball directly from a teammate at a free kick.

Free kick

A free kick is a shot on goal awarded after a foul or misconduct, and can be taken from any place in the goal area. It is classified as *direct* or *indirect*.

A direct free kick counts as a goal whether or not the ball touches a player from either team on its way to the goal. It is awarded for major offenses that are committed intentionally, such as the following:

- Playing the ball with the arm, from the shoulder to the fingertips (does not apply to goalkeeper)
- Tripping an opponent
- Pushing an opponent
- Holding an opponent by the body or uniform
- Jumping at an opponent, even if no contact is made
- Charging an opponent in a violent or dangerous manner, except for shoulder-to-shoulder contact
- Charging at an opponent from behind, except when the opponent is legally obstructing the ball
- Striking an opponent with the arm, hand or elbow
- Kicking an opponent with the foot or knee

An indirect free kick counts as a goal only if the ball touches a player on either team before crossing the goal line. It is awarded for less serious offenses, such as the following:

- Offside violations
- Dangerous play, such as kicking near an opponent's head, lying on the ball, jumping recklessly or trying to play a ball held by the goalkeeper
- Obstruction, such as blocking an opponent's movement when the ball is out of playing distance
- Charging an opponent when the ball is out of playing distance (more than one step away)
- Charging the goalkeeper by making body contact in the goal area that prevents the goalkeeper from playing the ball or retaining possession
- When the goalkeeper takes more than four steps while controlling the ball (by holding, throwing, bouncing or rolling it) before releasing it to another player; the goalkeeper cannot play the ball again until it has been touched by a teammate outside the penalty area

When a player takes a free kick inside his own penalty area, all opposing players must stay at least 10 yards from the ball and outside the area.

If a player takes a free kick outside his own penalty area, opponents must remain 10 yards. from the ball, except when the kick is taken within 10 yards of the goal line, in which case opposing players can stand on their own goal line between the goal posts.

A free kick awarded to the defending team within its own goal area may be taken from any point within that area.

An indirect free kick awarded to the attacking team within the opponents' goal area shall be taken from the part of the goal area that runs parallel to the goal line, at the point nearest to where the foul took place.

Ball placement is pointed out by the referee. A quick kick is permitted, but the ball must be stationary and at the proper spot.

Penalty kick

A direct free kick is awarded to the attacking team when an opposing player commits a major foul within his team's penalty area.

All players except the goalkeeper and the player taking the penalty kick must stand outside the penalty area, at least 10 yards from the ball. The goalkeeper must stand on the goal line between the goal posts and not move his feet until the ball is kicked. The kicker must place the ball, kick it forward and cannot play it again until the ball has been touched by another player.

If the ball is stopped by the goalkeeper or rebounds into the playing field, play continues. If the ball goes over the goal line (but not between the goal posts) after being touched by the goalkeeper, the attacking team gets a corner kick.

A penalty kick is retaken if:

- The defending team enters the penalty area before the kick is taken and no goal is scored
- An attacking player other than the kicker enters the penalty area before the kick and a goal is scored

- The kicker is penalized for an infringement after the ball is in play, in which case the defending team is awarded an indirect free kick from the place that the foul occurred

If a game is tied after regulation play, each team selects five players to try to make a goal in a penalty kick shootout. The team that scores the most goals wins. If the game remains tied, the shootout continues with different players until a team wins.

Goal kick

A goal kick is taken by any defending player, including the goalkeeper, after the ball goes over the end line (but not into the goal) in the air or on the ground and was last touched by an attacking player.

The ball must be stationary when kicked, and must be kicked into play beyond the penalty area from any point within the goal area. The kicker may not kick the ball a second time until it is touched by another player.

Kicking team players may be anywhere on the field; opponents must be outside the penalty area until the ball has cleared the penalty area.

The ball must be touched by another player before a goal is scored. If the goalkeeper catches the ball or picks it up off the ground, it may be thrown to a teammate or drop-kicked (dropped to the ground and kicked as it rebounds).

Corner kick

A corner kick is taken by an attacking player after the ball goes over the end line (but not into the goal) when it was last touched by a defensive player.

The ball is placed inside the corner kick area nearest to where it went out-of-bounds. The corner flag is not removed.

Any attacking team player may kick the ball, but cannot kick it again before it is touched by another player.

Attacking players may be anywhere on the field; defenders must be no closer than 10 yards from the ball.

A goal may be scored directly from a corner kick without another player touching the ball.

Advantage clause

The referee has the option of letting play continue after an apparent foul occurs if he believes the penalty would benefit the offending team. Referees generally call "Advantage, play on!" so that play continues without interruption.

Fouls and Misconduct

A foul is a rule violation that is penalized by a direct free kick or an indirect free kick, depending on the seriousness of the offense.

A *caution* (yellow card) is a formal warning to a player guilty of:

- Repeated disregard of game rules
- Unsportsmanlike conduct
- Entering or leaving the game without the referee's permission
- Disagreement with the referee's decision

Sending off (red card) is when the referee removes a player from the game for:

- Serious foul play
- Violent conduct
- Foul or offensive language
- A second misconduct after receiving a caution

After a send-off, play is resumed with a direct free kick or an indirect free kick (depending on the infringement) by an opposing player from the place of the misconduct.

Referee signals

Play on - advantage

Penalty kick

Indirect free kick

Direct free kick

Goal kick

Corner kick

Caution or expulsion

Linesman signals

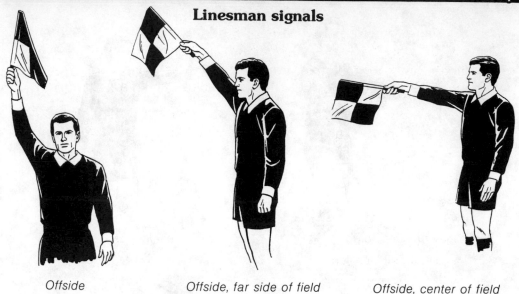

Offside

Offside, far side of field

Offside, center of field

Offside, near side of field

Throw-in

Corner kick

Substitution

Goal kick

If a player is sent off for a second offense due to a caution, the referee must show both the yellow and the red card at the same time. This is to make clear that the player is being sent off for the second offense and not for one requiring immediate expulsion.

If a ball is deliberately kicked to a goalkeeper by a teammate, the goalkeeper is not allowed to touch it with the hands. If it is touched, the opposing team is awarded an indirect free kick.

Officials

The referee:

- Enforces the rules
- Acts as timekeeper; starts, stops and restarts the game
- Cautions or ejects offenders of the rules by showing a yellow card for a warning and a red card for an ejection. (An ejected player cannot be replaced.)

Two linesmen assist the referee. Their responsibilities are to:

- Indicate where and when the ball goes out of play
- Determine which team is entitled to a throw-in, goal kick or corner kick.
- Signal by flag infringements not seen by the referee

History

Softball was first played inside and called indoor baseball. Its introduction in 1887 is credited to G. W. Handcock of the Farragut Boat Club in Chicago. He used a 17-inch ball with the seams on the outside. An outdoor version of the game using a 12-inch ball with a standard baseball cover appeared in Minneapolis in 1895. It was also known as indoor-outdoor, playground ball, diamond ball, kitten ball and mush ball. The game was standardized in 1923 and the Amateur Softball Association was organized 10 years later. Major differences from baseball include a smaller field, a larger ball, underhand pitching and seven-inning games. Participation is widespread as a recreation and as a competitive sport in schools, leagues and sponsored games.

Object of the Game

Two teams compete to score *runs* (points) by players safely moving around four bases on a diamond-shaped field. The highest score wins.

Note: The three common versions of softball are fast pitch (FP), slow pitch (SP) and 16-inch slow pitch (16SP); the rule differences are identified.

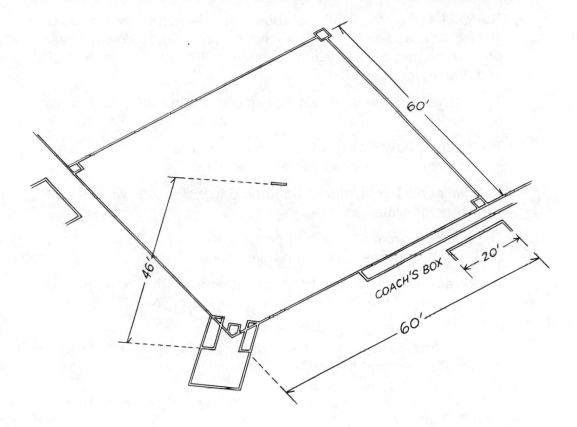

Playing Field

The field of play is shared by an infield and an outfield and is separated into fair and foul territory.

The *diamond* is 60 square feet (65 in SP, 55 in 16SP) with a base at each corner.

The *bases* include first, second and third base. They are made of canvas, are 15 square inches and up to five inches high. They are fastened in place.

Home plate is made of white rubber and is five-sided. It is 17 inches wide across the edge facing the pitcher, 8½ inches long on each side and 12 inches long on the sides of the point facing the catcher.

The *pitcher's plate* is made of rubber. It is 24 inches long and six inches wide, and level to the ground. It is set 46 feet from the rear point of home plate (40 feet for women in FP), 50 feet for all in SP and 38 feet for all in 16SP.

The *pitcher's circle* is 16 feet in diameter around the pitcher's plate (FP only).

The *batter's boxes* are six feet long and four feet wide. They are six inches from the outside edges of home plate.

The *catcher's box* is 10 feet long and 8 feet, 5 inches wide. It is behind home plate.

The *on-deck circle* for the next batter is five feet in diameter and between the player's bench and home plate.

The *three-foot line* is parallel to and three feet outside the baseline starting halfway from home plate and ending beyond first base to guide the runner.

The *coaches' boxes* are 10 feet wide by 20 feet long and set 15 feet outside the diamond behind first and third bases.

The outfield is the wide area of the field beyond the diamond and most distant from home plate.

The *foul lines* extend from home plate past first and third bases to the foul poles set at a boundary fence. *Fair territory* is the playing field within and including the foul lines; *foul territory* is the area outside the foul lines to a designated out of play area or fence.

Equipment

The **bat** is one piece of hardwood or laminated wood sections, metal, plastic, bamboo or a combination of materials. It cannot be more than 34 inches long, including a 15-inch maximum safety grip or be heavier than 38 ounces. It is smooth and round with a maximum diameter of 2¼ inches or three-sided with a hitting side 2¼ inches wide. Metal bats may be angular.

The **ball** is smooth-seamed and flat-surfaced and made of stitched horse or cowhide or a molded synthetic cover over a kapok, rubber, cork or poly mix center core. It is 12 inches in diameter (FP or SP) and weighs 6¼ to 7 ounces. For slow pitch, the ball is 16 inches and weighs 9 to 10 ounces. For women, the ball is 11 inches in diameter and weighs six ounces.

Gloves come in no standard size for outfielders. They generally are five-fingered. The catcher and first baseman use a *mitt* with thumb and body sections. Webbing cannot be more than five inches long.

Uniforms

All players wear the same design and style uniforms with a six-inch number on the back.

Shoes may have metal spikes ¾-inch long except in youth, co-ed or senior games, where spikes are not permitted.

Helmets are required for adult FP batters and base runners, are permitted for pitchers and catchers and are mandatory for youth batters, catchers and runners. All FP catchers must wear masks with throat guards; body protectors are recommended for adult catchers and must be worn by youth catchers. In SP, youths must wear masks.

General Rules

The game is divided into innings, during which each team has a turn *at bat* (to hit the ball) and to be in the field. A regulation game consists of seven innings.

The second half of the seventh inning does not have to be played if the team that bats last scores more runs in six innings or before the third out in the last of the seventh. If the game is tied, extra innings are played until one team has more runs at the end of a complete inning or until the team batting second scores more runs before a third out.

A game that is stopped (such as for rain or darkness) counts as complete if five innings have been played or if the team batting second has more runs after four innings than the other team has scored in five. A game is called a tie if the scores are even after five or more innings.

The *home* team is the team on whose field the game is played; the other team is the *visitor*. If the game is played in a neutral setting, one team is designated the home team.

The team at bat is allowed three *outs* (when batters or base runners are prevented from safely reaching or advancing bases) in an inning. After that, the side is *retired*, its players move to the field and the team that was in the field comes to bat.

One run is scored each time a base runner touches first, second and third base and home plate before the third out of an inning.

Fielders (defensive players), except for the pitcher and the catcher, can stand anywhere in *fair* territory. The pitcher must start on the pitcher's plate (fair territory) and the catcher in the catcher's box (foul territory.)

The fielding positions are as follows:

1 — pitcher	6 — shortstop
2 — catcher	7 — left fielder
3 — first baseman	8 — center fielder
4 — second baseman	9 — right fielder
5 — third baseman	10 — extra fielder (SP)

In FP, a *designated player* (DP) named before the game may bat for another team member, but must keep the same place in the batting order for the entire game. The DP can play defense, but the starting player and DP cannot be in the game at the same time.

In SP, an *extra player* (EP) named before the game may play as a batter but must play the entire game. All 11 players can interchange positions. In co-ed SP (five male, five female) there can be two EPs: 12 players bat and 10 play on defense.

All starting players, including DPs and EPs, may be substituted for and can re-enter the game one time but must bat in their original place. If substitutes are replaced, they cannot re-enter.

Officials

The umpire behind home plate controls the game. Responsibilities include pitching and hitting *calls* (judgments) and working with base umpires (who make decisions on plays at the bases) on fair and foul balls and other rulings.

Procedure

A coin toss determines which side bats at the *top* of the first inning. (The second half of an inning is the *bottom*.) The *visitors* bat first. Defensive players take their positions in the field. The plate umpire calls "play" to start the game.

Batting

Players bat in the order given to the plate umpire on the scoresheets.

The batter stands inside or on the batter's box lines.

The *strike zone* in FP is the rectangular space above home plate between the batter's armpits and the knee tops when in a natural batting stance; in SP, it is from the back shoulder top to the bottom of the front knee.

A *strike* is a pitch that:

- Is swung at by the batter and missed
- Is *called* by the umpire when the batter *takes* (does not swing at) a ball that enters the strike zone
- Hits a batter in the strike zone
- Is swung at, missed and touches the batter; the ball is dead
- Is *foul tipped* (hit no higher than the batter's head straight back to the catcher and caught without touching the ground); the batter is out if it is the third strike

Note: In FP, the ball is in play and any base runners may try to advance at the risk of being put out; in SP, the ball is *dead* (out of play) and the base runners cannot move.

A *foul ball* (also a strike) is a batted ball that:

- Is hit into an area outside the foul lines and not caught by a fielder (if caught, the batter is out); if the batter already has two strikes the strike count stays at two and the ball is dead. In SP, the batter is out if the foul ball is the third strike. Any ball caught in an out-of-play area, such as a seating area, is considered *no catch* and ruled a foul ball.
- Hits the bat or the batter while in the batter's box with less than two strikes
- Touches a player or umpire in foul territory
- Rolls into foul territory before reaching first or third base before being touched and comes to rest there

The batter is out after three strikes.

A *ball* is a pitch that:

- Is called by an umpire that does not pass through the strike zone and is not swung at by the batter. In FP, the ball is in play; in SP, the ball is dead.
- Hits the ground or home plate before going into the strike zone and is not swung at. In FP, the ball is in play; in SP, the ball is dead.
- In SP, hits the batter outside the strike zone and is not swung at. In FP, the batter goes to first base.

Also, a ball is called for every warm-up pitch over five (FP) or three (SP) or if the pitcher takes more than 20 seconds to deliver or if the catcher does not return the ball promptly to the pitcher.

Four balls allow the batter to go to first base, which is called a *walk* or *base on balls*.

A *fair ball* is a batted ball that:

- Lands or is touched by a player in fair territory (infield or outfield)
- Goes over the boundary fence on the fly in fair territory or after bouncing off the foul pole (both are *home runs*)
- First lands in foul territory, then rolls fair into the infield
- Bounces on a base or touches a player or an umpire while in fair territory

The batter is out and the ball is in play:

- After a called or swinging third strike is caught by the catcher (FP)
- On a third strike caught after a foul ball is hit (SP)
- If the third strike is missed and the batter is touched by the ball
- After a third strike with the runner on first and less than two outs (FP)
- If the fly ball is caught in fair or foul territory
- When the *infield fly rule* (a fly ball hit in the infield with runners on first and second base or first, second and third and before two outs) is called by the umpire

The batter is out and the ball is dead if:

- The fielder intentionally drops a fly ball or *line drive* (a ball hit on a straight line) with a runner on first base and less than two outs
- A *bunt* (a ball not fully swung at but lightly tapped to the infield) goes foul after a second strike (FP); bunts are not allowed in SP
- The ball is hit twice or is hit and touches the batter in fair territory after coming out of the batter's box

- The catcher drops a third strike but touches the batter with the ball or throws it to first base before the batter reaches the base
- The batter interferes with the catcher's play at the plate, brings an illegal bat into the box, or switches boxes after the pitcher begins to throw
- The base runner interferes with a fielder's play before reaching first base

On balls hit into fair territory in the air, the batter is out if the fielder catches the ball before it touches the ground or an outfield boundary fence.

On balls hit on the ground, the batter is out if the fielder can pick up the ball and throw it or run with it to first base before the batter arrives.

If the ball cannot be caught before touching the ground and cannot be received at first base before the batter arrives, the batter has a *single* base hit and may stay safely at first base or try to run to other bases.

If the defensive team can get the ball to second or third base and *tag* the batter (touch with the ball or with the ball in the glove) before the batter arrives at a base or between the bases, the batter is out.

A hit that allows the batter to safely reach second base is a *double*; a hit that allows the batter to reach third base is a *triple*.

On a home run, the batter runs around all the bases, crosses home plate and scores, as do any teammates already on base. A home run can also be made *inside the park* if the fielders cannot get the ball to home plate in time to tag the batter.

Base running

The batter becomes a base runner, with the ball in play, after:

- The ball is hit into fair territory
- Four balls are called (the ball is dead in SP)
- In FP, the catcher drops the third strike with less than two outs and first base is unoccupied or with two outs and first base occupied; the batter is safe on first if not tagged or beats the catcher's throw

The batter goes to first base and the ball is dead:

- After catcher or fielder interference
- If a fair ball strikes a base runner or umpire before the ball passes or touches a fielder
- In FP, if a pitch is not swung at and not a called strike and hits the batter in the box who is trying to avoid it

Note: If a fielder throws a glove at a thrown ball, the batter is given two bases; at a batted ball, three bases; at a ball going over the outfield boundary, a home run.

A runner has a right to be at each base by getting there before being put out and can stay until legally advancing to another base or by being *forced* (loses the right to be on a base and must move ahead) to leave by the batter or another base runner.

A runner must touch all the bases, including home plate, in the correct order to score.

Two runners cannot be on the same base at the same time. The first to legally arrive is safe; the other runner may be tagged out. If the first runner is forced to advance and two runners are on base, the second runner has the legal right to the base.

When the ball is in play, a runner may advance:

- After the ball is hit into fair territory or thrown into fair or foul territory
- After a ball leaves the pitcher's hand (FP) and after the ball crosses home plate or is hit (SP)
- After any fly ball is caught, although the runner must first *tag up* (touch the current base)
- On a *steal* (FP only) by running to the next base after the ball is pitched; runner is out if tagged
- In FP, on a *wild pitch* (the catcher cannot reach the pitch) or a *passed ball* (the catcher mishandles the pitch)
- When a fair ball hits the runner or umpire after passing a fielder or touches a fielder
- When a ball in play is blocked or overthrown into out-of-play territory or a pitch goes in or past the backstop
- When a fielder obstructs the runner and the runner does not run past a base which the umpire believes the runner would have reached if not obstructed

All runners advance one base with no risk of being put out when the batter walks, when the ball in play is blocked or overthrown into out-of-play territory or if a fielder obstructs a runner and the runner does not run past the base the umpire feels the runner would have made if not for the obstruction.

If the batter hits a home run, all runners score. If the batter hits a **ground rule double** (the ball bounces over a fair boundary fence or goes into an unplayable area), the hitter and any runners are awarded two bases.

The runner must return to a base after:

- Each pitch not hit by the batter
- A ball is caught on the fly
- A foul ball is not caught
- Batter, runner or umpire interference
- An intentionally dropped infield fly
- A batter is hit by a pitched ball that is swung at and missed

A run does not score if:

- The third out is from the batter being out before reaching first base
- Another base runner is forced out
- The base runner starts before the pitcher throws the ball to the batter (FP) or before the pitched ball reaches home plate (SP)

A base runner is out if the runner:

- Is tagged by a fielder with the ball or the fielder touches the base with the ball in hand before the runner arrives (a **force out**).
- Is tagged by a fielder while not safely standing on base when the ball is in play
- Runs past first base, turns toward second and is tagged
- Runs more than three feet outside of a direct line between the bases to avoid being tagged
- Interferes with a player fielding a batted ball or with a thrown ball; in a **double play** (two offensive players put out in the same action) attempt, both runners are out if interference prevents the second out
- Is hit by a fair ball while off base and before it passes any infielder, except the pitcher
- Passes another runner or arrives last while another runner is on a base

- Leaves base before a fly ball is caught or is tagged before returning
- Misses touching a base and the defensive player tags the runner or the base
- Purposely kicks the ball or runs the bases backward to confuse the defense

A base runner is not out if the runner:

- Runs outside the basepath to avoid interfering with a fielding attempt
- Is not tagged with the ball firmly held by the fielder
- Touches and runs past first base but returns directly to it
- Is hit with a batted ball while standing on base or with a ball batted past an infielder when there was no opportunity for an out
- Stays on base until a fly ball is touched, then tries to advance

Pitching

The pitcher stands facing the batter, with the catcher inside the catcher's box.

In FP, the pitch begins with the ball in both hands and both feet (women) or the pivot foot only (men) on the pitcher's plate for one to 10 seconds.

In SP, only one hand must be on the ball and one foot on the pitching plate for one to 10 seconds.

Any type of *windup* (motion before releasing the ball) is allowed, but the pitcher cannot stop or reverse after starting or continue after the ball leaves the hand.

In FP, a ball can pass the hip twice but cannot have more than one *windmill* (full revolution of the arm); in SP, no windmills are allowed and the ball is to be released the first time it passes the hip.

A ball must be thrown underhand to be a legal pitch. Also:

- The hand must stay below the hipline and the wrist not farther away from the body than the elbow.
- The ball must be released at the same time as any forward step (FP) or any step (SP).
- The other foot must stay on the pitching plate until the forward foot touches the ground.

- In SP, the ball must rise at least six feet — but no more than 12 feet — between the pitcher's hand and before crossing home plate.
- Only moderate pitching speed is allowed, based on the umpire's judgement.

Illegal pitches also include the following:

- Rolled or bounced balls
- Putting foreign substance on the ball or purposely damaging the balls
- Throwing the ball to a base while a foot is on the pitcher's plate; the pitcher must step on the plate
- A pitch in which the catcher leaves the catcher's box before the ball is released (FP) or the ball reaches the plate (SP)

An umpire may call a *no pitch*, which cancels any play after a pitch, if:

- The batter was not ready
- The pitch was made during a halt in play
- The ball slips out of the pitcher's hand (in FP, the ball is live, the batter is awarded a ball and the base runners can try to advance)
- A runner has not returned to a base after a foul ball or is called out for leaving a base too soon

Runners do not advance on illegal or no-pitches. In FP, if the batter hits an illegal pitch and reaches first base, all runners can advance at least one base; any play counts. In SP, if the batter swings at an illegal pitch, any play counts.

PLAYING FIELD MEASUREMENTS FOR YOUTHS

	Baselines		Pitching distance		Fence distance min/max	
	FP	SP	FP	SP	FP	SP
Boys under 18	60′	65′	46′	50′	200′/225′	275′
Girls under 18	60′	65′	40′	50′	200′/225′	225′
Boys under 16	60′	65′	46′	46′	200′/225′	275′
Girls under 16	60′	65′	40′	46′	200′/225′	225′
Boys under 14	60′	65′	46′	46′	175′/200′	150′
Girls under 14	60′	65′	46′	46′	175′/200′	150′/175′
Boys under 12	60′	60′	34′	40′	175′/200′	175′
Girls under 12	60′	60′	35′	40′	175′/200′	175′
Boys under 10	55′	50′	35′	35′	150′/175′	150′
Girls under 10	55′	50′	35′	35′	150′/175′	150′/175′

SPEED SKATING

History

Skating on ice is an ancient pastime. The technique derived from skiing and was widely practiced in parts of Northern Europe. The first skates were made of wood or bone and poles were needed as the absence of a sharp edge hampered the push-off. The first pair of all-iron skates were made in the 16th century and marked the beginning of speed skating as an organized sport. Races were held in Holland on frozen canals and waterways and by 1763 there were competitions in England. The first speed skate, a hollow metal blade attached to a leather boot, was introduced in the 1850s. The sport became popular in the U.S. and many events were staged after the Civil War. International racing began in 1892. Men's events were part of the first winter Olympics in 1924; women began to compete in 1960. Short track speed skating was introduced as a new Olympic event in 1992.

The Amateur Speedskating Union of the U.S. is the national organization that introduces boys and girls and men and women to the sport and promotes races through it regional associations. The U.S. International Speedskating Association controls the Olympic style competitions.

Object of the Sport

Skaters race over various distances around a course on ice; the fastest time (lowest point total) wins.

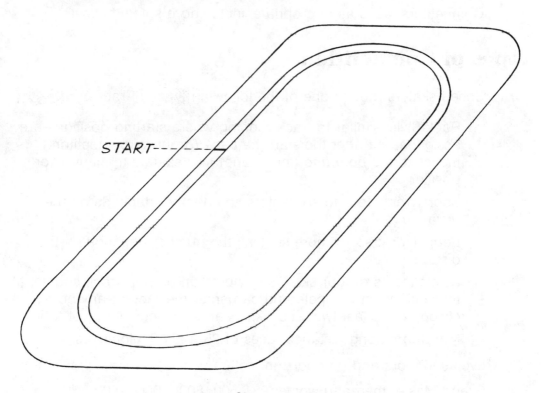

Short track

Field of Play

A **short track** is a 111.12-meter (365-foot) oval course in an indoor **rink** (contest area).

A **long track** is a 400-meter (437-yard) oval outdoor course.

A **pre-start line** is marked 75 centimeters (30 inches) behind the starting line.

A **finish line** usually is at the end of one straight side, depending on the event.

SPEED SKATING

Equipment

Skates have no official design; they usually are made of leather with thin, straight steel blades 12 to 18 inches long.

Competitors dress as appropriate, including a safety helmet.

Types of Competition

Speed skaters race in one of the following types of races:

Pack Style: similar to track running where starting positions are assigned, but after the start the *pack* (group of competitors) moves to the *pole line* (inner lane) and skaters maneuver for position

Short Track: four to six skaters; the number depends on the distance

Long Track: six or more skaters; the number depends on the distance

Relay: teams of four skaters compete on a short track course; all members must compete and can enter the race at any point, except in the last two laps; skater and replacement must touch

Marathon: Long distance races of 25 and 50 kilometers.

Events indoors and outdoors, in meters:

Grand Master men and women —50 years or older	500	800	1000	1500	
Master men and women —35 years or older	500	800	1000	1500	3000
Senior men and women —19-34 years	500	800	1000	1500	3000
Intermediate boys and girls —18 years or younger	500	800	1000	1500	3000
Junior boys and girls —15 years or younger	300	500	800	1000	1500
Juvenile boys and girls —13 years or younger	300	500	800	1000	
Midget boys and girls —11 years or younger	300	500	600	800	

Note: Local associations have divisions for 5 to 7 years and up.

General Rules

Skaters race counterclockwise with the left hands toward the center of the track.

The skater starting in the inner lane is drawn at random or determined by the skater with the best performance in the preceding race.

Two *false starts* (premature jumps over the starting line) disqualify a skater from an event.

Scoring

Points are awarded in final events by the order of finish, as follows:

> First place — 5 points
> Second place — 3 points
> Third place — 2 points
> Fourth place — 1 point

The overall winner is the skater with the greatest number of points won in all final events.

Procedure

At the official's call, the skaters stand motionless at the pre-start line.

On the "ready" command, skaters step up to the start line and take their starting position. Skates cannot be over the starting line.

The race begins with a whistle or shot.

The race may be re-started after a false start or if a skater falls within the first six meters on the long track or before the *apex* (center) of the first turn in the short track.

In the long track events, the skater on the inner lane has the right-of-way and must be passed on the right (outside), unless the inner skater has drifted and there is room to pass on the left. Indoors, passing can be done from either side. The passing skater is always responsible for collisions and shall not interfere with or slow an opponent's progress.

In the *home stretch* (final straight section skated), opponents must stay in their lanes until the finish, unless one skater has such a lead that changing lanes will not create interference.

A skater finishes the race when a skate first touches the finishing line.

Olympic style

This type of skating is done on the 400-meter track with two lanes. Two competitors skate against the clock; the fastest time over a single race or multiple races wins.

Other races cover various distances, as follows:

Men: 500, 1000, 1500, 5000 and 10,000 meters
Women: 500, 1000, 1500, 3000 and 5000 meters

Points are given based on a skater's time for the event. As an example, in a 500-meter event, each second counts one point. The winner is the skater with the fastest time; that is, the lowest number of points. Ties create co-winners.

Officials

The referee decides all disputes and protests, has authority to make decisions, monitors weather and ice conditions and can skate along and observe contestants from an inner track. The timekeeper clocks all events. Judges determine the order of skaters finishing and the scorer records the finishing positions and points scored. A starter begins each race; a lap counter keeps track of each skater's progress.

Penalties are signaled by a raised arm with a fist. Skaters can be disqualified for causing a collision while moving out from the inner lane, changing lanes on a curve, pushing opponent, skating backward, fighting or other unsportsmanlike conduct.

History

The game is a variation of the older sport of racquets and was originally played in the yards of taverns and inns in England. It was described by Charles Dickens in *The Pickwick Papers* as a game in debtor's prison. Racquets was first played on an indoor four-walled court at Harrow's School in England in 1822. Another game that followed used a softer ball than racquets, one that could be "squashed" in the hand; this gave the newer game its name. The sport spread to America in the mid-19th century. The rules were formalized in 1890 and many courts were built at private clubs. The United States Squash Racquets Association governs the amateur affairs of the sport.

Since World War II, the game has achieved wide popularity throughout the world. The North American hard ball game, described here, is different from that played overseas. The international version uses a wider court, a softer ball and has different scoring.

Object of the Game

Two players or teams using long-handled racquets play in a completely enclosed court and try to hit a ball off the front wall in a way that their opponents cannot properly return it. The side with the highest point total wins the game.

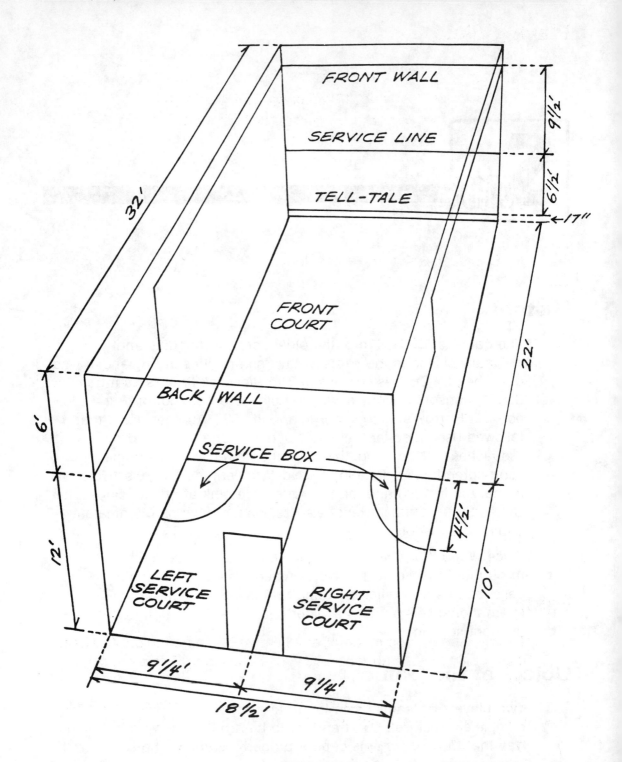

Singles court

Playing Field

The court's dimensions are as follows:

Singles: 32 feet long, 18½ feet wide, 18 feet high
Doubles: 45 feet long, 25 feet wide, 22 feet high

The *front wall line*:

Singles: 16 feet above the floor
Doubles: 20 feet above the floor

The *service line*:

Singles: 6½ feet above the floor
Doubles: 8 feet, 2 inches above the floor

The *back wall line*:

Singles: 6½ feet above the floor
Doubles: 7 feet above the floor

The *service court line*:

Singles: 22 feet from the front wall
Doubles: 30 feet from the front wall

The *telltale line* (a tin strip):

Singles and doubles: 17 inches high on the front wall

The *side wall lines* connect the front and back wall lines.

The *service boxes* have a radius of 4½ feet.

Equipment

The **racquet** can be made of any permissible material, but the head must be wood. It is approximately 27 inches long. The strings may not be metal.

The **ball** is made of a rubber compound and is hollow. Its diameter is approximately 1¾ inches and it weighs about 1.1 ounces.

Dress is informal; white or light clothing is preferred, and appropriate court shoes are required.

General Rules

Games can be played between two players (singles) or four players (doubles).

After hitting the ball, a player must move out of the way and allow an opponent a fair view of the ball and room to play it.

A five minute warm-up period is allowed.

Play is continuous from the first serve to the end of a game.

A rest period of two minutes is allowed between games, except for a five-minute break after the third game.

Points can be won by either the server or the receiver. Note: In international games, only the server scores points.

The first player or team to reach 15 points wins the game, unless the score is tied at 13. In that case, the first player to reach 13 has three choices, as follows:

- Set to five — the game is played to 18
- Set to three — the game is played to 16
- No set — the game is played to 15

The player must announce his decision before the next serve.

If there is a tie at 14 (and was no tie at 13), the first player to 14 may choose *set to three* and extend the game to 17, or select *no set* and have the game remain at 15 points.

The first player to win three games wins the match.

Procedure

A racquet spin (smooth or rough side) determines who serves and receives.

Serving

The server stands with at least one foot inside the service box area of the service court. The ball is to be thrown in the air or bounced once before being struck with the racquet.

In singles play, at the start of the game and when there is a new server, the ball is served by the winner of the previous point. The server may choose the service box and alternate boxes until the serve is lost or the game is over.

The ball is to be served onto the front wall, above the service line and below the front wall line, before it touches any other part of the court. The rebound may strike other walls, but the ball must first touch the floor inside the opposite service court if not volleyed.

A *fault* is a ball that:

• Hits the front wall on or below the service line

• Hits the front wall on or below the front wall line

• Bounces in front of or on the service court line

• Bounces into the server's court

• Is served without one foot inside the service box

If the first serve is a fault, another serve can be made. Two consecutive faults lose the point.

The following violations also result in a lost serve:

• The server hits the ball more than once during the motion

• The ball touches any part of the court before being hit

• The ball touches any part of the court before hitting the front wall

• The ball hits the telltale line or touches the server

In doubles play, the first server serves until losing a point; then the partner serves. After another point is lost, the serve moves over to the first player on the other side. When that player loses a point, the fourth player serves. Exception: at the start of each new game, the serving team changes after the loss of the first point.

Returns

The ball must be hit on a *volley* (before it hits the floor) or before it touches the floor twice to be a good return of a serve or from a following play. The ball must get to the front wall on the *fly* (in the air) and touch above the telltale line and below the front wall line. The return may touch any other walls before reaching the front wall but may only be stroked one time; no *double-hits*. All returns must be within the playing areas.

If the receiver does not make a good return, the server wins the point. If a good return of serve is made, players then alternate making returns. The player that fails to make a good return loses the point.

The ball may be hit many times during a rally (strokes between the players) until it has twice touched the floor before being returned or goes out of court.

A bad return is when the ball bounces twice before being hit, or if the ball is hit twice, touches the floor on its way to the front wall, hits the telltale or goes out of play.

Lets

A *let* is the replay of a point at the request of a player and ends the rally. Lets are given under the following circumstances:

- The receiver is not ready
- The player's movement to the ball is obstructed
- An opponent cannot help being hit with the ball
- The ball is damaged or strikes some object
- The players (without a referee) cannot agree on an action

A *let point* is awarded to a player not given the chance to play the ball and make a winning shot.

Officials

The referee controls the game. When there are two judges, a player may appeal to the referee, who in turn refers to the judges. If both judges overrule the referee, their decision is final.

History

Swimming was an essential part of the physical and military training for young men in ancient Greece and Rome. Plato wrote that a man's education was not complete until he could read, write and swim. By the Middle Ages, interest in swimming disappeared because of fear that disease was spread in the water. In Japan, swimming instruction was ordered by the Emperor in the 1800s and organized events were held. The first swimming club was formed in London in 1837; championships were held in England and Australia by mid-century.

Competitive swimming began to be popular in the U.S. in the late 1800s. The first modern Olympics in 1896 had events for men; those for women began in 1912. United States Swimming, the governing authority for the sport, has extensive training, development and competition programs for a broad range of classes and age groups.

Object of the Sport

Participants compete by moving their bodies through water with arm and leg motion. The first individual or team to finish a set distance using a *stroke* (swimming style) or combination of strokes is the winner.

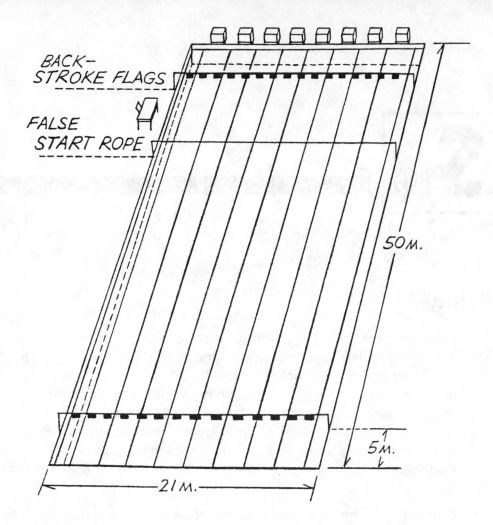

BACK-
STROKE FLAGS

FALSE
START ROPE

50 M.

5 M.

21 M.

Field of Play

The *long course* for major competitions is 50 meters (164 feet) long and 23 meters (75 feet) wide and two meters (6 feet, 7 inches) deep. The *short course* is 25 yards or 25 meters (82 feet) long and 18 meters (60 feet) wide. The minimum depth is 1.2 meters (four feet).

The pools includes six to eight *lanes*, numbered from right to left as the swimmers face the pool at the start. Each lane is 2.75 meters (nine feet) wide, separated by lane ropes with floats.

Dark *markers* are at the bottom of the pool in the center of each lane to a point two meters (6 feet, 7 inches) from the ends of the pool. T-shaped end wall targets are above and below the water line.

Numbered starting **blocks** (raised platforms) are placed approximately 0.75 meters (30 inches) above the water surface and set flush to the pool end wall. Grips are used for backstroke starts.

Triangular **flags** in contrasting colors are suspended on ropes five meters (16 feet, 5 inches) from each end to warn backstroke swimmers of the turn and the finish. They are placed 4.6 meters (15 feet) from the ends on the short course.

A **rope** is suspended across the pool 15 meters (49 feet) from the starting end to recall competitors who make a **false start** (begin to race before the signal). It is suspended 11 meters (36 feet) from the start of the short course.

The water temperature is 78 to 80 degrees.

Uniforms

Swimmers wear non-transparent and appropriate bathing suits. Goggles and caps are permitted; no speed or buoyancy devices are allowed.

General Rules

Competitors must stay in their assigned lanes and swim the complete distance of the event.

Competitors may be disqualified for the following violations:

- Late arrival at the start
- Interfering with another swimmer (such as splashing and lane crossing)
- Not touching the end wall at a turn or at the finish
- Swimming in another lane
- Walking on or jumping from the floor of the pool
- Entering the pool during a race or for unsportsmanlike conduct

Procedure

Lane assignments for final competitions are based on times recorded in preliminary **heats** (early rounds of an event). Advancement from heats to semi-finals to final is determined by finishing times.

The swimmer with the best time is given the center lane or lane to the right of the center. The other swimmers are assigned lanes in descending order of their times, alternately, to the left and right. The *spearhead principle* (arrangement of swimmers by times) has the fastest swimmers in the center and the slowest swimmers in the outside lanes.

The starter directs swimmers to step on the starting blocks (except for the backstroke or medley relay); both feet are the same distance back from the starting block. In the backstroke, swimmers start in the water facing the pool edge and holding it or hand grips and with their feet curled under the water surface.

After the referee's whistle, the starter commands, "Take your mark." Competitors step forward to the front end of platforms into the starting position. When all swimmers are motionless, the starting signal is given.

A *false start* occurs when swimmers leave their marks before the starting signal. In the backstroke, a false start occurs when a swimmer does not keep his hands or feet in the proper position.

A swimmer who makes a false start because of the movement of another competitor may not be charged for the offense.

A false starts brings automatic disqualification to the offender.

After a false start, the starter repeats the starting signal and a false start rope is lowered to signal the swimmers in the water.

Strokes and Relays

Breaststroke: After a diving start, the body is face down with the shoulders parallel to the water surface. The hands are pushed forward from the breast, with palms out, and brought back even to the hips with a simultaneous circular arm movement. The legs are drawn up together and then kicked back sideways (frog-like) with the feet turned outward. The head must break the surface during the arm and leg movement cycle. At the start and at turns, a swimmer may bring the arms back to the legs and make one leg kick while under water. The end wall touch must be made with both hands, but the turn can be done in any way. The head must break the water during the last full stroke cycle. The touch at the finish is to be made with both hands together.

Butterfly: After a diving start, the arms are pulled back one time under water, bringing the swimmer to the surface. Both arms are then brought forward at the same time above the water and pulled down back under water. The leg kick is *dolphin* (up and down together). No alternating movement of arms or legs is allowed. The turns may be made in any manner the swimmer desires. The end wall touch at the turns and the finish is to be with both hands, simultaneously.

Backstroke: The swimmer starts in the water, then pushes off and swims with the back down throughout the race, except during the turns. The arm stroke is windmill style in circular motion; the leg kick is *flutter* (alternating up and down, with the knees bent). The swimmer must touch the end wall. If a swimmer turns past a vertical position, the motion must be continuous (a freestyle-like flipturn). After the turn, the swimmer must have the back down before the feet leave the end wall. While on the back, any body part can touch the end wall to finish the race.

Freestyle: After a diving start, the swimmer may use any stroke. The preferred style is *front crawl* (body down, arms alternating up and into the water in a pulling motion, with a flutter kick). At the turns and finish, the end walls are to be touched by any body part.

Individual medley: The swimmers race four strokes of equal distances over the prescribed distance. The sequence: butterfly, backstroke, breaststroke, freestyle. Standard rules for strokes, turns and finish are to be followed.

Relay races: Four swimmers are on each team, and each swims one-fourth the event length. No swimmer swims more than one *leg* (equal distance). A teammate cannot leave the platform before an incoming swimmer has touched the end wall.

Freestyle relay: Each team has four swimmers, and each swims ¼ the event distance using any stroke, with a freestyle finish.

Medley relay: As above, but each swimmer swims a different stroke. Sequence: backstroke, breaststroke, butterfly, freestyle. The finish rule for each style applies.

SWIMMING

Events

Short course: meters or yards

Freestyle: 50/100/200/400 (500 yards) /800 (1000 yards) /1500

Backstroke: 100/200

Butterfly: 100/200

Breaststroke: 100/200

Individual medley: 200/400

Freestyle relay: 400/800

Medley relay: 400

Long course: meters

Freestyle: 50/100/200/400/800/1500

Backstroke: 100/200

Butterfly: 100/200

Breaststroke: 100/200

Individual medley: 200/400

Freestyle relay: 400/800

Medley relay: 400

13 to 18 years: meters or yards

Freestyle: 50/100/200/400 (500 yards) /800 (1000 yards) /1500

Backstroke: 100/200

Butterfly: 100/200

Breaststroke: 100/200

Individual medley: 200/400

Freestyle relay: 200/400/800

Medley relay: 200/400

11 to 12 years: meters or yards

Freestyle: 50/100/200/400 (500 yards)
Backstroke: 50/100
Butterfly: 50/100
Breaststroke: 50/100
Individual medley: 100/200
Freestyle relay: 200/400
Medley relay: 200/400

10 and under

As above, except 400 meter freestyle, medley relay and freestyle relay

Scoring

Points are awarded to teams based on the results of the events. Scoring values vary depending on the type of the meet (dual, triangular and so on), the number of lanes in the pool, mixed classes of swimmers and other situations. The local swimming committee is to establish and make available scoring information.

Officials

The referee is in charge of the *meet* (swimming competition) with authority over all other officials and swimmers, and decides all matters related to conduct of events.

The starter controls swimmers until a fair start is made, and gives participants specific instructions, signals the start and handles false starts.

Judges have authority over swimmers after the race has started. Stroke judges monitor the style of swimming as correct for the event. Turning judges watch all turns and relay changes and tell competitors how many laps remain in the race. Place judges call the order of finish.

Timekeepers time competitors in the lanes and record results.

The chief judge and chief timekeeper assign responsibilities to other officials and receive their reports.

Scorers record the order of finish and collect team and point scores.

History

The game originated in England in the early 1900s and was called by its trade name, *ping pong*. Known as table tennis since 1921, when an international group was formed, the sport had great popularity and growth. For many years the most outstanding players came from central Europe: Hungary, Czechoslovakia, Austria. By the 1950s, both the men's and women's events were dominated by Asians: Japanese, Chinese, Korean. Overseas, table tennis is considered a major competitive sport. In the United States, it has been more of a recreational game, but the development of the sport by the U.S. Table Tennis Association from training, local and regional events and televised tournaments has raised the level of play and increased participation.

Object of the Game

Players use paddles to hit a small ball across a table that is divided by a net. Points are won by making shots that cannot return.

Playing Field

The table is usually made of wood. It measures nine feet long by five feet wide and 30 inches high. Dark green is the preferred color, with white side, center and end lines.

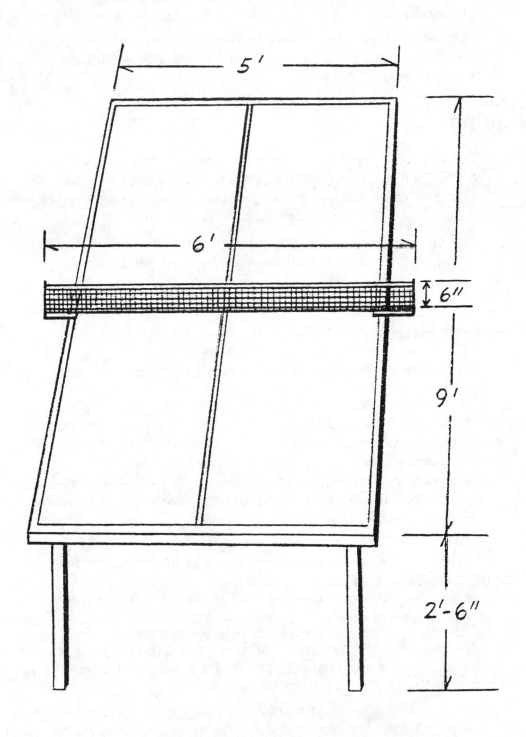

5'

6'

6"

9'

2'-6"

The table edges are part of the playing surface; the table sides are not.

The net is six feet long and six inches high and suspended across the center of the table by posts. The net should be dark green with a white line on the top.

Equipment

The **racquet** or **paddle** can come in any size, shape or weight; the *blade* (handle and center section) are to be made of wood. The side used to hit the ball should be covered with sponge rubber; the sides can be different colors, but one must be red.

The **ball** is made of celluloid or other plastic, and can be white or yellow. It is 1½ inches in diameter and weighs .09 ounces.

Players dress in active sportswear, in any color except white.

General Rules

Games are played between individuals (singles) or pairs (doubles).

A point is scored when an opponent:

- Does not make a good serve
- Fails to make a good return
- Hits the ball two times successively
- *Volleys* (hits the ball when it has not bounced in a player's court after an opponent has sent it over or around the net)
- Lets the ball bounce twice in own court
- Hits the ball with an illegal racquet surface
- Touches the playing surface with a *free hand* (not holding the racquet)
- Touches the net or moves the table while the ball is in play
- In doubles, hits the ball out of turn

The ball is judged as passing over or around the net if it goes under or outside the net supports or if it is hit after bouncing back over the net by its own force.

The first side to score 21 points wins the game, unless the score is tied at 20; then, the winner is the first side to score two points more than the opponent.

The winner of a match is the first side to win three or five games.

Play is continuous, but two minutes rest may be taken between games.

Procedure

The right to serve or receive and the choice of ends is decided by a coin toss. The winner may make the loser choose first.

In doubles, the serving side decides first who on the team will serve and the receiving side decides who will receive. After that, the order of serving and receiving is reversed from the previous game.

Serving

The ball is held in the open palm of the free hand with the fingers together and the thumb out. The hand must be higher than the table. The ball is thrown straight up, without spin, and cannot be hit until it starts to fall. At the time of the serve, the racquet must be behind the table end or an imagined extension. After hit by the racquet, the ball must touch the table on the server's side and go over or around the net and then bounce in the receiver's court.

In doubles, the ball must first touch the server's right hand court or center line and then the receiver's right hand court (diagonally opposite) or center line.

Returning

The return is to go over or around the net and bounce in the opponent's court. A return is good if the ball touches the net or its supports, or if it passes the net and returns back to the hitter before being struck by an opponent. The ball cannot bounce more than once or be hit twice successively before its return.

Order of play

In singles: The server makes a good service, the receiver makes a good return, then the server and receiver make alternate returns.

In doubles: The server makes a good service, and then the receiver, the server's partner and the receiver's partner each make good returns in that order. Play continues in sequence.

A change of service occurs after every five points. In singles, the server becomes the receiver. In doubles, the first receiver becomes the second server, the partner of the original server becomes the third server and the partner of the original receiver becomes the fourth server.

The sequence continues until the end of the game. If the score is 20-20, the server changes at every point.

The player who served first in a game receives first in the next game. In doubles, the order of receiving switches from the previous game.

The players change ends after each game and (in the final game of a match) when one player or team has scored 10 points. In doubles, the receiving team changes their order.

A *rally* is the time when the ball is served until the point is won.

A *let* is a rally when no point is scored. It includes the following circumstances:

- The ball touches the net or supports during the serve
- The receivers are not ready
- A serve is not made or received in the proper order
- The umpire determines a problem with the playing conditions or a disturbance

The ball is in play until it touches anything except the playing surface, the net and supports or a held racquet. Otherwise, a rally is decided by a point or a let.

Expedite system

At the end of 15 minutes (or sooner, if the players agree), a let is called to put a time limit on a game. The serve alternates after every point. The serving player or side has the service stroke and 12 additional strokes to win the rally or the point is given to the receiver. Once started, the system remains for the rest of the match and the players alternate serves.

Officials

An umpire, if available, decides the results of all play.

History

Tee Ball, the entry sport to baseball and softball for youngsters six to eight years old, has become a major youth recreational activity. The elimination of pitching and any fear of being hit by a pitched ball allows organized team participation at an early age. Young players learn the fundamentals and develop baseball skills in minimally competitive league play. The emphasis is on hitting, running and defensive teamwork.

Branch Rickey, the owner of the Brooklyn Dodgers in the early 1950s, is credited with the introduction of a flexible batting tee made from an automobile radiator hose. It was used by the great stars of that era, such as Duke Snyder and Gil Hodges. Rules for a tee-based game followed and, using a tee adapted from an inflation cup, a cow milking device, the sport was widely played in Canada during the 1960s. Little League Baseball has set guidelines for tee ball since 1974 and the game provides a natural transition to their Minor League program. Many local groups have developed their own playing rules and regulations.

Object of the Game

Members of two teams take turns hitting a ball off a tee set on home plate. Batters try to get on base and advance to home; fielders try to prevent that from happening. Scores are not kept, and there are no winners and losers.

Field of Play

The field is similar to the dimensions of a Little League field, but with only 50 feet between the bases.

The *playing line* is an imaginary line running between first base and third base. It also can be an arc, a curved circle extending out 40 feet from home plate.

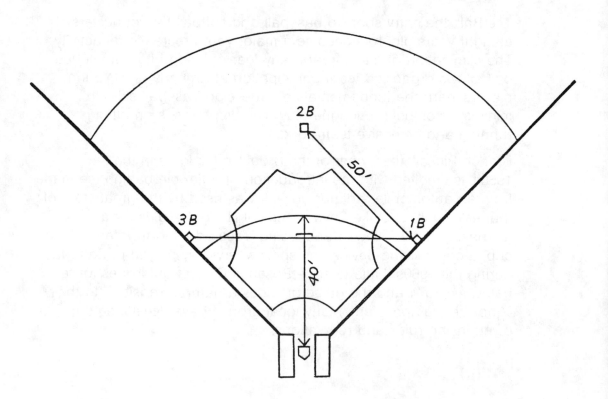

Equipment

The **bat** is a smooth, rounded stick of aluminum, fiberglass or wood (not laminated). It is approximately 27-33 inches long and 2¼ inches in diameter.

The **ball** is approximately nine inches in diameter and weights five ounces. It may be softer than a standard baseball.

The **tee** is a platform with an adjustable, flexible tube to support the ball.

Uniforms

Players dress in active sportswear, including soft-soled shoes. The batter, on-deck batter, base runners and coaches must wear helmets.

The catcher must wear protective gear: a mask, helmet, shin guards, and chest protector with collar.

The fielders wear gloves, the firstbaseman a glove or mitt and the catcher a mitt.

Team T-shirts and caps are suggested, but not mandatory.

General Rules

A tee ball *roster* (list of players on team) should not include more than 20 boys and girls; 15 is preferred. The roster may be changed anytime.

Players must be at least six years old and not turn nine before August 1st in the year in order to play. The "league age" is a player's age before August 1st.

Teams should try to have an equal number of players of the same league age.

Players are to be assigned to their teams by a cooperative effort by all concerned adults (managers, coaches, and others).

The game follows the general rules of baseball/softball, except for the following:

- The ball is hit off the tee, not pitched
- Bunting and half swings are not permitted
- The infield fly rule does not apply
- Unlimited substitutions are permitted for the defensive team

(See baseball/softball chapters for game basics, term definitions and so on.)

Only players, managers, coaches and umpires are allowed on the playing field before and during a game.

When a team is at bat, all players are to stay on their bench except the batter, the on-deck batter and any base runners. When a team is in the field, all reserve players must stay on their team's bench.

Managers and coaches may stand near players but not interfere with the game. They can ask the umpire for time to show or explain to a player what is to be done. Managers and coaches may also act as umpires, if needed.

Only one game is played per day.

Standings are not kept; there are no championships games or awards, except for participation.

Night games, admission charges and televising are not permitted.

Procedure

The starting lineup of each team should include all the players.

The catcher stands far enough behind home plate so as to not interfere with the batter.

The pitcher acts as an infielder and stays with both feet on the pitcher's plate until the ball is hit.

All other infielders play in their positions and shall not cross the playing line until the ball is hit. When this happens, the umpire calls, "time" and the ball is dead.

The basic outfield consists of left, left-center, center, right-center and right fielders.

Additional players may be used to fill in the infield.

When the defensive team is in place and ready, its manager tells the umpire, who then puts the ball on the tee and calls, "Play ball."

The entire roster of players bats in order.

As there is no pitching, there are no balls; therefore, no bases on balls.

Local organizers decide whether strikeouts are called.

A foul ball is called if the ball is hit into fair territory but travels less than 15 feet, or if the batter hits the tee, knocking the ball off.

If the hit ball does not cross the playing line (or arc), it is not in play and is treated like a strike.

The batter becomes a runner when the ball is hit hard enough into fair territory.

The runner is safe if the ball is not caught on the fly or is fielded and arrives at a base after the runner gets there.

Base runners cannot leave the base until the ball is hit.

If the fielder over-throws the ball, the runner is allowed one extra base.

After players have moved ahead on the bases as far as possible or after an out, the umpire calls "time" and puts the ball back on the tee.

The batting side is out when three outs are made, or all the players on the team have batted one time in the inning (the *bat around rule*).

The local league decides game length. The recommendation is four innings or a 90-minute time limit. Games should not exceed six innings.

History

Tennis originated during the 12th or 13th centuries in France, where it was called *jeu de paume* (game of the palm). The players used the front of their hand to hit a ball back and forth over a net on an indoor court. Major W. C. Clapton introduced a modern version of the sport in Wales to be played on grass. He published rules, took out a patent on the game and its equipment and named it *sphairistike* — Greek for playing ball. The sport quickly spread to England, replacing croquet as the most popular outdoor game. Now known as lawn tennis, the first major championship was played at Wimbledon in 1877.

The game was brought to the U.S. by an American sportswoman, Mary Ewing Outerbridge, in 1874. The Davis Cup award for team play was created by an American in 1900. The 1920s were an era of growth, with top players becoming well-known celebrities. Tennis participation continued to expand through the years before and after World War II. Beginning in the 1960s, sponsored events, television, high profile professionals and the accomplishments of young players together with the building of indoor and outdoor courts and the availability of new equipment moved tennis into the mainstream of American recreational and competitive sport. The United States Tennis Association is the national governing body and its programs are dedicated to advancing the game at all levels of play.

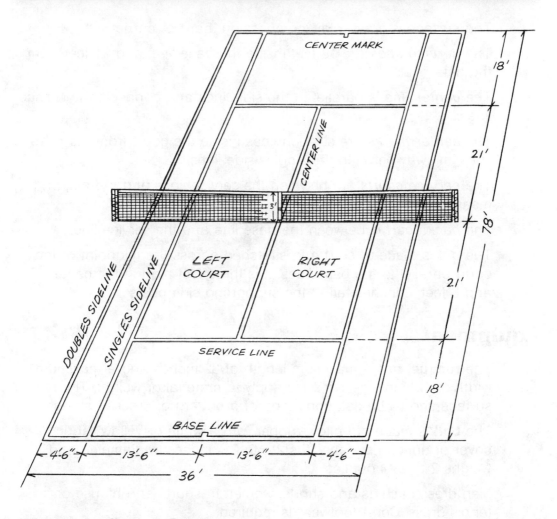

Object of the Game

Two or four players using regulation tennis racquets compete to score points by hitting a tennis ball over a net and out of an opponent's reach, or in such a way that it cannot be returned back across the net inside the court.

Playing Field

The court measurements are to the outside edge of the lines. The court measures 78 feet at the side line and 36 feet at the base line.

The *singles court* is 27 feet wide; the *doubles court* is 4½ feet wider on each side.

The *surface* is grass, clay, composition, hard or carpet.

The *service lines* are 18 feet inside the base line, and 21 feet from the net.

The *center line* is parallel to the side lines and connects the service lines.

The *center marks* are six-inch lines inside the court from the base lines, midway between the singles side lines.

The *service courts* are between the service lines and the net, and measure 21 × 13½ feet.

The *back court* is between the base line and the service line.

The *net* is made of cord and stretched across the midpoint of the court parallel to the base lines. It is three feet high in the center, and 3 feet, 6 inches tall at the supporting side posts.

Equipment

The **racquet** has a maximum length of 32 inches and a maximum width of 12½ inches. No rules apply to material or weight. The hitting surface should be flat, consisting of a pattern of crossed strings.

The **ball** is made of hollow rubber with a white or yellow fabric cover of uniform surface. It is 2½ to 2⅝ inches in diameter, and weighs 2 to 2¹⁄₁₆ ounces.

Men dress in shirts and shorts, women in shorts and blouse or tennis dress. Court footwear is required.

General Rules

The game may be played indoor or outdoors.

Games may be played between two players (singles), four players (doubles) or a male and female on each team (mixed doubles).

Scoring

Either the serving side or receiving side can score points.

A zero score is referred to as *love*. The first point is *15*, the second is *30*, the third is *40*. The fourth point scored (*game point*) wins the game unless the score is tied at *duece* (40-all).

One side must gain a lead of two points. The first point scored after duece is an **advantage** or **ad.** If the server goes ahead, it is **ad-in**; **ad-out** is when the receiver scores a point.

If the side with an advantage loses a point, the score returns to deuce. A game continues until one side wins.

The first player to score four points and lead by two wins the game.

The first player to win six games and lead by two or win a tiebreaker wins the set.

The first player to win two sets in a three-set match (women's and most men's) or three sets in a five-set match wins the match.

The tiebreaker is won by the first player or side to win seven points. If the score is tied at 6-all, play continues until one side has a two-point lead.

The server's score always is given first; for example, if the score is 30-15, the serving side has two points and the receiving side has one point). In a tiebreaker, points are given in numerical order; the above score would be 2-1.

Procedure

The winner of a coin toss or racquet spin chooses to serve or to receive and select at which end of the court to begin play.

In singles:

> Players serve from behind the righthand court to a service court diagonally opposite, and then from alternate courts after each point.

> Players keep the serve for a complete game, and alternate throughout the set.

> Players change ends after the first and third games and follow that sequence until the end of the set. If the total number of games played is even at that point, ends do not change until after the first game of the next set.

In doubles:

The players decide who serves first. The serve changes sides after every game and players on the same team alternate serving. For example, the partner of the first server serves the third game; the first server does not serve again until the fifth game. The players change ends after the second game and every two games that follow. Partners also decide who will receive the first serve, which is then taken in alternate turns. The order of serving and receiving shall be decided at the beginning of each set.

Serving

The ball is served to start every game and after a point is scored.

The server stands with both feet behind the base line and anywhere between an imaginary extension of the service mark and the singles side line.

The serve may be made overhand or underhand. The ball is thrown into the air and must be struck with the racquet before it hits the ground.

The server may catch the ball before striking it or may let it drop to the court without swinging and then toss it up again.

The ball must cross the net without bouncing and land in the receiver's service court.

A *service fault* occurs when the ball goes into the net or lands outside the receiver's court or is swung at and missed.

A *foot fault* occurs when the server steps on or over the base line with either foot or serves from beyond the center mark or runs or walks before hitting the ball. The server may cross the base line after the racquet strikes the ball.

If the first serve is a fault, the player is entitled to a second serve from behind the same half of the court. If another fault occurs, it is a *double fault* and the server loses a point.

An *ace* is a serve that the receiver cannot play.

A *let* is called if any serve touches the net but still lands within the service court or touches the receiver before it hits the ground or was served before the receiver was ready. The serve does not count, and the player serves again. A let may also be called if play has been interrupted.

Service during a tiebreaker proceeds as follows:

1. Side A serves point 1 from the righthand court
2. Side B serves points 2 and 3, alternating courts
3. Side A serves points 4 and 5 from the left and right
4. Side B serves point 6 from the left, and the players change ends
5. Side B serves point 7 from the right
6. Side A serves points 8 and 9, left and right
7. Side B serves points 10 and 11, left and right
8. Side A serves point 12 from the left
9. If the game is 6-all, ends are changed and the game continues, repeating the sequence as from the start

Receiving and play

The ball is in play from the time it is struck by the server's racquet until a point has been decided. A ball that lands on any line is good and is considered to be within the court area marked by the line.

The receiver must hit a properly served ball on the first bounce and return it across the net into the section between the base line and either the singles or doubles side lines, depending on the game.

After the serve has been returned, it then can be hit by either side as a *volley* (on the fly) or by a *ground stroke* (after one bounce) into the opponent's court, as above.

A return is good if:

- The ball touches and then goes over the net and lands within the court
- The ball rebounds back over the net (the intended receiver may reach over, but not touch the net, to hit the ball)
- The ball is hit from outside the posts, or If the player's racquet extends over the net after the ball was struck

A *rally* is a series of strokes between the players until a point is scored.

A side wins a point when an opponent commits one of the following violations after receiving the ball:

- Hits it into the net
- Lets it bounce twice before hitting
- Hits it outside the court
- Hits it before it crosses the net
- Hits it twice or carries it on the racket
- Throws the racket and hits the ball
- Touches the net

A side loses a point for any of the above actions and, on serve, for a double fault.

Game point decides the result of a game; ***set point*** determines the winner of a set; ***match point*** is the point on which the result of the match depends.

Officials

During tournaments, the referees include the following:

- A chair umpire in charge of the match
- A net cord judge with fingers on the net at the serve
- Line umpires to see if the ball lands inside or outside the court boundaries and to call foot faults on serves

TRACK & FIELD

History

Competition in track and field events, also known as *athletics*, is considered to be the oldest of organized sports. They were the central part of the ancient, male-only Olympic Games for over 1100 years, beginning in 776 B.C. (Women had their own Heraea Games every four years.) There are records of athletic events in the 12th and 16th centuries, but modern track and field dates from school and university contests in 19th century England.

Interest and participation in the sport grew rapidly in North America after the New York Athletic Club promoted indoor meets in the 1860s. In 1896, track and field became recognized internationally as it was part of the revived Olympics in Athens. Women began to compete in the early 1900s and entered the Olympics in 1928. Through the years, many outstanding athletes have become world-famous celebrities based on their performance achievements.

Many organizations are involved in various aspects of track and field. The Athletics Congress establishes rules and conducts national and other competitions in the U.S. New training methods, track and equipment improvements, and innovative techniques have all contributed to the development of the games. Today, track and field may be the most universally played of all the competitive sports.

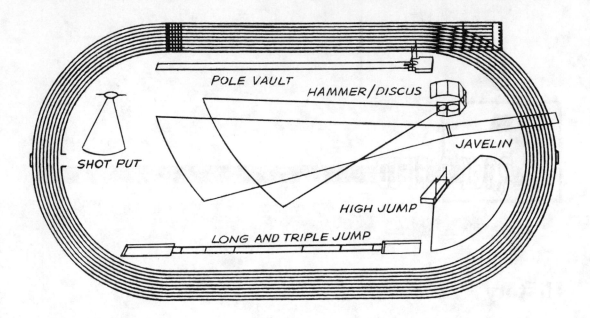

Object of the Games

Competitors try to run faster, jump higher and/or throw objects farther than their opponents. The first person to the finish line wins track events; the best height or distance wins field events.

Track Events

Field of Play

A standard outdoor running track is 400 meters (437 yards), with a synthetic or gravel surface. It consists of six to eight lanes, each 1.22 meters (48 inches) wide.

Indoor tracks are usually 200 meters, and made of wood boards or composition with curves that are often *banked* (raised from the inside edge).

Starting positions are marked at various points on the track based on the distance of the race; all finishes are at the same place.

Equipment

A **starting block** (an adjustable metal foot support, often with built-in detectors for illegal starts) is used in events up to and including 400 meters.

Electronic timers record finishes up to $\frac{1}{100}$ of a second. Otherwise, stop watches are used.

Competitors dress in shorts and jersey with numbers on the front and back.

Shoes are made of leather or synthetic material with up to 11 spikes. Running barefoot or with one shoe is permitted.

General Rules

Races of 110 meters or less are run on a straight course. Longer races run counter-clockwise; a runner's left hand is always toward the center of the track. A *lap* is one complete run around the track.

Heats (qualifying rounds) are held to provide the runners for a *final* (last round of an event).

The lane order is drawn randomly in the first round. After that, performances in the competition determine lane assignment. In *sprints* (shorter distance events), racers must stay in their lanes from start to finish or be disqualified. In the 800 meters, racers stay in their lanes until after the first turn. Longer events are not run in lanes.

In races where runners must stay in their lanes around the curves of the track, starting positions are *staggered* so that each runner travels the same distance.

In races where starting blocks are used, the starter calls:

1. "On your marks" to tell the racers to crouch with both hands touching the ground

2. "Set" to get the racers into their final, motionless positions

In the longer races, only "On your marks" is called; the runners remain standing.

After all racers are in a steady position, a pistol is fired to begin the race. It is a false start if a competitor commits one of the following violations:

- Does not get into set position
- Disturbs other racers
- Starts before the pistol is fired

After a false start, the race is recalled by a second pistol shot.

After a warning, a second false start disqualifies the competitor.

The winner is the runner whose torso (upper body from shoulders to waist, not the arms, legs or head) first reaches the vertical plane (imaginary boundary) of the finish line.

Running

Sprint races for men and women cover distances of 100, 200 and 400 meters.

Endurance races for men and women are run over distances of 800, 1500, 3000, 5000 and 10,000 meters.

Relays are events with four runners on a team; each runs a *leg* (one quarter of the full distance).

A starting block is used by the leadoff runners only.

Runners carry a *baton* (metal or wood tube, approximately one foot long and weighing two ounces) in one hand.

The baton is passed between team members in a *takeover zone* (marked area 20 meters long). Any exchange outside the zone disqualifies the team. If the baton is dropped, it must be picked up by the runner who dropped it.

Relay events cover two distances for both men and women:

- 4 × 100 meters: four runners, each runs 100 meters
- 4 × 400 meters: four runners, each runs 400 meters

A team member receiving the baton must not start running more than 10 meters behind the takeover zone in the 4 × 100 meter relay. In the 4 × 400 meter relay, the receiver must start in the takeover zone.

The 4 × 100 meter relay is run in lanes. In the 4 × 400 meter relay, the competitors may leave their lanes for an inside position after the second runner makes the first turn.

After passing the baton, runners must stay in their respective lanes until the track is clear of competitors.

Hurdles

Hurdles are sprint races in which the runner must jump over 10 barriers.

The hurdle is an L-shaped metal frame four feet wide with a wood top bar. The height and spacing of hurdles depends on the event. It is designed so that force applied to the center of the top edge is required to knock it over.

A runner must clear the hurdle with both legs, but is not penalized for knocking it over.

Runners are disqualified for running out of the lane, trailing a foot or leg alongside a hurdle or deliberately pushing over a hurdle.

Hurdle events (with hurdle heights) are as follows:

- 100 meter (33 inches) — women
- 110 meter (42 inches) — men
- 400 meter (30 inches) — women
- 400 meter (36 inches) — men

Steeplechase

The steeplechase is a 3000-meter event for men in which runners have to go over 28 hurdles and seven water jumps.

The dry hurdles are three feet high and 13 feet wide.

The water jumps are 12 feet long, with a maximum depth of 27½ inches.

No hurdles are placed in the first 200 meters; four hurdles and a water jump are placed in each of the next 400 meters.

Competitors may jump over, step on and push off or hand-vault over the hurdles.

Failing to go through the water or letting a foot drag alongside a hurdle disqualifies a competitor.

Note: The 2000-meter junior event has 18 hurdles and five water jumps.

Road Races

Road races are run on streets and roads and a variety of firm surfaces.

Participants dress in shorts, shirts or ventilated racewear and cushioned footwear. Headwear is optional.

Distances, for men and women, are as follows:

- 5, 8 and 10 kilometers
- Marathon (42.195 kilometers, or 26 miles, 385 yds)

Race Walking

Race walking is done on a road or track, with events for men and women.

The rules regarding form are as follows:

- Unbroken contact with the ground must be maintained throughout the race.
- The advancing (front) foot must touch the ground before the rear foot is fully lifted.
- The supporting (rear) leg must be straightened out (not bent) for a moment while the foot is on the ground.

A warning that the competitor appears to be running is given by a white flag; a disqualification is signaled by a red flag.

Events cover the following distances:

- 20 kilometers (12.4 miles)
- 50 kilometers (31.1 miles)

Field Events

General Rules

The order of jumping or throwing is drawn by lot.

No practice is allowed after the competition has started in an event.

A performance in any qualifying competition is not counted as part of the final competition.

Competitors are awarded the best of all jumps and throws, including tiebreakers in the high jump and pole vault.

High jump

In the high jump, men and women attempt to leap over a bar resting on two uprights. The bar is raised after each round.

Competition area

The *runway* is a fan-shaped area extending in front of the jump.

The *crossbar* is a round wood or metal rod with flat ends to rest on uprights. It has a maximum weight of two kilograms (4.4 pounds). It can be knocked off to fall frontward or backward.

The *uprights* are two rigid metal standards set four meters (13 feet, 3 inches) apart with a mechanism to raise the crossbar, as needed.

The *landing pit* is a foam rubber cushioned area, approximately 13 feet long × 16 feet wide.

Competitors wear spiked shoes with a ½-inch sole preferred.

Procedure

An official announces the starting setting of the bar height. After each round, the bar is raised not less than two centimeters (¾ of an inch).

Competitors may choose to jump at the height called or pass on the turn and try later at subsequent heights.

Competitors decide the length and direction of their run up to the bar. They must take off from one foot, but may jump with their chest up (*flop)* or down over the crossbar.

A jump is a failure if the bar is knocked off the uprights or a contestant touches an area beyond the uprights without first going over the bar.

After failing the first jump, competitors may decide not to attempt a second or third jump at that height and may still jump at a following height.

Three consecutive misses, at same or different heights, eliminates the competitor.

The measurement is made between the lowest part of the top edge of the bar and the ground.

Rounds continue until all but one contestant is eliminated. That contestant is the winner, and may attempt greater heights. If there is a tie, the jumper with the fewest attempts at the winning height (or the highest height) wins; if a tie remains, the jumper with the fewest total misses wins.

Pole Vault

Contestants (men only) use a flexible pole to *vault* (leap) over a crossbar resting on two uprights. The bar is raised between rounds.

Competition area

The *runway* has no set length, but 45 meters (148 feet) is preferred.

The *box* is an angled metal or wood structure, approximately 24 × 39 inches, sunken level with the ground in front of uprights to accept the pole.

The *pole* can be any material or size, but usually is fiberglass, at least 16 feet long and weighs 4.4 pounds.

The *crossbar* is a metal rod, 14 feet, 9 inches long and approximately five pounds.

The *crossbar* is a metal rod, 14 feet, 9 inches long and approximately five pounds.

The *uprights* are two metal standards set 14 feet apart with three-inch pegs to support the bar.

The *landing pit* is padded and five meters (16 feet, 5 inches) square.

Note: Competitors wear spiked shoes.

Procedure

An official announces the starting height of the bar. The bar is raised not less than five centimeters (two inches) after every round.

A jump is a failure if:

- The bar is knocked off the supports
- The contestant or pole touches an area beyond the uprights without clearing the bar
- The competitor, after leaving the ground, moves his lower hand above the upper one or moves the upper hand higher along the pole.

A competitor may jump at the height called or pass.

If the first jump fails, a competitor may choose not to jump again at that height but try again at following heights.

Competitors are eliminated after three consecutive misses at any height.

Measurement is made from the ground to the lowest part of the upper side of the bar (the point of the greatest sag).

Rounds continue until only one contestant remains. He may then decide to try at greater heights.

The winner is the contestant with the highest jump. If there is a tie, the vaulter with the fewest attempts at the winning height (the highest height) wins; if a tie remains, the vaulter with the fewest total misses wins.

Long Jump

Contestants (men and women) sprint down a runway, then jump from a board in the ground into a sandpit.

Competition area

The *runway* has no set length, but 45 meters (148 feet) is preferred.

The *take-off board* is a white wood board, eight inches wide and sunk level across the end of the runway.

The *take-off line* marks the legal end of board closest to the pit.

The *indicator board* is a plasticine sheet, four inches wide, set against a take-off board on the side toward the pit to show if the jumper has stepped beyond the take-off line.

The *landing area* is a moistened sandpit, three meters (9 feet, 9 inches) wide and nine meters (29 feet, 6 inches) long beginning at least one meter (39 inches) from the take-off line.

Note: Competitors wear spiked shoes.

Procedure

There is no limit to the length of the sprint down the runway.

The jump is a failure if the competitor:

- Touches the indicator board (an impression will be left in the soft surface)
- Jumps from outside the take-off board
- Somersaults
- Touches the ground outside the landing area closer to the take-off than to the nearest mark made by the jump within the pit
- Walks back through the landing area

The measurement is taken from the nearest edge of any *break* (mark) made in the sand by any body part to the take-off line.

Each jumper gets three qualifying trials and three final jumps.

The winner is the contestant with the longest jump. If the jumpers tie, the second-best jump determines the winner.

Triple Jump

Contestants (men only) sprint down a runway to a take-off board, then hop, step and jump into a landing area.

Competition area

The jumping area is the same as for the long jump, except there is an additional runway area between the take-off board and the landing pit.

Procedure

At take-off, the competitor pushes off on either foot and lands on the same foot (the hop), takes a leaping step and lands on the opposite foot, then jumps off that foot into the pit.

All other rules for take-off, landing, failures, measurements, winning and so on are the same as the long jump.

Throwing Events

Discus

A heavy disc is thrown (men and women) from inside a circled area out to a wedged-shaped marked section of the field.

Competition area

The *circle* is 2.5 meters (8 feet, 2½ inches) in diameter and has a non-slip surface; it is banded by a metal ring.

The *sector lines* are two white lines extending out from the circle at a 40-degree angle.

The *cage* is a metal structure with a net wall to protect the spectators.

Equipment

The **discus** is made of wood with a metal rim and a weighted interior. For men, it is 8.7 inches in diameter and weighs two kilograms (4 pounds, 6.55 ounces). For women, it is 7.1 inches in diameter and weighs one kilogram (2 pounds, 3.25 ounces).

Contestants dress in spikeless footwear; gloves are not allowed, but resin and a leather support belt are permitted.

Procedure

Contestants must observe the following rules:

- Begin from a stationary position with their back to a marked sector
- Avoid touching the top of the ring around the circle (the inside of the ring can be touched) or the ground outside it during the throw
- Stay within the circle until the discus has landed
- The throw can be interrupted and the discus set down if desired

The discus must fall between the sector lines.

Throws are measured from the nearest mark made by the discus to the inner edge of the circle's ring.

Three qualifying *trials* (throws) are taken, then the finalists make three final throws.

The winner is the contestant with the longest throw. Ties are broken by the second-best throw.

Hammer

A ball on a handled chain is thrown (men only) from a caged circle out to a marked area.

Competition area

The area is the same as for the discus, except the circle is seven feet in diameter.

Equipment

The **hammer** weighs 16 pounds and has three connected parts, as follows:

- The **head**, a solid or filled metal ball that is 4 to 4¾ inches in diameter
- The **wire**, approximately four feet long and made of steel, which is connected to the head by a swivel
- The **grip**, a handle with a single or double metal loop

Contestants dress the same as for the discus, but a palm and wrist glove is allowed; individual fingers may be taped.

Procedure

The procedure is the same as for the discus, except the hammer head can touch the ground during the throw.

If the hammer breaks during the throw, the throw does not count.

Measurement is taken from the nearest part of the head to the inner edge of the ring around the circle.

Three qualifying throws are taken, then the finalists make three throws.

The winner is the contestant with the longest throw. Ties are broken by the second-best throw.

Shot Put

A *shot* (heavy ball) is *put* (thrown) by men and women from inside a circled area out to a marked area.

Competition Area

The *circle* is seven feet in diameter, made of concrete or a similar non-slip surface, with a raised *stop board* (curved wooden edge, four inches tall) at the front of the circle.

Equipment

The **shot** is a solid or filled metal ball with a smooth surface. For men, it is 4¾ inches in diameter and weighs 16 pounds. For women, it is four inches in diameter and weighs four kilograms (8.8 pounds).

Competitors dress the same as for the discus or hammer throw.

Procedure

The procedure is the same as for the discus and hammer throw, except for the following:

- Only one hand may be used
- The put is from the shoulder with the shot held close to the chin
- The hand must not be lowered below the starting position and the shot must not be thrown from behind the shoulder line

Measurement of the throw is from the nearest mark made by the shot to the inside of the metal ring on the circle.

The winner is the contestant with the longest put. Ties are decided by the second-best put.

Javelin

A slender metal shaft is thrown (men and women) from behind a curved line at the end of a runway to land within a marked section.

Competition area

The *runway* is 36 to 40 yards long and approximately four meters (approximately 13 feet) wide.

The *arc* (front edge of the runway) is a white curved wood or metal strip, or a painted line.

The *sector lines* begin from a point eight meters (26 feet, 3 inches) behind the arc and extend out to flag markers at a 29-degree angle.

Equipment

The **javelin** is metal with cord grips. For men, it is 8 feet, 10 inches long and weighs 800 grams (1.8 pounds). For women, it is 7 feet, 6 inches long and weighs 600 grams (1.3 pounds).

Contestants dress in spiked shoes; resin is allowed but gloves are not.

Procedure

Contestants are permitted two practice throws. They must follow proper procedure, as follows:

- Start in a stationary position, holding the javelin in one hand at the grip
- Throw the javelin from over one shoulder or the upper part of the throwing arm
- Face forward until the javelin is thrown and not touch or go beyond the runway boundary lines or the arc
- Stay within the runway until the javelin has landed

The javelin must fall within the sector lines and land point down.

Throws are measured from the mark made by the tip of the javelin to the inside edge of the arc.

Contestants make three qualifying throws and then three final throws.

The winner is the contestant with the longest throw; ties are broken by the second-best throw.

Decathlon

Men compete in a combination of 10 track and field events over two days.

Points are based on a scoring table and are awarded for the times and distances performed. In general, rules, equipment and procedures are the same as for the individual events. The highest total score wins.

The first-day events are as follows:

1. 100 meter sprint
2. Long jump
3. Shot put
4. High jump
5. 400 meter sprint

The second-day events are as follows:

1. 110 meter hurdles
2. Discus
3. Pole vault
4. Javelin throw
5. 1500 meter run

Heptathlon

Women compete in a combination of seven events over two days. The rules are the same as for the decathlon and the individual events.

The first-day events are as follows:

1. 100 meter hurdles
2. High jump
3. Shot put
4. 200 meter sprint

The second-day events are as follows:

1. Long jump
2. Javelin throw
3. 800 meter run

History

Volleyball was developed in 1895 by William G. Morgan, a YMCA physical instructor in Holyoke, Mass. It was intended as an activity for older players seeking a less strenuous sport than basketball. The original game had some baseball-like rules including innings and outs with nine players on a side. As a net game, it differed from tennis as it was a team sport and played without racquets.

American missionaries took the game to the Far East; U.S. troops help to internationalize the game during World Wars I and II. The Federation Internationale de Volleyball reports that 250 million people, age 15 to 50 years old, are taking part in official tournaments and that, worldwide, over 800 million play for recreation. Men and women's volleyball became an Olympic sport in 1964.

In 1928, the United States Volleyball Association became the governing body for the sport in this country. Today, 35 million Americans participate, including almost 12 million beach volleyball players. There are more than 45,000 YMCA teams. The key to volleyball's popularity is that it is based on a simple concept, does not require expensive equipment and can be played indoors or out by men and women, boys and girls of all ages and skills.

Object of the Game

Two teams of six players try to score points by hitting a ball over a net so that the opposing team cannot return the ball or stop it from hitting the ground in its court. The game (*set*) winner is decided by the point total; a match is won by the team that wins the most sets.

Playing Field

The court measures 29 feet, 6 inches wide by 59 feet long, with marked boundaries. The lines are part of the area they mark.

The *center line* runs the width of the court under the net.

The *attack lines* run the width of the court, 9 feet, 10 inches behind the center line.

The *service areas* are behind the boundary lines at the right ends. They measure 9 feet, 10 inches wide by 6 feet, 6 inches deep.

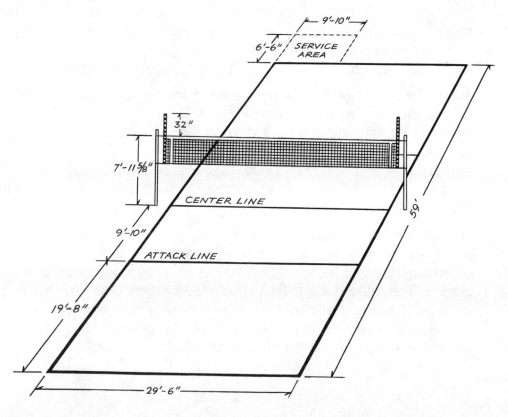

Equipment

The **ball** has a leather or leatherlike cover, has no laces and is light in color. It measures 25 to 27 inches in circumference, weighs 9 to 10 ounces, and has 4.5 to 6 pounds of air pressure per square inch.

The **net** is made of square mesh. It is a minimum of 32 feet long and 39 inches wide with a two-inch canvas band at the top.

For men, the net is 7 feet, 11⅝ inches high. For women, it is 7 feet, 4⅛ inches high.

Alternate net heights are as follows:

Age	Girls	Boys/coed
under 18	7'4⅛"	7'11⅝"
under 16	7'4⅛"	7'11⅝"
under 14	7'4⅛"	7'4⅛"

Grade	Girls	Boys/coed
Senior HS	7'4⅛"	7'11⅝"
Junior HS	7'4⅛"	7'11⅝"
Middle	7'4⅛"	7'4⅛"
Elementary	6'1"	6'1"

The **antenna** are flexible uprights, 32 inches in height, attached to the net directly above the side line boundaries.

Players dress in shirts, shorts and pants of the same design and color with numbers on front and back of the jerseys. Footwear may vary by player, but soft-soled court shoes are required.

General rules

The winner of a coin toss chooses to serve or receive or select the end of the court in which to begin play. If the winner elects to serve or receive, the loser gets choice of court.

The teams change sides, including benches, after each game except in a deciding game when the change is made after one team scores eight points.

Timeouts last 30 seconds. Each team is permitted two per game, when the ball is dead.

Teams consist of six players, one of whom is designated the captain.

Each player is noted by position (such as right front or center back) but does not have to stay in that court area after the serve.

The following rules apply to substitutions:

- The ball must be dead
- Teams are limited to six substitutes per set
- Replaced players may only re-enter the game once and in their original position in the serving order
- A substitute can only be replaced by the player whose position was taken and cannot return in the same game

Note: Certain competition levels (such as seniors, women's college, high school, youth and recreation) allow more substitutes, up to 12 in a set, and permit substitutes to enter the game three times.

Scoring

Points can only be scored by the serving team, except in the deciding game in a match.

One point is scored when:

- The ball hits the floor of the opponents' court inbounds
- The opponents cannot return the ball in three hits
- The opponents hit the ball out of bounds
- The opponents commit a *fault* (foul)

A *side-out* (loss of service) is called when the serving team does not score.

When the receiving team wins the *rally* (exchange of hits over the net), it gets to serve but does not earn a point.

During the deciding game of a match, a point is scored and ball possession is earned on every serve.

The serving team get points when the receiving team faults. If the serving team faults, the opponents get service and a point.

If one team is given a penalty, the other gets service and a point.

The winning team does not have to be serving to win.

The first team to score 15 points and lead by two points wins the game. Play continues until one team gets a two-point advantage, but there is a 17-point cap; a team can win by one point, 17-16.

Alternate rule: A team that gains a two-point lead after eight minutes of play wins the game.

The team that wins the best of three or best of five games wins the match.

Procedure

All players except the server must be within the court markings.

Each team has three players in a row (*front line*) near the net and three others (*back line*) standing behind them.

Serving

The server stands in the service area behind the end base line (right rear corner) and must remain there until the ball is hit. The server's feet cannot be on the line.

The server may bounce the ball before the serve and jump off the ground during the serve.

The server may use the hand, fist or any part of the arm to hit the ball into play. One re-serve is allowed if the ball is missed.

A serve is good when the ball enters the opposite court without a *service fault*, which occurs if the ball:

- Goes under or touches the net
- Touches the antenna or overhead obstruction
- Lands out of bounds
- Hits a teammate before crossing the net

A player keeps serving until the other team wins the right to serve.

Team players rotate one position in a clockwise pattern after the opponents have lost serve and before new service begins.

Teams change ends after each game. The serve goes to the team that was receiving at the end of the previous game.

VOLLEYBALL

Play

After the serve, players can move about on their side of the net but cannot completely step over the center line.

The ball can be hit with any part of the body above the waist.

One or both hands may be used, in an underhand or overhand motion, open or fisted; hands also may be clasped together.

The ball may be *spiked* (hit sharply downward into the opponent's court from a jump position). Front line players may spike from anywhere on the court but back line players must jump from behind the attack line.

Each team may contact the ball three times before returning it over the net. The first contact is a *dig*. A pass to a teammate nearer the net to attempt a spike is also called a *set*.

During an attempt to be the first to hit a ball coming from an opponent, double contact may be made by a player unless the fingers are used. No other player can touch the ball twice or between the first player's contacts.

Any body contact with the ball is considered as playing the ball.

A player may not hit the ball two times in succession.

When two players on the same team touch the ball at the same time, it counts as two hits and neither player may play the next ball.

A ball stopped between opposing players is to be replayed.

An *attack hit* (a ball aimed into the opponent's court) can be made by front line players at any time. Back line players can make an attack hit when behind the attack line or in front of the line if the ball is lower than the top of the net. Serves are not attack hits.

The ball can touch the top of the net and enter the opponents' court, except on a serve.

Players cannot attack a ball while it is on the opposite side of the net.

A ball in play that hits the net stays in play unless a team's three hits have been taken.

A referee's whistle means a *dead ball* when the ball hits the ground, goes under or outside an antenna or if a served ball touches the net and a point or side-out is awarded.

A ball landing on a line is within the playing area.

Blocking

Blocking is when one or more front line players try to stop the ball before, as or after it crosses the net and force it back.

The blocking players are close to each other; at least one must have some body part higher than the net.

A player can reach over the net to block but cannot attack the ball or interfere with the ball from the opponents' side.

A ball contacted in a block simultaneously by one or more players does not count as one of the team's three hits.

A player in a block can play the ball after a touch on the block, which does count as the first of the team's three hits.

Back line players cannot block or participate in a legal block.

Serves cannot be blocked.

There is no block without ball contact.

A returned blocked ball is played as if it crossed the net; the attacking team again has three hits.

Faults

Service is lost or a point gained if:
- The ball touches the ground
- The ball is played more than three times
- The ball hits a player below the waist
- The ball is held or does not clear the net
- The ball passes outside the antenna or under the net
- A player hits the ball twice in a row (except after a block)
- A player touches the net or deliberately touches an opponent
- A player reaches over the net (except in block) or under the net and contacts the ball

327

- A player assists a teammate to hit the ball over the net
- A player fully crosses the center line with a foot or touches the opponents' court with any other part of the body
- A rule violation is called, such as for an illegal serve, being out of position on the court, making an illegal substitution, attacking or blocking from the back row or committing a personal penalty

Sanctions

A *yellow card* is a warning to a participant for a minor offense. If the same offense occurs, a red card is given.

A *red card* is a penalty for serious offenses. The serving team loses the serve; the receiving team loses a point.

A *red/yellow card* means that the participant is removed from the game if another similar offense occurs. No other penalty is necessary.

Timing

Occasionally, games may be determined by a time limit. In this case, each game consists of eight minutes of live ball action. The clock starts with each serve and runs until the ball is whistled dead.

The team with the highest score wins but must be ahead by two points. (See Scoring section.)

Two 30-second timeouts are allowed per team; a three-minute break is taken between games.

Versions of Play

Co-ed play

The following rules apply to games played between teams consisting of both men and women:

- Male and female players alternate the serving order and court position
- When a ball is played more than once, at least one hit must be made by a female (blocks do not count)

- If only one male player is on the front line, a male back line player may move ahead of the attack line to block
- A female back line player may block
- The net height is 7 feet, 11⅝ inches

Reverse co-ed

The rules are the same as for co-ed games, but one male must hit the ball on each possession, one female back liner is allowed to come forward to block and no male back liner can come forward to block.

The net height is 7 feet, 4⅛ inches

Beach and grass play

The rules are the same as for hard court games, with the following exceptions:

- The boundary lines to be marked by brightly colored anchored rope
- Attack lines can be tape or elastic line
- The center line is unmarked but divides the court directly under the net
- The ball has 18 panels, with air pressure of five pounds per square inch
- Teams can consist of two, three, four or six players each
- Games are played to 11 or 15 points, with a two-point advantage needed to win
- Teams change ends after five and 10 points in a 15-point game and after four and eight in an 11-point game
- In games with fewer than six players, the serve can be made from anywhere behind the end line, and the other players can be anywhere on the court

Officials

The first referee controls the match from a raised position at one end of the net and calls the match. The second referee assists from the opposite end and calls net, center line and back faults, but not ballhandling faults.

A scorer sits behind the second referee. Line judges, if there are only two, work from opposite corners of the court.

Side out

Ball in

Ball in bounds/line violation

Ball out (player in adjacent court);
outside the antenna

Serving error

Ball contacted by player
and going out-of-bounds

Four hits

Crossing center line

Held/thrown/lifted ball

Double hit

Ball contacted
below waist

End of game or match

Time out

Substitution

Delay of service

Ball in net at serve/player
touching net

Ball not released
at time of service

Double fault/play over

Illegal block or screen

Out of position

Back line spiker

Over the net

Ball touches object overhead

Warning/penalty/
expulsion/disqualification

Team delay

Point

Illegal contact

Service

History

Modern water polo began as a football-like sport played in lakes and rivers with teams trying to carry a rubber ball across to their opponent's side. In 1870, the first rules were developed in London for football to be played in swimming pools. The games were a contest of strength with little passing or teamwork. A player would often put the ball inside his swimsuit and go underwater to the other end. He might be jumped on there by the goalie, who was allowed to stand on the edge of the pool.

The rules were altered to make the game more like soccer and with a caged goal. By 1888, the game had come to America but the style of play changed dramatically; it became one of the roughest of all sports with fierce underwater battles. By the turn of the century, water polo was an established popular spectator sport. It was introduced into the 1900 Olympics and the English-style rules were adopted by all member nations. United States Water Polo, Inc. supervises the sport, provides information and training materials and encourages high standards of play and increased participation.

Object of the Game

Two teams playing in a swimming pool compete to score points by putting a ball into their opponent's goal.

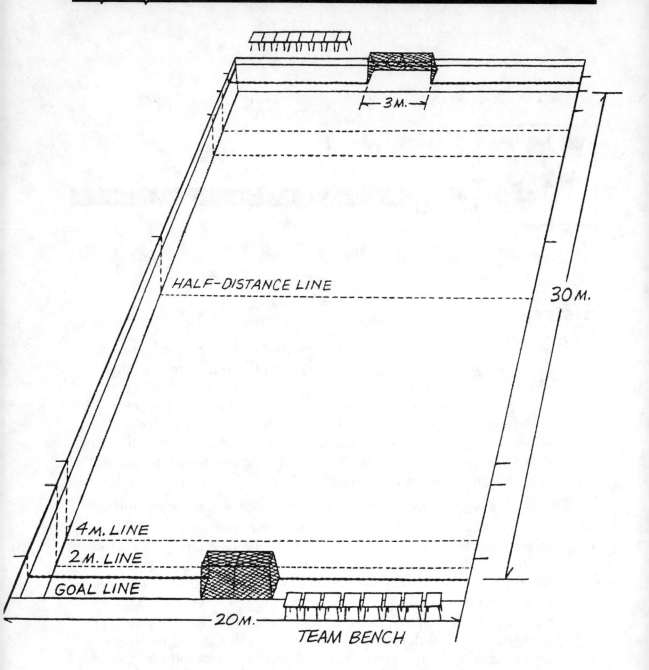

Playing Field

The *pool* is rectangular, 20 to 30 meters (66-99 feet) long and 17 to 20 meters (56-66 feet) wide. For women and juniors, it is 25 meters (82 feet) long and 17 meters (56 feet) wide, maximum.

The *markings* include the following:

- Goal lines, white, 30 centimeters (12 inches) from each end of the pool
- Two-meter lines, red, 6 feet, 7 inches from the goal lines
- Four-meter lines, yellow, 13 feet, 2 inches from the goal lines
- A half-distance line, white, at mid-pool
- A colored sign at each end of the field of play, two meters from the corner

The *goal* is rigid, white and netted. It measures three meters (9 feet, 9 inches) wide and is centered between the pool sides.

The crossbar over the goal line is 90 centimeters (35 inches) above the water surface when the water is more than 1.5 meters (5 feet, 11 inches) deep; it is 2.4 meters (4 feet, 7 inches) from the pool bottom if the water is less deep.

Equipment

The **ball** is inflated, waterproof and round. It is 22 centimeters (8¾ inches) in diameter and weighs approximately 16 ounces.

Players dress in caps numbered 2 to 13; one team wears dark blue and the other white. The goalkeepers wear a red cap with the number 1. The caps are tied under the chin. Men wear swim trunks and women wear one-piece suits. Players may not put oil or grease on their bodies.

General Rules

Each team has seven players (a goalkeeper, three forwards and three backs) and six substitutes.

The game length is four periods, each seven minutes of actual play. There are two-minute breaks between periods when teams change ends.

Teams cannot keep the ball for more than 35 seconds without making a *shot* (scoring attempt) at the opponents' goal. The 35-second count starts over if the shooting team recaptures the ball, if opponents get possession or after a *foul* (rule violation).

The goalkeeper may use both hands, punch the ball with the fist, stand, walk or jump up from the pool floor when inside the four meter line. The goalkeeper can shoot at an opponents' goal if within his own half of the pool, but cannot go beyond or touch the ball beyond the half-distance line. The goalkeeper cannot hold on to the gutter or any part of the end of pool.

The other players cannot touch the ball with both hands at the same time or punch it with a fist. They may trap or catch the ball, lift it up, hold it while not swimming, *dribble* (push it in front of the body), pass the ball to another player or shoot.

Substitutes can only enter the game between periods, after a goal, for an injured player or if a teammate has been *excluded* (made to leave) for bad conduct.

Scoring

Teams receive one point when the ball fully crosses the goal line between the goal uprights and under the crossbar if two players (other than a goalkeeper) have touched it after the start or a restart of play. The ball may be thrown, dribbled and moved by any body part, but not punched, into the goal. To score at a period's end, the ball must have fully left the hand of the shooter before the signal sounds. A goal scored during a foul does not count.

The team with the most points wins. If the score is tied, there is a five-minute break followed by *extra time* (two three-minute periods) with a one-minute rest between periods. The system continues until a decision is reached; there is no sudden death.

Procedure

Games begin with a coin toss; the winner chooses the pool end or team color.

At the start, players line up behind their own goal line, one meter (39 inches) apart and at least one meter from the goal uprights and with no more than two players under the crossbar.

The referee blows a whistle and throws the ball into the center of the playing area. Time starts when the first player touches the ball.

After a goal, players can begin anywhere on their side of the pool. The referee blows the whistle and one player from the team scored upon restarts play from the center of the pool by passing the ball to a teammate behind the half-distance line.

If a ball thrown by an attacker crosses the opponents' goal line, but does not go between the uprights, a *goal throw* (taken from anywhere behind the two meter line) is given to the defending goalkeeper.

When a ball crosses the defender's goal line, but does not go between the uprights, and is last touched by a defender, a *corner throw* (from the two meter mark on the side of the goal where the ball went out) is given to the attacking team. Only the defending goalkeeper can be within the two meter line.

A ball is out of play if it is sent over the side of the pool or hits the side and bounces back into the water. The ball is then given to a player on the opposite team who makes a *free throw* (toss or dribble) from a place nearest to where the ball went out of play or from the two-meter mark, if the ball went out between the two-meter mark and the goal line.

If players from both teams commit fouls at the same time, the referee makes a *neutral throw* (to a place that gives both sides an equal chance to reach the ball).

Fouls and Penalties

An *ordinary foul* occurs when one of the following violations are committed:

- Holding the ball under water when tackled
- Hitting the ball with the fist
- Holding on to or pushing off the goal, pools ends or sides during play
- Touching the ball with both hands at the same time or punching it
- Jumping up from, standing or walking on the bottom of the pool
- Swimming ahead of own goal line before the referee's signal
- Pushing an opponent or preventing the movement of an opponent who does not have the ball
- Moving inside the defender's two-meter line and not behind the line of the ball

- Moving beyond or touching the ball beyond the half-distance line (goalkeepers only)
- Keeping the ball for more than 35 seconds without shooting

The penalty for ordinary fouls is a free throw, but two players other than the defending goalkeeper must touch the ball before any goal is made. The throw is taken from where the foul occurred unless within the two-meter line, in which case it is made at that line.

A *major foul* occurs when a player pulls an opponent or holds one that does not have the ball, kicks or hits an opponent, illegally prevents a goal within the four-meter line, interferes with any throw, splashes water in an opponent's face, enters the water improperly, uses violence or foul language or repeats misconduct.

The penalty for a major foul is a *personal fault*. The offending player is sent out of the water for 20 seconds or until a goal is scored or until the defending team gets the ball — whichever happens first. When a player has left the water, play restarts with an opponent's free throw. If a player has three personal faults or commits a serious violation, the player is excluded, but a substitute may be entered before the free throw.

A *penalty throw* (a free throw from the four-meter line by any member of team awarded the penalty) is given for a major foul committed within an opponents' four-meter line. A shot must be made directly at the goal. The goalkeeper stands on the goal line; all other players stay outside the area.

Officials

Referees control the game, start and play the game, call fouls and throws. They may use the *advantage rule*, which is not stopping play for a foul that would benefit the offending team. They use sticks with blue and white flags to signal fouls and ball possession.

Goal judges signal corner throws (with a red flag), goal throws (red flag) and goals (both flags). Timekeepers record the exact periods of actual play and monitor the 35-second rule. A secretary maintains all game records, including scores and fouls.

History

One of the oldest and widely practiced of all sports, wrestling was illustrated in Babylonian and Egyptian art and other ancient cultures. Wrestling was not only an Olympic event from 776 B.C., but an important part of Greek lifestyle. With few variations, it has been contested throughout the ages, all over the world.

Wrestling was popular in the American frontier; Abraham Lincoln was reportedly a noted local wrestler. By the end of the 19th century, two styles were used in competition. *Greco-Roman* (holds only above the waist) were in the Olympics of 1896 and *catch-as-catch-can* (renamed *freestyle*, with many holds allowed) was added in 1904. Rule changes with an emphasis on control and scoring points has contributed greatly to the sport's popularity. There are several variations for scholastic (especially high school), collegiate and international amateur events.

The Amateur Athletic Union is the governing body in the United States for all levels of the sport. The AAU youth and adult programs provide safe and healthy athletic competition without overemphasizing excellence and winning.

WRESTLING

Object of the Sport

Two opponents of similar weight try to *pin* (touch) each other's shoulders to the floor by using various *holds* (grips and movements). The contestant with the most points in a *bout* (timed event) wins.

Field of Play

The *mat* is a cushioned canvas or synthetic material. It measures 39 feet, 3 inches square and is about two inches thick.

The *center circle* is 39 inches in diameter with a thin red outside border

The *central wrestling area* is 22 feet, 9 inches in diameter.

It is surrounded by a *passivity zone*, a red band that is 39 inches wide with a diameter of 29 feet, 6 inches.

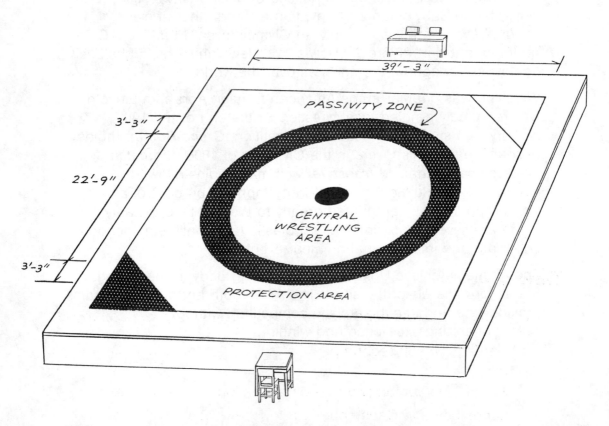

It is set inside a *protection area*, a safety zone that has a minimum width of 48 inches, with one corner marked red and the other blue.

A *platform*, if used, has a maximum height of 43 inches.

Uniforms

Contestants wear a *singlet* (a tight-fitting, one-piece outfit) in red or blue, as assigned, a protective supporter, handkerchief and soft and lightweight sport shoes without soles or buckles. Knee pads are permitted. Headgear should conform to local standards. Wrist bandages, jewelry and body grease are prohibited. Contestants should be closely shaven or have a mature beard.

Age and Weight Categories

Wrestlers are categorized by age and weight. The classifications are as follows:

Division	Age	Weight classes
Bantam	7-8 years	8 classes from under 45 pounds to over 70
Midget	9-10	12 classes from under 50 to over 112
Junior	11-12	15 classes from under 55 to over 148
Schoolboy	13-14	18 classes from under 66 to over 185
Cadet	15-16	14 classes from under 83½ to 242
Elite	17-18	12 classes from under 98 to 275
Espoir	19-20	10 classes from under 105½ to 286
Senior	open	10 classes from under 105½ to 286

Competitors enter an event in their weight class or in one class above their weight.

Time of bouts

The length of bouts depends on the age group. They are as follows:

Bantam: two 90-second periods with a 30-second rest between periods

Midget and Junior: two two-minute periods, 30-second rest

Schoolboy and Cadet: one four-minute period

Elite, Espoir, Senior: one five-minute period

Masters: two two-minute periods, one-minute rest

Masters over age 60: two 90-second periods, one-minute rest

Senior/International and Olympic categories

	pounds
Light flyweight	105½
Flyweight	114½
Bantamweight	125½
Featherweight	136½
Lightweight	149½
Welterweight	163
Middleweight	180½
Light heavyweight	198
Heavyweight	220
Heavyweight plus	286

General Rules

The rules depend on the type of competition.

Freestyle: Wrestlers may use their legs to grasp the opponent's arms or legs, to trip or as part of any action.

Greco-Roman: Wrestlers may not use their legs or grasp the opponent below the hips.

Procedure

Competitors are weighed prior to the contest.

Participants are divided into two groups by weight and paired up by drawing lots. The top three finishers from each group in the elimination rounds wrestle against each other in the finals, unless they met earlier. If so, the previous point score is used.

Competitors are called by name and go to corners with the same colors as their singlets, meet at the center for inspection by the referee and then return to their corners. At the whistle, they approach and face each other.

The period begins with the wrestlers standing.

Holds begin in the central wrestling area and can end there or in the passivity zone or in the protection area. If they end in that area, the wrestlers go back to the center.

Timeouts for injury (up to two minutes for each wrestler) can be called by the referee; a competitor is out of the match if the time limit expires.

The timekeeper signals the end of the bout; the referee also blows a whistle.

A bout ends at a *fall*, which occurs when a wrestler is held to the mat with both shoulders touching long enough for the referee to say "tomber" (tom-bay), raise his hand for confirmation from the judge or mat chairman, slap the mat with his hand and then blow a whistle.

If there is no fall, the wrestler with the most points wins.

Scoring

The scoring is as follows:

5 points: Executing a *grand technique*, a move from the mat that takes an opponent off the ground and then to a position where his shoulders are in immediate danger (of being pinned). If the move does not cause immediate danger, it only scores two points.

3 points: Lifting an opponent from the mat, or a standing move that puts the opponent in *danger* (of a fall) with his back to the mat.

2 points: Putting the opponent in danger from various ground moves (for example, rolling an opponent across the shoulders).

1 point: Executing a *takedown* (bringing an opponent to the mat but not in danger), executing a *reversal* (moving from underneath an opponent to above and gaining control), forcing an opponent down on to one or both arms, a hold illegally blocked, an opponent leaving the mat, and others.

A 15-point lead stops the contest. A bout also can be won by *technical superiority*.

In a *tie* (each wrestler has the same number of points) there is an immediate overtime, with no rest period. The first point scored wins the bout.

After each bout, *positive* points are given to determine the contestants' standing in their group. For example, four points are awarded to the winner and 0 to the loser if the bout ended in a fall or by technical superiority; 3.5 points to the winner if the bout ends with a margin of 12 to 14 points; three points to the winner and one for the loser if the bout ends with a margin of 1 to 11 points and if the loser scored at least one technical point.

Illegal Holds/Penalties

Forbidden holds and moves include throat holds, bending an opponent's arms behind his back, a *full nelson* (arms under an opponent's armpits with hands clasped behind the opponent's head) not done from the side, a *chicken wing* (pressure on an opponent's arm behind his back) or holds with a *headlock* (arms and hands held on the opponent's head).

Prohibited actions include pulling an opponent's hair or ears, pinching, finger twisting, causing pain or hurt, punching or kicking, head butting, touching the opponent's face between the mouth and eyebrows, forcing elbows or knees into the opponent's chest or stomach, grabbing the bottom of a foot and holding on to the mat.

A wrestler whose illegal hold prevents his opponent from completing an action is given a caution warning and the opponent is awarded two points. If the illegal hold did not affect the opponent's move, a caution is given and one point is awarded.

Passivity is a wrestler's attitude that stalls the progress of a bout by not actively competing. Examples include not attempting holds, lying flat on the mat, pushing or holding an opponent's hands and leaving the mat. The penalty is a caution; three cautions, including any for illegal holds, disqualify the offender.

Officials

A referee works on the mat with the wrestlers and is in charge of the bout. The referee wears a red band on the left wrist and a blue band on the other to signal — by raising the arm — which competitor has scored points. The referee starts, interrupts and stops the bout. A judge, a *mat chairman* (head official) and a *controller* (timekeeper) observe, evaluate and record actions from off the mat.

Note: Doctors or other medical attendants may stop the bout at any time by declaring a competitor unfit to continue.

1993

SPORTS ALMANAC

AND

SCHEDULE

OF

EVENTS

Compiled and Edited By

Vincent M. Mallozzi

The following results are from sporting events which occurred between September 15, 1991 and September 15, 1992.

ARCHERY

U.S. Champions

Women's Freestyle — Sherry Block, Colorado Springs, Colo.

Men's Freestyle — Allen Rasor Jr., Los Angeles, Calif.

Senior Women's Freestyle — Denise Parker, South Jordan, Utah.

Senior Men's Freestyle — Jay Barrs, Mesa, Ariz.

Women's Olympic Style — Judi Adams, Phoenix, Ariz.

Men's Olympic Style — Jay Barrs.

Men's Compound Unlimited — Kirk Ethridge, Rogersville, Tennessee.

Women's Compound Unlimited — Inga Low, Roseville, Calif.

Men's Barebow — Bob Burns, Rough and Ready, Calif.

Women's Barebow — Jacquie Low, Santa Cruz, Calif.

World Champions

Women's Barebow — Nadine Visconti, France.

Men's Barebow — Andera Rosenberg, Sweden.

Women's Freestyle — Carole Ferriou, France.

Men's Freestyle — Jay Barrs, United States.

Women's Compound — Susanne Kessler, Denmark.

Men's Compound — Morgan Lundin, Sweden.

Olympics

Men's 70-Meter Individual

Gold — Sebastien Flute, France.

Silver — Chung Jae-Hun, South Korea.

Bronze — Simon Terry, Britain.

Team

Gold — Spain (Juan Holgado Romero, Antonio Vazquez Megido, Alfonso Menendez Vallin).

Silver — Finland (Ismo Falck, Jari Lipponen, Tomi Poikolainen). Bronze — Britain (Richard Priestman, Steven Hallard, Simon Terry).

Women 70-Meter Individual

Gold — Cho Youn-Jeong, South Korea.

Silver — Kim Soo-Nyung, South Korea.

Bronze — Natalia Valeeva, Unified Team.

Team

Gold — South Korea (Lee Eun-Kyung, Cho Youn-Jeong, Kim Soo-Nyung).

Silver — China (Wang Hong, Wang Xiaozhu, Ma Xiangjun).

Bronze — Unified Team (Natalia Valeeva, Lioudmila Arjannikova, Khatouna Kvrivichvili).

AUTO RACING

Formula One — Nigel Mansell, Great Britain.

CART PPG-Indy Car — Michael Andretti, Nazareth, Pa.

Nascar Winston Cup — Dale Earnhardt, Mooresville, N.C.

S.C.C.A. Trans-Am — Scott Sharp, Camaro, East Norwalk, Conn.

World of Outlaws Sprint Cars — Steve Kinser, Bloomington, Ind.

Indianapolis 500 — Al Unser, Jr., Albuquerque, New Mexico.

Daytona 500 — Davey Allison, Hueytown, Ala.

LeMans 24 Hours — Peugeut: Yannick Dalmas, France, Derek Warwick and Mark Blundell, Britain.

IMSA Camel G.T. — Geoff Brabham, Electramotive Nissan.

N.H.R.A. Top Fuel — Joe Amato, Old Forge,Pa.

N.H.R.A. Funny Car — John Force, Yorba Linda, Calif.

N.H.R.A. Pro Stock — Darrell Alderman, Morehead, Ky.

BADMINTON

U.S. Champions

Men's Singles — Chris Jogis, Palo Alto, Calif.

Women's Singles — Joy Kitzmiller, Manhattan Beach, Calif.

Men's Doubles — Ben Lee, Daly City, Calif., and Tom Reidy, Tempe, Ariz.

Women's Doubles — Joy Kitzmiller and Linda French, Elmhurst, Ill.

Mixed Doubles — Andy Chong, Chicago, Ill., and Linda French.

Collegiate Champions

Men's Singles — Tom Reidy, Arizona State.

Women's Singles — Andrea Andersson, Arizona State.

Men's Doubles — Tom Reidy and Martin Flores, Arizona State.

Women's Doubles — Jenny Chan and Andrea Andersson, Arizona State.

Mixed Doubles — Tom Reidy and Jenny Chan, Arizona State.

World Champions

Men's Singles — Zhao Jianhua, China.

Women's Singles — Tang Jiuhong, China.

Men's Doubles — Park Joo Bong and Kim Moon Soo, Korea.

Women's Doubles — Nong Qunhua and Guan Weizhen, China.

Mixed Doubles — Park Joo Bong and Chung Myung Hee, Korea.

Olympics

Men's Singles

Gold — Alan Budi Kusuma, Indonesia.

Silver — Ardy Wiranata, Indonesia

Bronze — Thomas Stuer-Lauridsen, Denmark, and Hermawan Susanto, Indonesia.

Men's Doubles

Gold — Kim Moon-Soo and Park Joo Bong, South Korea.

Silver — Eddy Hartono and Rudy Gunawan, Indonesia.

Bronze — Li Yongbo and Tian Bingyi, China, and Sidek Razif and Sidek Jalani, Malaysia.

Women's Singles

Gold — Susi Susanti, Indonesia.

Silver — Bang Soo Hyun, South Korea.

Bronze — Huang Hua, China, and Tang Jiuhong, China.

Women's Doubles

Gold — Hwang Hye Young and Chung So Young, South Korea.

Silver — Guan Weizhen and Nong Qunhua, China.

Bronze — Gil Young-Ah and Shim Eun-Jung, South Korea, and Lin Yanfen and Yao Fen, China.

BANDY

World Champion — Sweden

BARREL JUMPING

World Champion — Patrick Le Clerc, St. Bruno, Canada.

BASEBALL
(1991 SEASON)

Major League

World Series

Minnesota Twins defeated Atlanta Braves, 4 games to 3.

Division Champions

American League — East: Toronto Blue Jays; West: Minnesota.

National League — East: Pittsburgh Pirates; West: Atlanta.

All-Star Game

American League defeated National League, 4-2.

American League Standings

Eastern Division

	W	L	Pct	GB	Home	Away
Toronto	91	71	.562	—	46-35	45-36
Boston	84	78	.519	7	43-38	41-40
Detroit	84	78	.519	7	49-32	35-46
Milwaukee	83	79	.512	8	43-37	40-42
New York	71	91	.438	20	39-42	32-49
Baltimore	67	95	.414	24	33-48	34-47
Cleveland	57	105	.352	34	30-52	27-53

Western Division

	W	L	Pct	GB	Home	Away
Minnesota	95	67	.586	—	51-30	44-37
Chicago	87	75	.537	8	46-35	41-40
Texas	85	77	.525	10	46-35	39-42
Oakland	84	78	.519	11	47-34	37-44
Seattle	83	79	.512	12	45-36	38-43
Kansas City	82	80	.506	13	40-41	42-39
California	81	81	.500	14	40-41	41-40

National League Standings

Eastern Division

	W	L	Pct	GB	Home	Away
Pittsburgh	98	64	.605	—	52-32	44-32
St. Louis	84	78	.519	14	52-32	32-46
Philadelphia	78	84	.481	20	46-36	32-48
Chicago	77	83	.481	20	46-37	31-46
New York	77	84	.478	20 ½	40-43	37-41
Montreal	71	90	.441	26 ½	33-35	38-55

Western Division

	W	L	Pct	GB	Home	Away
Atlanta	94	68	.580	—	48-33	46-35
Los Angeles	93	69	.574	1	54-27	39-42
San Diego	84	78	.519	10	42-39	42-39
San Francisco	75	87	.463	19	43-38	32-49
Cincinnati	74	88	.457	20	39-42	35-46
Houston	65	97	.401	29	37-44	28-53

Individual Leaders

Batting Average: American League — Julio Franco, Texas, .341; National League — Terry Pendleton, .319

Runs Batted In: American League — Cecil Fielder, Detroit, 133; National League — Howard Johnson, Mets, 117.

Home Runs: American League — Jose Canseco, Oakland and Cecil Fielder, Detroit, 44; National League — Howard Johnson, Mets, 38.

Stolen Bases: American League — Rickey Henderson, Oakland, 58; National League — Marquis Grissom, Montreal, 76.

Slugging: American League — Tartabull, Kansas City, .593; National League — Clark, San Francisco, .536.

Hits: American League — Molitor, Milwaukee, 216; National League — Pendleton, 187.

Runs: American League — Molitor, 133; National League — Butler, Los Angeles, 112.

351

Bases on Balls: American League — Thomas, Chicago, 138; National League — Butler, 108.

On-Base: American League — Thomas, 453; National League — Bonds, Pittsburgh, 410.

Doubles: American League — Palmeiro, Texas, 49; National League — Bonilla, Pittsburgh, 44.

Triples: American League — Johnson, Chicago, 13; National League — Lankford, St. Louis, 15.

E.R.A.: American League — Roger Clemens, Boston, 2.62.; National League — Dennis Martinez, Montreal, 2.39.

Saves: American League — Bryan Harvey, California, 46; National League — Lee Smith, St. Louis, 47.

Won-Lost: American League — Erickson, Minnesota, 20-8; National League — Smiley, Pittsburgh, 20-8.

Games: American League — Ward, Toronto, 81; National League — Jones, Montreal, 77.

Innings: American League — Clemens, 271.0; National League — Maddux, Chicago, 263.0.

Strikeouts: American League — Clemens, 241; National League — Cone, New York, 241.

Complete Games: American League — McDowell, Chicago, 15; National League — Glavine, Atlanta, 9.

Shutouts: American League — Clemens, 4; National League — De. Martinez, Milwaukee, 5.

Awards

Cy Young: American League — Roger Clemens, Boston. National League — Tom Glavine, Atlanta.

Rookie of the Year: American League — Chuck Knoblauch, Minnesota. National League — Jeff Bagwell, Houston.

M.V.P.'s: American League — Cal Ripken, Baltimore Orioles. National League — Terry Pendleton, Atlanta.

Collegiate Champions

N.C.A.A. Division I — Pepperdine.

N.C.A.A. Division II — University of Tampa.

N.C.A.A. Division III — William Patterson.

N.A.I.A. — Lewis Clark St., Idaho.

Little League

World Series — Long Beach, CA (Philippines team disqualified for illegal players.)

Olympics

Gold — Cuba.

Silver — Taiwan.

Bronze — Japan.

BASKETBALL
(1991-1992 SEASON)

N.B.A.

Champions — Chicago Bulls.

Final Standings

EASTERN CONFERENCE Atlantic Division

	W	L	Pct	GB
Boston	56	26	.683	—
Philadelphia	44	38	.537	12
New York	39	43	.476	17
Washington	30	52	.366	26
New Jersey	26	56	.317	30
Miami	24	58	.293	32

Central Division

	W	L	Pct	GB
Chicago	61	21	.744	—
Detroit	50	32	.610	11
Milwaukee	48	34	.585	13
Atlanta	43	39	.524	18
Indiana	41	41	.500	20
Cleveland	33	49	.402	28
Charlotte	26	56	.317	35

WESTERN CONFERENCE Midwest Division

	W	L	Pct	GB
San Antonia	55	27	.671	—
Utah	54	28	.659	1
Houston	52	30	.634	3
Orlando	31	51	.378	24
Minnesota	29	53	.354	26
Dallas	28	54	.341	27
Denver	20	62	.244	35

Pacific Division

	W	L	Pct	GB
Portland	63	19	.768	—
L.A. Lakers	58	24	.707	5
Phoenix	55	27	.671	8
Golden State	44	38	.537	19
Seattle	41	41	.500	22
L.A. Clippers	31	51	.378	32
Sacramento	25	57	.305	38

Individual Leaders

Scoring — Michael Jordan, Chicago, 30.1.

Rebounds — Dennis Rodman, Detroit Pistons, 18.7.

Assists — John Stockton, Utah Jazz, 13.7.

Blocked Shots — David Robinson, San Antonio Spurs, 4.49.

Awards

Playoff M.V.P. — Michael Jordan, Chicago.

Regular Season M.V.P. — Michael Jordan.

Rookie of the Year — Larry Johnson, Charlotte Hornets.

Coach of the Year — Don Nelson, Golden State Warriors.

N.C.A.A.

Men's Division I — Duke.

Division II — Virginia Union.

Division III — Calvin (Mich.).

Women's Division I — Stanford.

Division II — Delta State.

Division III — Alma (Mich.).

Other College Champions

N.A.I.A. Men — Oklahoma City University.

N.A.I.A. Women — Arkansas Tech.

N.I.T. — Virginia.

National Jr. College — Three Rivers, Mo.

Women's N.J.C.A.A. — Louisburg, N.C.

Olympics

Men

Gold — United States.

Silver — Croatia.

Bronze — Lithuania.

Women

Gold — Cuba.

Silver — China.

Bronze — United States.

BIATHLON

U.S. Champions

Men's 10k — Josh Thompson, Gunnison, Colo.

Men's 20k — Josh Thompson.

Women's 7.5k — Joan Guestchow, Minnatonka, Minn.

Women's 15k — Angie Stevenson, Bend, Ore.

Olympics

Men's 10k

Gold — Marc Kirchner, Germany.

Silver — Ricco Gross, Germany.

Bronze — Harri Eloranta, Finland.

Men's 20k

Gold — Yevgeny Redkine, Unified Team.

Silver — Mark Kirchner.

Bronze — Mikael Lofgren, Sweden.

Men's 4x7.5k Relay

Gold — Germany.

Silver — Unified Team.

Bronze — Sweden.

Women's 7.5k

Gold — Anfissa Restsova, Unified Team.

Silver — Antje Misersky, Germany.

Bronze — Yelena Belova, Unified Team.

Women's 15k

Gold — Antje Misersky.

Silver — Svetlana Pecherskaia, Unified Team.

Bronze — Myriam Bedard, Canada.

Women's 3x7.5K Relay

Gold — France.

Silver — Germany.

Bronze — Unified Team.

BILLIARDS

World Champions

Men's 9-Ball — Johnny Archer, United States.

Women's 9-Ball — Franziska Stark, Germany.

Junior Division — Hui-Kai Hsia, Taiwan.

3-Cushion — Torbjorn Blomdahl, Sweden.

Snooker — Stephen Hendry, Scotland.

BOBSLEDDING

World Champions

2-Man World Cup — Gunther Huber, Italy.

4-Man World Cup — Wolf Hoppe, Germany.

2-Man & 4-Man Combined — Wolf Hoppe.

2-Man Junior World Championship-Winterberg — Kurt Einberger, Australia.

4-Man Junior World Championship — Stephan Rausch, Germany.

Olympics

2-Man Bobsled

Gold — Switzerland.

Silver — Germany I.

Bronze — Germany II.

4-Man Bobsled

Gold — Austria I.

Silver — Germany I.

Bronze — Switzerland I.

BOWLING

P.B.A. Tour

BPAA U.S. Open — Robert Lawrence, Austin, Texas.

Firestone Tournament of Champions — Marc McDowell, Madison, Wisc.

Bud Light P.B.A. National Championship — Eric Forkel, Chatsworth, Calif.

Bud Light Touring Players Championship — Dave Ferraro, Kingston, N.Y.

Ebonite P.B.A. Senior Championship — Gene Stus, Allen Park, Mich.

L.P.B.T.

BPAA U.S. Open /M Tish Johnson, Panorama City, Calif.

Sam's Town Invitational /M Lorri Nichols, Algonquin, Ill.

Women's International Bowling Congress Queens — Cindy Coburn-Carroll, Buffalo, NY.

Gold Rush Mixed Doubles — Robin Romeo and Rick Easley, Van Nuys, Calif.

National Doubles — Stacy Rider and Anne Marie Duggan, LaHabra, Calif.

A.B.C.

Singles — Gary Blatchford, Phoenix, Ariz., and Bob Youker, Syracuse, N.Y. (tie).

Doubles — Gene Stus and Dave Bernhardt, Detroit, Mich.

All Events — Mike Tucker, Fountain Valley, Calif.

Regular team — Coors Light, Reading, Pa.

Booster team — Suburban Lanes, Meade, Ks.

Team All Events — Reebs Funeral Home, Toledo, Ohio.

Masters Tournament — Ken Johnson, Fort Worth, Texas.

W.I.B.C

Championship Tournaments

Open Singles — Patty Ann Meyaguez, Puerto Rico.

Open Doubles — Nancy Fehr, Cincinnati, and Lisa Wagner, Palmetto, Fla.

Open Team Event — Hoinke Classic, Cincinnati.

Open All-Events — Mitsuko Tokimoto, Tokyo.

Queen's Tournament — Cindy Coburn-Caroll, Tonawanda, N.Y.

Division One Singles — Linda Lesniak, Evergreen Park, Ill.

Division One Doubles — Mary Piche, Burlington, Ont., and Karen Nicol, Hamilton, Ont.

Division One Team — Rubber Mill, Medford, Ore.

Division One All-Events — Shari Ellison, Columbus, Ga.

Division Two Singles — Barb Davis, Mount Morris, Ill.

Division Two Doubles — Jenelle Paksi, St.
Johns, Mich., Jo Lynn Wendling, St. Johns,
Mich.

Division Two Team — Put Togethers, Muncie,
Ind.

Division Two All-Events — Sandy Woelk,
Kingsville, Ont.

BOXING

Heavyweight — Evander Holyfield, Atlanta, Ga.,
undisputed.

Cruiserweight — Bobby Czyz, Totowa, N.J.,
W.B.A.; Anaclet Wamba, France, W.B.C.;
James Warring, Miami, I.B.F.

Light heavyweight — W.B.A. title is vacant, Jeff
Harding, Australia, W.B.C., Charles Williams,
Grand Rapids, Mich., I.B.F.

Super middleweight — Victor Cordova, Panama,
W.B.A.; Mauro Galvano, Italy, W.B.C.; Iran
Barkley, PLACE, I.B.F.

Middleweight — Reggie Johnson, PLACE,
W.B.A.; Julian Jackson, Virgin Islands, W.B.C.;
James Toney, Detroit, I.B.F.

Junior middleweight — Vinny Pazienza,
Cranston, R.I., W.B.A.; Terry Norris, San Diego,
W.B.C.; Gianfranco Rossi, Italy, I.B.F.

Welterweight — Meldrick Taylor, Philadelphia,
W.B.A.; James McGirt, Brentwood, L.I., W.B.C.;
Maurice Blocker, Germantown, Maryland,
I.B.F.

Junior Welterweight — Akinobu Hiranaka,
Japan, W.B.A.; Julio Cesar Chavez, Mexico,
W.B.C.; Rafael Pinieda, Colombia, I.B.F.

Lightweight — All three titles are vacant.

Junior Lightweight — Ganaro Hernandez, Los
Angeles, W.B.A.; Azumah Nelson, Ghana,
W.B.C.; John Molina, Puerto Rico, I.B.F.

Featherweight — Park Yung-Kyun, South Korea,
W.B.A.; Paul Hodkinson, Great Britain, W.B.C;
Manuel Medina, Mexico, I.B.F.

Junior Featherweight — Wilfredo Vazquez,
Puerto Rico, W.B.A.; Thierry Jacob, France,
W.B.C.; Welcome Ncita, South Africa, I.B.F.

Bantamweight — Eddie Cook, PLACE, W.B.A.;
Joichiro Tatsuyoshi, Japan, W.B.C.; Orlando
Canizales, Houston, Texas, I.B.F.

Junior bantamweight — Katzuya Onizuka,
Japan, W.B.A.; Sunkil Moon, South Korea,
W.B.C.; Robert Quiroga, San Antonio, I.B.F.

Flyweight — Kim Yong-kang, South Korea,
W.B.A.; Muangchai Kittikasem, Thailand,
W.B.C.; Rodolfo Blanco, Colombia, I.B.F.

Junior flyweight — Hi Ioka, Japan, W.B.A.;
Humberto Gonzalez, Mexico, W.B.C.; Michael
Carbajal, Phoenix, I.B.F.

Strawweight — Choi Hi-yong, South Korea,
W.B.A.; Ricardo Lopez, Mexico, W.B.C.;
FahLan Lookmingkwan, Thailand, I.B.F.

World Amateur Championships

106 lbs. — Eric Griffin, United States.

112 lbs. — Istvan Kovacs, Hungary.

119 lbs. — Serafim Todorov, Bulgaria.

125 lbs. — Kirkor Kikorov, Bulgaria.

132 lbs. — Marco Rudolph, Germany.

139 lbs. — Konstantin Tszyu, Soviet Union.

147 lbs. — Juan Hernandez, Cuba.

156 lbs. — Juan Lemus, Cuba.

165 lbs. — Tommaso Russo, Italy.

178 lbs. — Torsten May, Germany.

201 lbs. — Felix Savon, Cuba.

Heavyweight — Roberto Balado, Cuba.

Olympics

48 Kg (106 pounds)

Gold — Rogelio Marcelo, Cuba.

Silver — Daniel Bojinov, Bulgaria.

Bronze — Jan Quast, Germany and Roel
Velasco, Philippines.

51 Kg (112 pounds)

Gold — Su Choi-Chol, North Korea.

Silver — Raul Gonzalez, Cuba.

Bronze — Timothy Austin, United States and
Istvan Kovacs, Hungary.

54 Kg (119 pounds)

Gold — Joel Casamayor, Cuba.

Silver — Wayne McCullough, Ireland.

Bronze — Li Gwang Sik, North Korea and
Mohamed Achik, Morocco.

57 Kg (126 pounds)

Gold — Andreas Tews, Germany.

Silver — Faustino Reyes, Spain.

Bronze — Hocine Soltani, Algeria and Ramazi Paliani, Unified Team.

60 Kg (132 pounds)

Gold — Oscar De La Hoya, United States.

Silver — Marco Rudolph, Germany.

Bronze — Hong Sung Sik, North Korea and Namjil Bayarsaikhan, Mongolia.

63.5 Kg (140 pounds)

Gold — Hector Vinent, Cuba.

Silver — Mark Leduc, Canada.

Bronze — Jyri Kjall, Finland and Leonard Doroftei, Romania.

67 Kg (148 pounds)

Gold — Michael Carruth, Ireland.

Silver — Juan Hernandez, Cuba.

Bronze — Anibal Acevedo Santiago, Puerto Rico and Arkom Chenglai, Thailand.

71 Kg (157 pounds)

Gold — Juan Lemus, Cuba.

Silver — Orhan Delibas, Netherlands.

Bronze — Gyorgy Mizsei, Hungary and Robin Reid, Britain.

75 Kg (165 pounds)

Gold — Ariel Hernandez, Cuba.

Silver — Chris Byrd, United States.

Bronze — Chris Johnson, Canada and Lee Seung Bae, South Korea.

81 Kg (179 pounds)

Gold — Torsten May, Germany.

Silver — Rostislav Zaoulitchnyi, Unified Team.

Bronze — Zoltan Beres, Hungary and Wojciech Bartnik, Poland.

91 Kg (201 pounds)

Gold — Felix Savon, Cuba.

Silver — David Izonritei, Nigeria.

Bronze — Arnold Van Der Lijde, Netherlands and David Tua, New Zealand.

91 Kg-plus (201-plus pounds)

Gold — Roberto Balado, Cuba.

Silver — Richard Igbineghu, Nigeria.

Bronze — Brian Nielsen, Denmark and Svilen Roussinov, Bulgaria.

CANOEING

U.S. Sprint National Champions

Canoe

500 meters — Jim Terrell, Milford, Ohio.

1,000 meters — Greg Steward, Williamsburg, Ohio.

10,000 meters — James Ross, Bethesda, Md.

Men's Kayak

500 meters — Norman Bellingham, Washington, D.C.

1,000 meters — Greg Barton, Bellingham, Washington.

10,000 meters — Greg Barton.

Women's Kayak

500 meters — Sheila Conover, Newport Beach, Calif.

5,000 meters — Sheila Conover.

Olympics

Men's Single Canoe Slalom

Gold — Lukas Pollert, Czechoslovakia.

Silver — Gareth Marriott, Britain.

Bronze — Jacky Avril, France.

Double Canoe Slalom

Gold — United States (Scott Strausbaugh and Joe Jacobi).

Silver — Czechoslovakia (Miroslav Simek and Jiri Rohan).

Bronze — France (Franck Adisson and Wilfrid Forgues).

Single Kayak Slalom

Gold — Pierpaolo Ferrazzi, Italy.

Silver — Sylvain Curinier, France.

Bronze — Jochen Lettmann, Germany.

Kayak 500 Singles

Gold — Mikko Yrjoe Kolehmainen, Finland.

Silver — Zsolt Gyulay, Hungary.

Bronze — Knut Holmann, Norway.

Kayak 500 Doubles

Gold — Germany (Kay Bluhm and Torsten Rene Gutsche).

Silver — Poland (Maciej Freimut and Wojciech Kurpiewski).

Bronze — Italy (Antonio Rossi and Bruno Dreossi).

Kayak 1,000 Singles

Gold — Clint Robinson, Australia.

Silver — Knut Holmann, Norway.

Bronze — Greg Barton, United States.

Kayak 1,000 Doubles

Gold — Germany (Kay Bluhm and Torsten Gutsche).

Silver — Sweden (Gunnar Olsson and Karl Sundqvist).

Bronze — Poland (Grzegorz Kotowicz and Dariusz Bialkowski).

Kayak 1,000 Quads

Gold — Germany (Mario Von Appen, Oliver Kegel, Thomas Reineck, and Andre Wohllebe).

Silver — Hungary (Ferenc Csipes, Zsolt Gyulay, Laszlo Fidel, and Attila Abraham).

Bronze — Australia (Kelvin Graham, Ian Rowling, Steven Wood, and Ramon Andersson).

Canoe 500 Singles

Gold — Nikolai Boukhalov, Bulgaria.

Silver — Mikhail Slivinski, Unified Team.

Bronze — Olaf Heukrodt, Germany.

Canoe 500 Doubles

Gold — Unified Team (Alexandre Masseikov and Dmitri Dovgalenok).

Silver — Germany (Ulrich Papke and Ingo Spelly).

Bronze — Bulgaria (Martin Marinov and Blagovest Stoyanov).

Canoe 1,000 Singles

Gold — Nikolai Boukhalov, Bulgaria.

Silver — Ivans Klementjevs, Latvia.

Bronze — Gyorgy Zala, Hungary.

Canoe 1,000 Doubles

Gold — Germany (Ulrich Papke and Ingo Spelly).

Silver — Denmark (Arne Nielsson and Christian Frederiksen).

Bronze — France (Didier Hoyer and Olivier Boivin).

Women's Kayak Slalom

Gold — Elisabeth Micheler, Germany.

Silver — Danielle Woodward, Australia.

Bronze — Dana Chladek, United States.

Kayak 500 Singles

Gold — Birgit Schmidt, Germany.

Silver — Rita Koban, Hungary.

Bronze — Izabella Dylewska, Poland.

Kayak 500 Doubles

Gold — Germany (Ramona Portwich and Anke Von Seck).

Silver — Sweden (Susanne Gunnarsson and Agneta Andersson).

Bronze — Hungary (Rita Koban and Eva Donusz).

Kayak 500 Quads

Gold — Hungary (Eva Donusz, Kinga Czigany, Erika Meszaros, and Rita Koban).

Silver — Germany (Katrin Borchert, Birgit Schmidt, Anke Von Seck, and Ramona Portwich).

Bronze — Sweden (Anna Olsson, Maria Haglund, Susanne Rosenqvist, and Agneta Andersson).

CASTING

United States Champions

Men's all-around — Steve Rajeff, Poulsbo, Wash.

Men's all-distance — Steve Rajeff.

Men's all-accuracy — Steve Rajeff.

Women's all-accuracy — Brenda Banks, Toronto.

World Champion

International Casting Federation European All-Around — Henri Ostertag, Sweden.

CHESS

United States Champions

Men — Gata Kamsky, New York City.

Women — Tie: Esther Epstein, Brookline, Mass.; Irina Levitina, Teaneck, N.J.

World Champions

Men — Garry Kasparov, Soviet Union.

Women — Xie Jun, China.

COURT TENNIS

World — Wayne Davies, New York City.

U.S. Open — Lachland Deuchar, Australia.

U.S. Open Doubles — Julian Snow, Great Britain and Rob Fahey, Australia.

U.S. Amateur — Julian Snow.

U.S. Amateur Doubles — Julian Snow and Ralph Howe, Palm Beach, Florida.

British Amateur — Julian Snow.

CRICKET

World Cup — Pakistan.

CROQUET

World — Robert Fulford, England.

U.S. Singles — John C. Osborn, New York City.

U.S. Doubles — Debbie Cornelius, England and Reid Fleming, Boston.

U.S. International Rules — David Openshaw, England.

National Amateur Singles Championship — Tom Huhn, Palm Beach Gardens, Fla.

CROSS-COUNTRY

United States Champions

Men — Todd Williams, Knoxville, Tenn.

Women — Lynn Jennings.

N.C.A.A. Men

Team

Division I Team — University of Arkansas.

Division II Team — University of Massachusett at Lowell.

Division III Team — University of Rochester.

Individual

Division I — Sean Dollman, Western Kentucky University.

Division II — Martin Lyons, Edinboro University.

Division III — Sandu Rubenciuc, Augustana College.

N.C.A.A. Women

Division I Team — Villanova.

Division II Team — California Poly State, San Louis Obispo.

Division III Team — University of Wisconsin (Oshkosh).

Individual

Division I — Sonia O'Sullivan, Villanova. Division II — Christie Allen, Pittsburg State University Division III — Laura Horejs, University of Wisconsin (Oshkosh).

World Champions

Men's — John Ngugi, Kenya.

Women — Lynn Jennings, United States.

Men's Junior — Ismael Kirui, Kenya.

Women's Junior — Paula Radcliffe, Great Britain

CURLING

United States Champions

U.S. Men — Doug Jones, Seattle, Wash.

U.S. Women — Lisa Schoeneberg, Madison, Wisc.

World Champions

Men — Markus Eggler, Switzerland.

Women — Elisabet Johansson, Sweden.

CYCLING

Men's Pro Road — Gianni Bugno, Italy.

Men's Amateur Road — Viktor Pyaksinsky, Soviet Union.

Junior Men's Road — Jeff Evanshine, United States.

Women's Road — Leontien Van Moorsel, Netherlands.

Men's Pro Sprint — None (Carey Hall, Australia, disqualified after positive drug test).

Men's Amateur Sprint — Jens Fiedler, Germany.

Women's Sprint — Ingrid Haringa, Netherlands.

Men's Pro Pursuit — Francis Moreau, France.

Men's Amateur Pursuit — Jens Lehmann, Germany.

Women's Pursuit — Petra Rossner, Germany.

Men's Pro Points Race — Vyacheslav Ekimov, Soviet Union.

Men's Amateur Points Race — Bruno Risi, Switzerland.

Women's Points Race — Ingrid Haringa, Netherlands.

Men's Amateur 1K Time Trial — Jose Moreno, Spain.

Men's Keirin — Michael Hue, Britain.

Men's Pro Motor Paced — Danny Clark, Australia.

Men's Amateur Motor Paced — Roland Konigshoffer, Austria.

World Mountain Bike

Men's Cross-Country — John Tomac, United States.

Women's Cross-Country — Ruthie Matthes, United States.

Men's Downhill — Albert Iten, Switzerland.

Other Professional

World Cup — Maurizio Fondriest, Italy

Tour de France — Miguel Indurain, Spain.

Tour of Italy — Miguel Indurain.

Tour of Switzerland — Luc Roosen, Belgium.

U.S. Pro Road — Bart Bowen, United States.

Tour Du Pont — Greg LeMond, United States.

U.S. Cycling Federation Olympic Trials and National Championships

Men's Kilometer Time Trial — Erin Hartwell, Indianapolis, Ind.

Men's Sprint — Ken Carpenter, La Mesa, Calif.

Women's Match Sprint — Connie Paraskevin-Young, Indianapolis, Ind.

Men's National Road Race — Chann McRae, Plano, Tex.

Men's Olympic Road Race — Timothy Peddie, Boulder, Colo.

Women's National Road Race — Jeanne Golay, Glenwood Springs, Colo.

Women's Olympic Road Race — Inga Thompson, Reno, Nev.

Men's Points Race — James Carney, Annandale, N.J.

Women's Points Race — Janie Eickhoff, Los Alamitos, Calif.

Men's Pursuit — Carl Sundquist, Pembroke Pines, Fla.

Men's Team Pursuit — U.S. National Team/Skittles.

Women's Pursuit — Rebecca Twigg, San Diego, Calif.

Men's Time Trial — John Stenner, Boulder, Colo.

Women's Time Trial — Jeanne Golay.

Men's Criterium — David McCook, Cocoa, Fla.

Women's Criterium — Laura Charameda, Marshall, Mich.

Men's Team Time Trial — Team U.S.A. Number 2/Skittles.

Men's Mountain Bike National Champion — Ned Overend, Durango, Colo.

Women's Mountain Bike National Champion — Juliana Furtado, Boulder, Colo.

World Cup

Men's Overall World Cup Mountain Bike — Thomas Frischknecht, Switzerland.

Women's Overall World Cup Mountain Bike — Juliana Furtado, Boulder, Colo.

Men's Mountain Bike World Cup Finals — Ned Overend, Durango, Colo.

Women's Mountain Bike World Cup Finals — Ruthie Matthes, Boulder, Colo.

Olympics

Men's Individual Pursuit

Gold — Chris Boardman, Britain.

Silver — Jens Lehmann, Germany.

Bronze — Gary Anderson, New Zealand.

Individual Sprint

Gold — Jens Fiedler, Germany.

Silver — Garry Neiwand, Australia.

Bronze — Curtis Harnett, Canada.

Individual Points Race

Gold — Giovanni Lombardi, Italy.

Silver — Leon Van Bon, Netherlands.

Bronze — Cedric Mathy, Belgium.

Individual Road Race

Gold — Fabio Casartelli, Italy.

Silver — Erik Dekker, Netherlands.

Bronze — Dainis Ozols, Latvia.

1 Km Time Trial

Gold — Jose Moreno, Spain.

Silver — Shane Kelly, Australia.

Bronze — Erin Hartwell, United States.

4,000-Meter Team Pursuit

Gold — Germany (Michael Gloeckner, Jens Lehmann, Stefan Steinweg, Guido Fulst).

Silver — Australia (Brett Aitken, Stephen McGlede, Shaun O'Brien, Stuart O'Grady).

Bronze — Denmark (Ken Frost, Jimmi Madsen, Jan Bo Petersen, Klaus Kynde Nilsen).

Road Race

Gold — Germany (Bernd Dittert, Christian Meyer, Uwe Peschel, Michael Rich).

Silver — Italy (Flavio Anastasia, Luca Colombo, Gianfranco Contri, Andrea Peron).

Bronze — France (Herve Boussard, Didier Faivre-Pierret, Philippe Gaumont, Jean Louis Harel).

Women's Individual Road Race

Gold — Kathryn Watt, Australia.

Silver — Jeannie Longo-Ciprelli, France.

Bronze — Monique Knol, Netherlands.

Individual Sprint

Gold — Erika Salumae, Estonia.

Silver — Annett Neumann, Germany.

Bronze — Ingrid Haringa, Netherlands.

Individual Pursuit

Gold — Petra Rossner, Germany.

Silver — Kathryn Watt, Australia.

Bronze — Rebecca Twigg, United States.

DARTS

U.S. Champions

Men — Dave Kelly, Boston, Mass.

Women — Stacy Bromberg, Los Angeles, Calif.

DIVING

United States Indoor Champions

Men's 1 Meter — Mark Lenzi, Fredericksburg, Va.

Men's 3M — Mark Lenzi.

Men's 1OM — Patrick Jeffrey, Fort Lauderdale, Fla.

Women's 1M — Julie Ovenhouse, Howell, Mich.

Women's 3M — Julie Ovenhouse.

Women's 1OM — Cokey Smith, Ann Arbor, Mich.

United States Outdoor Champions

Men's 1M — Mark Lenzi.

Men's 3M — Mark Lenzl.

Men's 1OM — Scott Donie, Fort Lauderdale, Fla.

Women's 1M — Kristen Kane, Kingston, Wash.

Women's 3M — Veronica Ribot-Canales, Miami.

Women's 1OM — Mary Ellen Clark, Fort Lauderdale, Fla.

Olympics

Men's Platform

Gold — Sun Shuwei, China.

Silver — Scott Donie, United States.

Bronze — Xiong Ni, China.

Men's Springboard

Gold — Mark Lenzi, United States.

Silver — Tan Liangde, China.

Bronze — Dmitri Saoutine, Unified Team.

Women's Platform

Gold — Fu Mingxia, China.

Silver — Elena Mirochina, Unified Team.

Bronze — Mary Ellen Clark, United States.

Women's Springboard

Gold — Gao Min, China.

Silver — Irina Lachko, Unified Team.

Bronze — Brita Pia Baldus, Germany.

DOG SHOWS

Westminster, New York City — Ch. Registry's Lonesome Dove, Wire Fox Terrier, owned by Marion and Samuel Lawrence, Orlando, Fla.

Westchester, Tarrytown, N.Y. — Ch. Salilyn's Condor, English Springer Spaniel, owned by Donna and Dr. Roger Herzig, Louisville, Ky., and Julie Gasow, Troy, Mich.

Houston K.C., Houston, Tex. — Ch. Registry's Lonesome Dove.

Louisville K.C., Louisville — Ch. Registry's Lonesome Dove, Wire Fox Terrier.

Bucks County, Erwinna, Pa. — Ch. Salilyn's Condor, English Springer Spaniel, owned by Donna and Dr. Roger Herzig, Louisville, Ky., and Julie Gasow, Troy, Mich.

EQUESTRIAN

United States Champions

Jumping — Lisa Jacquin, Collegeville, Pa.

Dressage — Carol Lavell, Fairfax, Vt.

World Champions

Team Jumping — United States.

Team Pairs Driving — United States.

World Cup Jumping — Thomas Fruhmann, Austria.

World Cup Dressage — Isabell Werth, Germany.

Olympics

Individual Jumping

Gold — Ludger Beerbaum, Germany.

Silver — Piet Raymakers, Netherlands.

Bronze — Norman Dello Joio, United States.

Team Jumping

Gold — Netherlands (Piet Raymakers, Bert Romp, Jan Tops, and Jos Lansink).

Silver — Austria (Boris Boor, Joerg Muntzner, Hugo Simon, and Thomas Fruhmann).

Bronze — France (Herve Godignon, Hubert Bourdy, Michel Robert, and Eric Navet).

Individual Dressage

Gold — Nicole Uphoff, Germany.

Silver — Isabelle Werth, Germany.

Bronze — Klaus Balkenhol, Germany.

Team Dressage

Gold — Germany (Nicole Uphoff, Monica Theodorescu, Isabelle Werth, and Klaus Balkenhol).

Silver — Netherlands (Anky Van Grunsven, Annemarie Sanders, Tineke Bartels, and Ellen Bontje).

Bronze — United States (Charlotte Bredahl, Michael Poulin, Robert Dover, and Carol Lavell).

Individual Three-Day Event

Gold — Matthew Ryan, Australia.

Silver — Herbert Blocker, Germany.

Bronze — Robert Tait, New Zealand.

Team Three-Day Event

Gold — Australia (David Green, Gillian Rolton, Andrew Hoy, and Matthew Ryan).

Silver — New Zealand (Andrew Nicholson, Victoria Latta, Robert Tait, and Mark Todd).

Bronze — Germany (Matthias Baumann, Cord Mysegaes, Ralf Ehrenbrink, and Herbert Blocker).

FENCING

U.S.F.A. Champions

Men

Foil— Nick Bravin, Los Angeles, Calif.

Epee — Rob Stull, Austin, Tex.

Saber — Michael Lofton, New York City.

Team Foil — New York Fencers Club.

Team Epee — New York Athletic Club.

Team Saber — New York Fencers Club.

Women

Foil — Caitlin Bilodeaux, Concorde, Mass.

Epee — Barbara Turpin, Minneapolis, Minn.

Team Foil — Women's Fencers Club.

Team Epee — D.C. Fencers Club.

College Champions

Men

Foil — Nick Bravin, Stanford.

Team Foil — Yale.

Epee — Harald Bauder, Wayne St. (Detroit).

Saber — Tom Strzalkowski, Penn State.

Team Epee — Columbia.

Team Sabre — Penn State.

Women

Foil — Olga Chernyak, Penn State.

Team Foil — Temple.

Olympics

Men's Individual Foil

Gold — Philippe Omnes, France.

Silver — Serguei Goloubitski, Unified Team.

Bronze — Elvis Gregory, Cuba.

Team Foil

Gold — Germany (Udo Wagner, Ulrich Schreck, Thorsten Weidner, Alexander Koch, and Ingo Weissenborn).

Silver — Cuba (Elvis Gregory, Guillermo Betancourt, Ostar Garcia, Tulio Diaz, and Hermenegildo Garcia).

Bronze — Poland (Marian Sypniewski, Piotr Kielpikowski, Adam Krzesinski, Cezary Siess, and Ryszard Sobczak).

Individual Sabre

Gold — Bence Szabo, Hungary.

Silver — Marco Marin, Italy.

Bronze — Jean-Francois Lamour, France.

Team Sabre

Gold — Unified Team (Grigorij Kirienko, Alexandre Chirchov, Gueorgui Pogossov, Vadim Gouttsait, and Stanislav Pozdniakov).

Silver — Hungary (Bence Szabo, Csaba Koves, Gyorgy Nebald, Peter Abay, and Imre Bujdoso).

Bronze — France (Jean-Francois Lamour, Jean-Philippe Daurelle, Franck Ducheix, Herve Granger-Veyron, and Pierre Guichot).

Individual Epee

Gold — Eric Srecki, France.

Silver — Pavel Kolobkov, Unified Team.

Bronze — Jean-Michel Henry, France.

Team Epee

Gold — Germany (Elmar Borrmann, Robert Felisiak, Arnd Schmitt Uwt Proske, and Vladimir Reznitchenko).

Silver — Hungary (Ivan Kovacs, Krisztian Kulcsar, Ferenc Hegedus, Erno Kolczonay, and Gabor Totola).

Bronze — Unified Team (Pavel Kolobkov, Andrei Chouvalov, Serguei Kravtchouk, Serguei Kostarev, and Valeri Zakharevitch).

Women' Individual Foil

Gold — Giovanna Trillini, Italy.

Silver — Wang Huifeng, China.

Bronze — Tatiana Sadovskaia, Unified Team.

Team Foil

Gold — Italy (Giovanna Trillini, Margherita Zalaffi, Francesca Bortolozzi, Diana Bianchedi, and Dorina Vaccaroni).

Silver — Germany (Sabine Christiane Bau, Zita-Eva Funkenhauser, Annette Dobmeier, Anja Fichtel-Mauritz, and Monika Weber-Koszto).

Bronze — Romania (Reka Szabo, Claudia Grigorescu, Elisabeta Tufan, Laura Badea, and Roxana Dumitrescu).

FIELD HOCKEY

N.C.A.A. Women

Division I — Old Dominion.

Division III — Trenton State.

National Club Championships

Men — Rye Field Hockey Club, Rye, N.Y.

Women's Indoor Tournament — The Pick-ups, Virginia.

Women's Hockey Festival — Holland Tunnel.

Olympics

Men

Gold — Germany.

Silver — Australia.

Bronze — Pakistan.

Women

Gold — Spain.

Silver — Germany.

Bronze — Britain.

FIGURE SKATING

United States Champions

Men — Christopher Bowman, Los Angeles, Calif.

Women — Kristi Yamaguchi, Freemont, Calif.

Pairs — Calla Urbanski, Chicago, Ill., and Rocky Marval, New Egypt N.J.

Dance — April Sargent-Thomas, Ogdensburg, N.Y., and Russ Witherby, Cincinnati, Ohio.

European Champions

Men — Petr Barna, Czechoslovakia.

Women — Surya Bonaly, France.

Pairs — Natalia Mishkutionok and Artur Dmitriev, Unified Team.

Dance — Marina Klimova and Sergei Ponomarenko, Unified Team.

World Champions

Men — Viktor Petrenko, Unified Team.

Women — Kristi Yamaguchi, United States.

Pairs — Natalia Mishkutionok and Artur Dmitriev, Unified Team.

Dance — Marina Klimova and Sergei Ponomarenko, Unified Team.

Olympics

Men

Gold — Viktor Petrenko, Unified Team.

Silver — Paul Wylie, United States.

Bronze — Petr Barna, Czechoslovakia.

Ice Dancing

Gold — Klimova/Ponomarenko, Unified Team.

Silver — Duchesnay/Duchesnay, France.

Bronze — Usova/Zhulin, Unified Team.

Pairs

Gold — Mishkutienok/Dmitriev, Unified Team.
Silver — Bechke/Petrov, Unified Team.
Bronze — Brasseur/Eisler, Canada.

Women

Gold — Kristi Yamaguchi, United States.
Silver — Midori Ito, Japan.
Bronze — Nancy Kerrigan, United States.

FOOTBALL
(1991 SEASON)

National Football League

Super Bowl — Washington Redskins 37, Buffalo Bills 24.

Division Champions

A.F.C. Champion — Buffalo Bills.
N.F.C. Champion — Washington Redskins.

Standings

American Conference

Eastern Division

	W	L	Pct	PF	PA	Home	Away
Buffalo	13	3	.813	458	318	7-1	6-2
Jets	8	8	.500	314	293	4-4	4-4
Miami	8	8	.500	343	349	5-3	3-5
New England	6	10	.375	211	305	4-4	2-6
Indianapolis	1	15	.063	143	381	0-8	1-7

Central Division

Houston	11	5	.688	386	251	7-1	4-4
Pittsburgh	7	9	.438	292	344	5-3	2-6
Cleveland	6	10	.375	293	298	3-5	4-4
Cincinnati	3	13	.188	263	435	3-5	0-8

Western Division

Denver	12	4	.750	304	235	7-1	5-3
Kansas City	10	6	.625	322	252	6-2	4-4
L.A.Raiders	9	7	.563	298	297	5-3	2-6
Seattle	7	9	.438	276	261	5-3	2-6
San Diego	4	12	.250	274	342	3-5	1-7

National Conference

Eastern Division

	W	L	Pct	PF	PA	Home	Away
Washington	14	2	.875	485	224	7-1	7-1
Dallas	11	5	.688	342	310	6-2	5-3
Philadelphia	10	6	.625	285	244	4-4	6-2
Giants	8	8	.500	281	297	5-3	3-5
Phoenix	4	12	.250	196	344	2-6	2-6

Central Division

Detroit	12	4	.750	339	295	8-0	4-4
Chicago	11	5	.688	299	269	6-2	5-3
Minnesota	8	8	.500	301	306	4-4	4-4
Green Bay	4	12	.250	273	313	2-6	2-6
Tampa Bay	3	13	.188	199	365	3-5	0-8

Western Division

New Orleans	11	5	.688	341	211	6-2	5-3
Atlanta	10	6	.625	361	338	6-2	4-4
San Francisco	10	6	.625	393	239	7-1	3-5
L.A.Rams	3	13	.188	234	390	2-6	1-7

Awards

Super Bowl M.V.P. — Mark Rypien, Washington.
M.V.P. — Thurman Thomas, Buffalo.
Offensive Player of the Year — Thurman Thomas.
Defensive Player of the Year — Pat Swilling, New Orleans Saints.
Offensive Rookie of the Year — Leonard Russell, New England Patriots.
Defensive Rookie of the Year — Mike Croel, Denver Broncos.
Coach of the Year — Wayne Fontes, Detroit Lions.

Canadian Football League

Grey Cup — Toronto Argonauts d. Calgary Stampeders.
M.V.P. — Raghib Ismail, Toronto.

N.C.A.A.

Division I-AA — Youngstown State.
Division II — Pittsburg State (Kansas).
Division III — Ithaca.
N.A.I.A. Division I — Central Arkansas.

Bowl Games

Aloha — Georgia Tech 18, Stanford 17.

Blockbuster — Alabama 30, Colorado 25.

California — Bowling Green 28, Fresno St. 21.

Cotton — Florida State 10, Texas A&M 2.

Copper — Indiana 24, Baylor 0.

Fiesta — Penn State 42, Tennessee 17.

Florida Citrus — California 37, Clemson 13.

Freedom — Tulsa 28, San Diego State 17.

Gator — Oklahoma 48, Virginia 14.

Hall of Fame — Syracuse 24, Ohio State 17.

John Hancock — UCLA 6, Illinois 3.

Holiday — Iowa 13, Brigham Young 13.

Independence — Georgia 24, Arkansas 15.

Liberty — Air Force 38, Mississippi State 15.

Orange — Miami (Florida) 22, Nebraska 0.

Peach — East Carolina 37, North Carolina State 34.

Rose — Washington 34, Michigan 14.

Sugar — Notre Dame 39, Florida 28.

Awards

Heisman Trophy — Desmond Howard, Michigan.

Lombardi Trophy — Steve Emtman, Washington.

Outland Trophy — Steve Emtman.

FRISBEE

World Ultimate Championships

Open Divison — Sweden.

Women — Japan.

Masters Division — United States.

Ultimate Players Association

Men's Open — New York Ultimate.

Women's Open — Lady Godiva (Boston).

Men's Masters — Red Menace (Boston).

Women's Masters — Hot Flashes (Missouri).

GOLF

P.G.A.

U.S. Open — Tom Kite, Austin, Tex.

The Masters — Fred Couples, West Palm Beach, Fla.

P.G.A. Championship — Nick Price, Orlando, Fla.

British Open — Nick Faldo, England.

Vardon Trophy — Corey Pavin, Oxnard, Calif.

The Players Championship — Davis Love III, Sea Island, Ga.

Senior Player's Championship — Dave Stockton, Mentone, Calif.

Awards

Leading money winner — Corey Pavin, Oxnard, Calif.

P.G.A. player of the year — Fred Couples, West Palm Beach, Fla.

P.G.A Senior Championship — Lee Trevino, Jupiter Island, Fla.

U.S.G.A. — Men

Public Links — Warren Schutte, Las Vegas, Nev.

Senior Open — Larry Laoretti, Palm City, Fla.

Amateur — Justin Leonard, Dallas, TX.

Senior Amateur — Bill Bosshard, Copley, Ohio.

Mid-Amateur — Jim Stuart, Macon, Ga.

Junior — Eldrick Woods, Cypress, Calif.

L.P.G.A.

U.S. Open — Patty Sheehan, Reno, Nev.

L.P.G.A. Championship — Betsy King, Limekiln, Pa.

U.S.G.A. — Women

U.S.G.A. Public Links — Amy Fruhwirth, Phoenix, Ariz.

U.S.G.A. Open — Patty Sheehan.

U.S.G.A. Amateur — Vicki Goetze, Watkinsville, Ga.

U.S.G.A. Senior — Phyllis Preuss, Colorado Springs, Colo.

U.S.G.A. Mid-Amateur — Sarah LaBrun Ingram, Nashville, Tenn.

U.S.G.A. Junior — Fuma Jamie Koizumi, Kailua-Kona, Hawaii.

N.C.A.A.

Men

Division I Individual — Warren Schutte, U.N.L.V.

Team — Oklahoma State.

Division II — Clete Cole, Columbus.

Team — Florida Southern.

Division III — Lee Palms, Emory.

Team — Methodist.

Women

Division I Individual — Annika Sorenstam, Arizona.

Team — U.C.L.A.

GYMNASTICS

U.S. Championships

U.S. Men's All-Around — John Roethlifberger, Minneapolis, Minnesota.

U.S. Women's All-Around — Kim Zmeskal, Houston.

McDonald's American Cup, Men — Jarrod Hanks, Norman, Oklahoma.

McDonald's American Cup, Women — Kim Zmeskal.

1992 World Championships

Men

Floor Exercise — Igor Korobchinski, Unified Team.

Parallel Bars — Li Jing, China and Alexei Voropaev, Unified Team.

Pommel Horse — Pae Gil Fu, Korea; Vitaly Scherbo, Unified Team and Li Jing, China.

Still Rings — Vitaly Scherbo.

Vault — You Ok Youl, Korea.

High Bar — Grigori Misutin, Unified Team.

Women

Floor Excercise — Kim Zmeskal, United States.

Uneven Bars — Lavinia Milosovici, Romania.

Balance Beam — Kim Zmeskal.

Vault — Henrietta Onodi, Hungary.

Olympics — Men

All-Around

Gold — Vitali Scherbo, Unified Team.

Silver — Grigori Misutin, Unified Team.

Bronze — Valeri Belenki, Unified Team.

Floor Exercise

Gold — Li Xiaosahuang, China.

Silver — Grigori Misutin, Unified Team and Yukio Iketani, Japan.

Horizontal Bar

Gold — Trent Dimas, United States.

Silver — Andreas Wecker, Germany, and Grigori Misutin, Unified Team.

Parallel Bars

Gold — Vitali Scherbo, Unified Team.

Silver — Li Jing, China.

Bronze — Igor Korobtchinski, Unified Team, Guo Linyao, China, and Masayuki Matsunaga, Japan.

Pommel Horse

Gold — Vitaly Scherbo, Unified Team and Pae Gil-Su, North Korea.

Bronze — Andreas Wecker, Germany.

Rings

Gold — Vitaly Scherbo, Unified Team.

Silver — Li Jing, China.

Bronze — Andreas Wecker, Germany, and Li Xiaosahuang, China.

Vault

Gold — Vitaly Scherbo, Unified Team.

Silver — Grigori Misutin, Unified Team.

Bronze — Yoo Ok Ryul, South Korea.

Team

Gold — Unified Team (Vitali Scherbo, Valeri Belenki, Grigori Misutin, Igor Korobtchinski, Aleksei Voropaev, Roustam Charipov).

Silver — China (Li Xiaosahuang, Li Chunyang, Guo Linyao, Li Jing, Li Dashuang, Li Ge).

Bronze — Japan (Yukio Iketani, Yoshiaki Hatakeda, Takashi Chinen, Daisuke Nishikawa, Yutaka Aihara, Masayuki Matsunaga).

Women

All-Around

Gold — Tatiana Gutsu, Unified Team.

Silver — Shannon Miller, United States.

Bronze — Lavinia Milosovici, Romania.

Balance Beam

Gold — Tatiana Lisenko, Unified Team.

Silver — Lu Li, China and Shannon Miller, United States.

Floor Exercise

Gold — Lavinia Milosovici, Romania.

Silver — Henrietta Onodi, Hungary.

Bronze — Shannon Miller, United States; Cristina Bontas, Romania; and Tatiana Gutsu, Unified Team.

Uneven Bars

Gold — Lu Li, China

Silver — Tatiana Gutsu, Unified Team

Bronze — Shannon Miller, United States

Vault

Gold — Henrietta Onodi, Hungary, and Lavinia Milosovici, Romania.

Bronze — Tatiana Lisenko, Unified Team.

Team

Gold — Unified Team (Oksana Tchoussovitina, Tatiana Lisenko, Elena Groudneva, Svetlana Boguinskaia, Roza Galieva, Tatiana Gutsu).

Silver — Romania (Gina Gogean, Maria Neculita, Mirela Pasca, Cristina Bontas, Vanda Hadarean, Lavinia Milosovici).

Bronze — United States (Wendy Bruce, Kerri Strug, Kim Zmeskal, Betty Okino, Shannon Miller, Dominique Dawes).

N.C.A.A. Champions

Men's Division I — Stanford.

All-Around — John Roethlisberger, Minnesota.

Women's Division I — Utah.

All-Around — Missy Marlowe, Utah.

HANDBALL

U.S. Handball Association

One-Wall

Men — Joe Durso, Brooklyn.

Women — Dori Ten, Brooklyn.

Three-Wall

Men — John Bike, Albequerque, N.M.

Women — Anna Engele, St. Paul, Minn.

Four-Wall

Men — Octavio Silveyra, Commerce, Calif.

Women — Lisa Fraser, Winnipeg.

HANG GLIDING

World Championship

Pre-World — John Pendry, Great Britain.

Pre-World Team — United States.

U.S. Pilot — Chris Arai, Oakland, Calif.

HARNESS RACING

Triple Crown Race Winners

Trotters

Yonkers Trot — Dead Heat: McCluckey and Magic Lobell.

Hambletonian — Alf Palema.

Kentucky Futurity — Whiteland Janice.

Pacers

Cane Pace — Western Hanover.

Little Brown Jug — Precious Bunny.

Messenger Stakes — Die Laughing.

Breeders Crown

3-Year-Old Colt Pace — Three Wizzards.

3-Year-Old-Filly Pace — Miss Easy.

3-Year-Old-Colt Trot — Giant Victory.

3-year-Old-Filly Trot — Twelve Speed.

2-year-Old-Colt Pace — Digger Almahurst.

2-year-Old-Filly Pace — Hazleton Kay.

2-year-Old Colt Trot — King Conch.

2-year-Old Filly Trot — Armbro Keepsake.

Horse Pace — Camluck.

Horse Trot — Billjojimbob.

Mare Pace — Delinquent Account.

Mare Trot — Me Maggie.

Other Major Stakes Races

Elitlopp — Billjojimbob.

North America Cup — Safely Kept.

Meadowlands Pace — Carlsbad Cam.

HOCKEY
(1991-1992 SEASON)

National Hockey League

Stanley Cup

Pittsburgh Penguins d. Chicago Blackhawks.

Standings

WALES CONFERENCE Patrick Division

	W	L	T	Pts	GF	GA
Rangers	50	25	5	105	321	246
Washington	45	27	8	98	330	275
Pittsburgh	39	32	9	87	343	308
Devils	38	31	11	87	289	259
Islanders	34	35	11	79	281	299
Philadelphia	32	37	11	75	252	273

Adams Division

	W	L	T	Pts	GF	GA
Montreal	41	28	11	93	267	207
Boston	36	32	12	84	270	275
Buffalo	31	37	12	74	289	299
Hartford	26	41	13	65	247	283
Quebec	20	48	12	52	255	318

CAMPBELL CONFERENCE Norris Division

	W	L	T	Pts	GF	GA
Detroit	43	25	12	98	320	256
Chicago	36	29	15	87	257	236
St. Louis	36	33	11	83	279	266
Minnesota	32	42	6	70	246	278
Toronto	30	43	7	67	234	294

Smythe Division

	W	L	T	Pts	GF	GA
Vancouver	42	26	12	96	285	250
Los Angeles	35	31	14	84	287	296
Edmonton	36	34	10	82	295	297
Winnipeg	33	32	15	81	251	244
Calgary	31	37	12	74	296	305
San Jose	17	58	5	39	219	359

Awards

M.V.P. — Mark Messier, N.Y. Rangers.

Stanley Cup M.V.P. — Mario Lemieux, Pittsburgh.

Top Defenseman — Brian Leetch, N.Y. Rangers.

Rookie of the Year — Pavel Bure, Vancouver Canucks.

Scoring Champion — Mario Lemieux.

Vezina Trophy — Patrick Roy, Montreal Canadiens.

Goals Against Average — Patrick Roy.

Lady Blng — Wayne Gretzky, Los Angeles Kings.

Coach of the Year — Pat Quinn, Vancouver.

College

Division I — Lake Superior St.

N.C.A.A. Division III — Plattsburgh (N.Y.).

E.C.A.C. Division I — St. Lawrence University.

Hockey East — Maine.

E.C.A.C. East Champion — Babson College (Wellesley, Mass.)

E.C.A.C. West Champion — Plattsburgh.

E.C.A.C. North Champion — Fitchburg St. (Mass.)

E.C.A.C. South Champion — Amherst.

E.C.A.C. Women — Providence.

E.C.A.C. Division III Women — St. Lawrence, Canton, N.Y.

Olympics

Gold — Unified Team.
Silver — Canada.
Bronze — Czechoslovakia.

HORSE RACING

Race Winners

Breeders' Cup Juvenile — Arazi.
B.C. Juvenile Fillies — Pleasant Stage.
B.C. Mile — Opening Verse.
B.C. Distaff — Dance Smartly.
B.C. Turf — Miss Alleged.
B.C. Classic — Black Tie Affair.
B.C. Sprint — Sheikh Albadou.
Florida Derby — Technology.
Santa Anita Handicap — Best Pal.
Santa Anita Derby — A.P. Indy.
Wood Memorial — Devil His Due.
Kentucky Derby — Lil E. Tee.
Preakness Stakes — Pine Bluff.
Epsom Derby — Dr. Devious.
Belmont Stakes — A.P. Indy.
Irish Derby — St. Jovite.
Haskill Invitational — Technology.
Travers Stakes — Thunder Rumble.
Arlington Million — Tight Spot.

HORSESHOE PITCHING

World Champions

Men — Kevin Cone, Iowa.
Women — Sue Snyder, Indiana.

HORSE SHOWS

National Championships

U.S.E.T. Show Jumping Championship —
Michael Matz, Collegeville, Pa., riding Rhum
IV.
U.S.E.T. National Dressage Championship —
Guenter Seidel, Carlsbad, Calif., riding Numir.

U.S. League Volvo World Cup — Carol Lavell,
riding Gifted.
U.S.E.T. Spring Three-Day Event Championship
— Todd Trewin, Woodenville, Wash. riding
Sandscript.

Awards

A.G.A. Rider of the Year — Margie Goldstein,
Miami.
Leading Horse of the Year — For the Moment.
Leading Rookie of the Year — McLain Ward,
Bruster, N.Y.

International Championship

Show Jumping World Cup Finals — Thomas
Fruhmann, Austria, riding Genius.
Volvo Dressage World Cup Finals — Isabell
Werth, Germany, riding Fabienne.
HCS Nations' Trophy Team World
Championship — U.S Equestrian Team (Leslie
Lenehan, riding Pressurized; Debbie Shaffner,
riding Volan; Joan Scharffenberger, riding
Victor; Greg Best, riding Gem Twist).

ICEBOATING

World Champions

World D.N. Class — Karol Jablonski, Germany.
European D.N. Class — Karol Jablonski.
North American Championship — Ron Sherry,
Mount Clemens, Mich.

JAI-ALAI

Florida Tournament of Champions

Singles — Joey, Dania Jai-Alai.
Doubles — Benny and Ecenarro, Miami Jai-Lai.

JUDO

U.S. Champions

Men's Open — Christophe Leininger, Colorado
Springs.
Women's Open — D'Anaya Bierria, Colorado
Springs.

Men's Heavyweight — Damon Keeve, San Francisco, Calif.

Women's Heavyweight — Carol Scheid, Nevada, Idaho.

Olympics

Men 60 Kg (132 pounds)

Gold — Nazim Gousseinov, Unified Team.

Silver — Yoon Hyun, South Korea.

Bronze — Tadanori Koshino, Japan and Richard Trautmann, Germany.

Men 65 Kg (143 pounds)

Gold — Rogerio Sampaio Cardoso, Brazil.

Silver — Josef Csak, Hungary.

Bronze — Udo Quellmalz, Germany and Israel Hernandez, Cuba.

Men 71 Kg (157 pounds)

Gold — Toshihiko Koga, Japan.

Silver — Bertalan Hajtos, Hungary.

Bronze — Chung Hoon, South Korea and Shay Smadga, Israel.

Men 78 Kg (172 pounds)

Gold — Hidehiko Yoshida, Japan.

Silver — Jason Morris, United States.

Bronze — Bertrand Damaisin, France and Kim Byung-Joo, South Korea.

Men 90 Kg (198 pounds)

Gold — Waldemar Legien, Poland.

Silver — Pascal Tayot, France.

Bronze — Hirotaka Okada, Japan and Nicolas Gill, Canada.

Men 95 Kg (209 pounds)

Gold — Antal Kovacs, Hungary.

Silver — Raymond Stevens, Britain.

Bronze — Dmitri Sergeev, Unified Team and Theo Meijer, Netherlands.

Men 95 Kg-plus (209-plus pounds)

Gold — David Khakhaleichvili, Unified Team.

Silver — Naoya Ogawa, Japan.

Bronze — David Douillet, France and Imre Csosz, Hungary.

Women 48 Kg (106 pounds)

Gold — Cecile Nowak, France.

Silver — Ryoko Tamura, Japan.

Bronze — Hulya Senyurt, Turkey and Amarilis Savon, Cuba.

Women 52 Kg (115 pounds)

Gold — Almudena Martinez, Spain.

Silver — Moriko Mizoguchi, Japan.

Bronze — Li Zhongyun, China and Sharon Rendle, Britain.

Women 56 Kg (123 pounds)

Gold — Miriam Blasco Soto, Spain.

Silver — Nicola Fairbrother, Britain.

Bronze — Chiyori Tateno, Japan and Driulis Gonzalez, Cuba.

Women 61 Kg (134 pounds)

Gold — Calherine Fleury, France.

Silver — Yael Arad, Israel.

Bronze — Zhang Di, China and Elena Petova, Unified Team.

Women 66 Kg (146 pounds)

Gold — Odalis Reve, Cuba.

Silver — Emanuela Pierantozzi, Italy.

Bronze — Kate Howey, Britain and Heidi Rakels, Belgium.

Women 72 Kg (159 pounds)

Gold — Kim Mi-Jung, South Korea.

Silver — Yoko Tanabe, Japan.

Bronze — Irene De Kok, Netherlands and Laetitia Meignan, France.

Women 72 Kg-plus (159-plus pounds)

Gold — Zhuang Xiaoyan, China.

Silver — Estela Rodriguez, Cuba.

Bronze — Natalia Lupino, France and Yoko Sakaue, Japan.

KARATE

Men's U.S. Champions

Advanced Kumite — Carlos Quintero, Hialeah, Fl.

Advanced 80+ kg. — Jay Farell, Beaverton, Ore.

Advanced 75 kg. — Chris Nicholas, Akron, Ohio.

Advanced -80 kg. — Doug Selchon, N. Huntington, Pa.

Advanced -70 kg. — Ferdie Allas, Ironton, Ohio.

Advanced -65 kg — William Chadrow, Redmond, Wa.

Advanced -60 kg. — Bismark Leon, New York.

Women's U.S. Champions

Advanced 60+ kg. — Tina Franks, Florence, Ky.

Advanced -60 kg. — Tracey Day, Coram, N.Y.

Advanced -53 kg — Christina Mucini, Douglastown, N.Y.

Advanced — Edna Loeber, New York.

LACROSSE

N.C.A.A.

Division I — Princeton.

Division III — Nazareth.

Women Division I — Maryland.

Women Division III — Trenton State.

N.J.C.A.A. — Herkimer College (N.Y.)

Major Indoor League — Buffalo Bandits.

LUGE

U.S. Champions

Men — Duncan Kennedy, Lake Placid, N.Y.

Women — Cammy Myler, Lake Placid, N.Y.

Men's Doubles — Chris Thorpe and Gordy Sheer, Croton-on-Hudson, N.Y.

World Cup Champions

Men — Markus Prock, Austria.

Women — Susi Erdmann, Germany.

Men's Doubles — Hansjorg Raffl and Norbert Huber, Italy.

Olympics

Men's Singles

Gold — Georg Hackl, Germany.

Silver — Markus Prock, Austria.

Bronze — Markus Schmidt, Austria.

Women's Singles

Gold — Doris Neuner, Austria.

Silver — Angelica Neuner, Austria.

Bronze — Susi Erdmann, Germany.

Men's Doubles

Gold — Stefan Krausse and Jan Behrendt, Germany.

Silver — Yves Mankel and Thomas Rudolph, Germany.

Bronze — Hansjorg Raffi and Norbert Huber, Italy.

MARATHON

New York, Men — Salvador Garcia, Mexico.

New York, Women — Liz McColgan, Scotland.

Boston, Men — Ibrahim Hussein, Kenya.

Boston, Women — Olga Markova, Russia.

London Marathon, Men — Antonio Pinto, Portugal.

London Marathon, Women — Katrin Dorre, Germany.

MODERN PENTATHLON

United States

Men — Mike Gostigian, Newtown Square, Pa.

Women — Terry Lewis, San Antonio.

Junior Men — Scott Christie, San Antonio.

Junior Women — Lauren Riester, San Antonio.

RESULTS

Olympics

Individual

Gold — Arkadiusz Skrzypaszek, Poland.

Silver — Attila Mizser, Hungary.

Bronze — Edouard Zenovka, Unified Team.

Team

Gold — Poland (Maciej Czyzowicz, Arkadiusz Skrzypaszek, and Dariusz Gozdziak).

Silver — Unified Team (Anatoli Starostine, Dmitri Svatkovski, and Edouard Zenovka).

Bronze — Italy (Gianluca Tiberti, Carlo Massullo, and Roberto Bomprezzi).

MOTORCYCLE RACING

U.S. Champions

U.S. Pro — Scott Parker, Swartz Creek, Mich.

Daytona 200 — Scott Russell, Santa Anna, Calif.

Camel Supercross — Jeff Stanton, Sherwood, Mich.

World Champions

Road Race

125 cc — Loris Capirossi, Italy.

250 cc — Luca Cadalora, Italy.

500 cc — Wayne Rainey, United States.

Motocross — Trampas Parker, United States.

ORIENTEERING

U.S. Champions

1992 Intercollegiate Champion (Men and Women Combined) — United States Military Academy.

U.S. Long Course Championship — Mikell Platt, Rockhill, S.C.

Women's U.S. Long Course Championship — Hannah North, Boise, Idaho.

World Champions

Men's Ski — Vidar Benjaminsen, Norway.

Women's Ski — Annika Zell, Sweden.

Sprint Ski Championship — Vidar Benjaminsen.

Women's Sprint Ski Championship — Arja Hannus, Sweden.

Men's World Ski Relay Championship — Finland.

Women's World Ski Relay Championships — Sweden.

PADDLEBALL

National Champions

Men's Open — Andy Kasalo, Kalamazoo, Mich.

Women's Open — Caprice Dehner, New Buffalo, Mich.

Men's Open Doubles — Andy Kasalo and Andy Mitchell, Kalamazoo, Mich.

Women's Open Doubles — Carla Teare, Clarkston, Mich., and Anna Thomas, Flint, Mich.

Men's B Divison — Doug Quick, Clarkston, Mich.

Women's Novice — Heather O'Connor, Pontiac, Mich.

PADDLE TENNIS

U.S. Champions

Men's Singles — Scott Freedman, Culver City, Calif.

Women's Singles — Nicole Marois, Los Angeles, Calif.

Men's Doubles — Sol Hauptman, Venice Beach, Calif. and Scott Freedman.

Women's Doubles — Ingrid Fields, Westchester, Calif., and Alex Chistolini, Culver City, Calif.

PARACHUTE JUMPING

Men's Paraski Nationals — Brett Pendleton, Salt Lake City, Utah.

Women's Paraski Nationals — Lynda Forney, Salt Lake City, Utah.

Paraski-team — Switzerland.

8-Way — U.S. Army Golden Knights, Fort Bragg, N.C.

4-Way — The Fource, Coolidge, Ariz.

PLATFORM TENNIS

U. S. Men's Singles — Scott Staniar, Greenwich, Conn.

U. S. Women's Singles — None.

U. S. Men's Doubles — Steve Baird, Harrison, N.Y., and Rich Maier, Scarsdale, N.Y.

U.S. Women's Doubles — Robin Fulton, Stamford, Conn., and Diane Tucker, Bedford, N.Y.

U.S. Mixed Doubles — David Ohlmuller, Montclair, N.J., and Patty Hogan, Summit N.J.

POLO

U.S. World Cup on Snow — Bernie's, St. Moritz.

U.S.T.A. Rolex Gold Cup — Revlon.

Lexus International Gold Cup — Revlon.

Regina World Cup — Rolex A&K.

POWERBOATING

National Champions

Grand National Hydro — Frank Richardson, Ogdensburg, N.Y.

6 Liter — Jerry Hale, Hayward, Calif.

2.5 Liter Modified — Jerry Hale.

5 Liter — Mark Weber, St. Clair Shores, Mich.

Formula Cobra — Mark Weber.

1 Liter Modified — John Wiggins, Gadsen, Al.

1 Ltr Stock — Joe Longo, Mt. Ephraim, N.J.

Jersey Speed Skiff — Ken Germershausen, Pasadena, Md.

Super Stock — Gee McClain, Cambridge, Md.

K-Racing Runabout — Gee McClain.

Competition Jet — Kenneth Niemann, Poulsbo Wa.

Grand Prix — Alan Schide, Centerville, Ohio.

Gold Cup — Chip Hanauer (Miss Budweiser).

POWER LIFTING

U.S.P.F.

Women

97 lbs — Ann Leverett, Savannah, Ga.

105 lbs — Glynis Ramarez-Bierra, Colorado Springs, Colo.

114 lbs — Mary Jeffrey, Parkersburg, W.V.

123 lbs — Carrie Graffam, Salem, Ore.

132 lbs — Rachel Mathis, Indianapolis, Ind.

148 lbs — Vickie Steenrod, Albuqerque, N.M.

165 lbs — Sara Roberson, France.

181 lbs — Veronica Mercer, Parkersburg, W.V.

198 lbs — Shelby Corson, Waterville, Maine.

Super Heavyweight — Juanita Trujillo, Grand Junction, Colo.

Men

114 lbs — Phil Hile, Madison, W.V.

123 lbs — Tim Taylor, Grand Forks Air Force Base, N.D.

132 lbs — Lamar Gant, Denver, Colo.

148 lbs — Dan Austin, Las Vegas, Nev.

165 lbs — Dave Ricks, Japan.

181 lbs — Greg Jones, Atlanta, Ga.

198 lbs — Sly Anderson, Shelby, Miss.

220 lbs — Steve Goggins, Fort Worth, Tex.

242 lbs — Dave Jacoby, Akron, Ohio.

275 lbs — Kirk Karwaski, Crofton, Md.

Super Heavyweight — Harold Collins, Pembroke, N.C.

QUARTER HORSE RACING

All-American Futurity — Royal Quick Dash.

All-American Derby — See Me Gone.

Rainbow Futurity — Deceptively.

Rainbow Derby — Ed Grimley.

Kansas Futurity — Deceptively.

Kansas Derby — Dash Master Miss.

RACQUETBALL

United States Champions

Men's Amateur Singles — Chris Cole, Flint, Mich.

Women's Amateur Singles — Michelle Gilman-Gould, Ontario, Ore.

Men's Pro Series — Drew Kachtik, Dallas, Texas.

Men's Pro Singles — Mike Ray, Hilton Head, South Carolina.

Women's Pro Singles — Jackie Paraiso-Gibson, San Diego, Calif.

RACQUETS

Unites States and World

U.S. Open — Neil Smith, England.

U.S. Pro — Neil Smith.

U.S. Amateur — James Male, England.

World — James Male.

RHYTHMIC GYMNASTICS

U.S. Champions

All-Around — Bianca Sapetto, San Pedro, Calif.

Junior All-Around — Christi Tucay, Burbank, Calif.

World Champions

All-around— Oksana Skaldina, Soviet Union.

Rope — Alexandra Timochenko, Soviet Union.

Hoop — Oksana Skaldina.

Ball — Oksana Skaldina.

Clubs — Maria Petrova, Bulgaria.

Olympics

Gold — Alexandra Timoshenko, Unified Team.

Silver — Carolina Pascual Gracia, Spain.

Bronze — Oksana Skaldina, Unified Team.

RODEO

U.S. College — Casey Minton, West Hills College, Calif.

World All-Around — Ty Murray, Stephenville, Tex.

ROLLER HOCKEY

U.S. Championships

Midget Division — Reynoldsville (Pa.) Lazers.

Freshman Division — Deptford (N.J.) Devils.

Sophomore Division — Deptford (N.J.) Devils.

Senior Women's Division — Chowchilla (Calif.) Rollin' Tuff.

Senior Bronze Division — Deptford (N.J.) Devils.

Senior Silver Division — Paducah (KY) Knights.

Senior Gold Division — Port Neches (Tex.) Champions.

Olympics

Gold — Argentina.

Silver — Spain.

Bronze — Italy.

ROLLER SKATING

U.S. Champions

Men's Singles — Heath Medeiros, Warwick, RI.

Women's Singles — April Dayney, Maumee, Ohio.

Men's Figures — Richard Saucedo, Hayward, Calif.

Women's Figures — Jennifer Rodriguez, Ft. Lauderdale, Fla.

Pairs — John Fetrow and Jodi Davidson, Flint, Mich.

Dance — Doug Wait and Deanna Monahan, San Jose, Calif.

Men's Senior In-Line — Dante Muse, West Des Moines, Iowa

Women's Senior In-Line — Vicci Ping, Puyallup, Wash.

Men's Senior Quad — James Wilterdink, Downington, PA.

Women's Senior Quad — Sandie Peeded, Greensboro, N.C.

World Champions

Men's Speed — Tony Muse, United States.

Men's Freestyle — Scott Cohen.

Women's Freestyle — Raffaella Del Vinaccio, Italy.

Men's Figures — Justin Bates.

Women's Figures — Raffaella Del Vinaccio.

Pairs — Larry McGrew and Tina Jerue.

Dance — Gregory Goody and Jodee Viola.

Women's Speed — Maria Eva Richardson, Argentina.

ROQUE

National Champion — Jack Roegner, Richmond, Indiana.

ROWING

U.S. CHAMPIONS

Women's Lightweight Four — University of Iowa.

Women's Varsity Eight — Boston University.

Men's Varsity Eight — Harvard.

Men's Lightweight Eight — Cornell.

Junior and Lightweight World Championships

Junior Men's

Single Sculls — Erik Tul, Slovenia.

Double Sculls — Germany.

Quadruple Sculls — Czechoslovakia.

Pair without Coxswain — Germany.

Pair with Coxswain — Germany.

Four without Coxswain — Great Britain.

Four with Coxswain — Germany.

Eight — United States.

Junior Women's

Single Sculls — Kathrin Rutschow, Germany.

Double Sculls — Germany.

Quadruple Sculls — Russia.

Pair without Coxswain — Austria.

Four without Coxswain — Czechoslovakia.

Eight — Germany.

Lightweight Men's

Single Sculls — Jens Mohr Ernst, Denmark.

Double Sculls — Australia.

Quadruple Sculls — Italy.

Four without Coxswain — Great Britain.

Eight — Denmark.

Lightweight Women's

Singles Sculls — Denmark.

Double Sculls — Germany.

Four without Coxswain — Australia.

Olympics

Men' Single Sculls

Gold — Thomas Lange, Germany.

Silver — Vaclav Chalupa, Czechoslovakia.

Bronze — Kajetan Broniewski, Poland.

Double Sculls

Gold — Australia (Stephen Hawkins and Peter Antonie).

Silver — Austria (Arnold Jonke and Christoph Zerbst).

Bronze — Netherlands (Henk-Jan Zwolle and Nico Rienks).

Quadruple Sculls

Gold — Germany (Andre Willms, Andreas Hajek, Stephan Volkert, and Michael Steinbach).

Silver — Norway (Lars Bjonness, Rolf Thorsen, Kjetil Undset, and Per Saetersdal).

Bronze — Italy (Gianluca Farina, Rossano Galtarossa, Alessandro Corona, and Filippo Soffici).

RESULTS

Coxed Pairs

Gold — Britain (Jonathan Searle, Greg Searle, and Garry Herbert).

Silver — Italy (Carmine Abbagnale, Giuseppe Abbagnale, and Giuseppe Di Capua).

Bronze — Romania (Dimitrie Popescu, Nicolaie Taga, and Dumitru Raducanu).

Coxless Pairs

Gold — Britain (Steven Redgrave and Matthew Pinsent).

Silver — Germany (Peter Hoeltzenbein and Colin Von Ettingshausen).

Bronze — Slovenia (Iztok Cop and Denis Zvegelj).

Coxed Fours

Gold — Romania (Viorel Talapan, Iulica Ruican, Dimitrie Popescu, Nicolaie Taga, Dumitru Raducanu).

Silver — Germany (Uwe Kellner, Ralf Brudel, Thoralf Peters, Karsten Finger, Hendrik Reiher).

Bronze — Poland (Jacek Streich, Wojciech Jankowski, Tomasz Tomiak, Maciej Lasicki, Michal Cieslak).

Coxless Fours

Gold — Australia (Andrew Cooper, Michael McKay, Nicholas Green, and James Tomkins).

Silver — United States (Doug Burden, Jeff McLaughlin, Thomas Bohrer, and Patrick Manning).

Bronze — Slovenia (Janez Klemencic, Saso Mirjanic, Milan Jansa, and Sadik Mujkic).

Coxed Eights

Gold — Canada (John Wallace, Bruce Robertson, Michael Forgeron, Darren Barber, Robert Marland, Michael Rascher, Andrew Crosby, Derek Porter, and Terrence Paul).

Silver — Romania (Ioan Iulian Vizitiu, Danut Dobre, Claudiu Gabriel Marin, Iulica Ruican, Viorel Talapan, Vasile Dorel Nastase, Valentin Robu, Vasile Ionel Mastacan, and Marin Gheorghe).

Bronze — Germany (Frank Richter, Thorsten Streppelhoff, Detlef Kirchhoff, Armin Eichholz, Bahne Rabe, Hans Sennewald, Ansgar Wessling, Roland Baar, and Manfred Klein)

Women's Single Sculls

Gold — Elisabeta Lipa, Romania

Silver — Annelies Bredael, Belgium

Bronze — Silken Laumann, Canada

Double Sculls

Gold — Germany (Kerstin Koeppen and Kathrin Boron).

Silver — Romania (Veronica Cochelea and Elisabeta Lipa).

Bronze — China (Gu Xiaoli and Lu Huali).

Quadruple Sculls

Gold — Germany (Kerstin Mueller, Sybille Schmidt, Birgit Peter, and Kristina Mundt).

Silver — Romania (Constanta Pipota, Doina Ignat, Veronica Cochelea, and Anisoara Dobre).

Bronze — Unified Team (Ekaterina Khodotovitch, Antonina Zelikovitch, Tatiana Oustioujanina, and Elena Khloptseva).

Coxless Pairs

Gold — Canada (Marnie McBean and Kathleen Heddle).

Silver — Germany (Stefani Werremeier and Ingeburg Schwerzmann).

Bronze — United States (Anna Seaton and Stephanie Pierson).

Coxless Fours

Gold — Canada (Kirsten Barnes, Brenda Taylor, Jessica Monroe, and Kay Worthington).

Silver — United States (Shelagh Donohoe, Cindy Eckert, Amy Fuiler, and Carol Feeney).

Bronze — Germany (Antje Frank, Gabriele Mehl, Birte Siech, and Annette Hohn).

Coxed Eights

Gold — Canada (Kirsten Barnes, Brenda Taylor, Megan Delehanty, Shannon Crawford, Marnie McBean, Kay Worthington, Jessica Monroe, Kathleen Heddle, and Lesley Thompson).

Silver — Romania (Doina Snep, Doina Robu, Ioana Olteanu, Victoria Lepadatu, Julia Bobeica, Viorica Neculai, Adriana Bazon, Maria Padurariu, and Elena Georgescu).

Bronze — Germany (Annegret Strauch, Sylvia Doerdelmann, Kathrin Haacker, Dana Pyritz, Cerstin Petersmann, Ute Wagner, Christiane Harzendorf, Judith Zeidler, and Daniela Neunast).

RUGBY

United States Champions

Club — Old Blues, Berkeley, Calif.

Women's Club — Bay Area SheHawk, Bay Area, Calif.

Men's College — California.

Women's College — Boston College.

Seven-A-Side — Old Puget Sound Beach, Seattle.

Military — Pensacola, Fla.

Schoolboy — Highlands H.S., Salt Lake City.

Men's Division II Club — The Battleship R.F.C., Mobile, Ala.

Local Union All-Stars Championship — Pacific Northwest.

World Champions

Five Nations — England.

Bledisloe Cup — Australia.

Hong Kong Sevens — Fiji.

SHOOTING

Amateur Trapshooting Association

Men's Clay Target Championship — Dr. William J. Godschalk, Hartford City, Indiana.

Women's Clay Target Championship — Janet Loebs, Shore Wood, Ill.

Men's Grand American Handicap — Mark T. Wade, Kenilworth, N.J.

Women's Grand American Handicap — Kelly Doll, Hanover, Pa.

Men's Doubles Championship — Larry Bumstead, Conrad, Iowa.

Women's Doubles Championship — Cathy Wehinger, Monroe, Wisc.

Men's High All Around Championships — Leo Harrison III, Hannibal, Mo.

Women's High All Around Championships — Nora Martin, Midway, Ky.

Olympics

Open Skeet

Gold — Zhang Shan, China.

Silver — Juan Jorge Giha Yarur, Peru.

Bronze — Bruno Rossetti, Italy.

Open Trap

Gold — Petr Hrdlicka, Czechoslovakia.

Silver — Kazumi Watanabe, Japan.

Bronze — Marco Venturini, Italy.

Men's Air Pistol

Gold — Wang Yifu, China.

Silver — Serguei Pyjianov, Unified Team.

Bronze — Sorin Babii, Romania.

Men's Free Pistol

Gold — Konstantine Loukachik, Unified Team.

Silver — Wang Yifu, China.

Bronze — Ragnar Skanaker, Sweden.

Men's Rapid Fire Pistol

Gold — Ralf Schumann, Germany.

Silver — Afanasijs Kuzmins, Latvia.

Bronze — Vladimir Vokhmianine, Unified Team.

Men's Running Game Target

Gold — Michael Jakosits, Germany.

Silver — Anatoli Asrabaev, Unified Team.

Bronze — Lubos Racansky, Czechoslovakia.

Men's Air Rifle

Gold — Iouri Fedkine, Unified Team.

Silver — Franck Badiou, France.

Bronze — Johann Riederer, Germany.

RESULTS

Men's Free Rifle

Gold — Lee Eun-Chul, South Korea.

Silver — Harald Stenvaag, Norway.

Bronze — Stevan Pletikosic, Yugoslavia.

Men's Three-Position Rifle

Gold — Gratchia Petikiane, Unified Team.

Silver — Bob Foth, United States.

Bronze — Ryohei Koba, Japan.

Women's Sport Pistol

Gold — Marina Logvinenko, Unified Team.

Silver —- Li Duihong, China.

Bronze--Dorzhsuren Munkhbayar, Mongolia.

Women's Air Pistol

Gold — Marina Logvinenko, Unified Team.

Silver — Jasna Sekaric, Yugoslavia.

Bronze — Maria Grousdeva, Bulgaria.

Women's Air Rifle

Gold — Yeo Kab-Soon, South Korea.

Silver — Vesela Letcheva, Bulgaria.

Bronze — Aranka Binder, Yugoslavia.

Women's Three-Position Rifle

Gold — Launi Meili, United States.

Silver — Nonka Matova, Bulgaria.

Bronze — Malgorzata Ksiazkiewicz, Poland.

SHUFFLEBOARD

National Champions

Men — Glenn Peltier, Canada.

Women — Mary Eldridge, St. Petersburg, Fla.

SKATEBOARDING

Skateboard Association

Vertical — Tony Hawk, Fallbrook, Calif.

Street Style — Chris Senn, Grass Valley, Calif.

Thrasher Skater of the Year — Danny Way, Vista, Calif.

SKELETON

World Championship

Men's Singles — Bruce Sandford, New Zealand.

SKIING

Collegiate Champions

N.C.A.A.

Team — Vermont.

Men's slalom — Einar Bohmer, University of Vermont.

Women's slalom — Katja Lesjak, Utah.

Men's giant slalom — Eric Archer, Colorado.

Women's giant slalom — Sally Knight, Vermont.

Olympics

Women's Combined

Gold — Petra Kronberger, Austria.

Silver — Anita Wachter, Austria.

Bronze — Florence Masnada, France.

Women's Downhill

Gold — Kerrin Lee-Gartner, Canada.

Silver — Hilary Lindh, United States.

Bronze — Veronika Wallinger, Austria.

Women's Giant Slalom

Gold — Pernilla Wiberg, Sweden.

Silver — Diann Roffe, United States and Anita Wacbter.

Women's Slalom

Gold — Petra Kronberger.

Silver — Annelise Coberger, New Zealand.

Bronze — Blanca Fernandez-Ochoa, Spain.

Women's Super Giant Slalom

Gold — Deborah Compagnoni, Italy.

Silver — Carole Merle, France.

Bronze — Katja Seizinger, Germany.

Men's Combined

Gold — Josef Polig, Italy.
Silver — Gianfranco Martin, Italy.
Bronze — Steve Locher, Switzerland.

Men's Downhill

Gold — Patrick Ortlieb, Austria.
Silver — Franck Piccard, France.
Bronze — Gunther Mader, Austria.

Men's Giant Slalom

Gold — Alberto Tomba, Italy.
Silver — Marc Girardelli, Luxembourg.
Bronze — Kjetil Andre Aamodt, Norway.

Men's Super Giant Slalom

Gold — Kjetil Andre Aamodt.
Silver — Marc Girardelli.
Bronze — Jan Einar Thorsen, Norway.

Men's Slalom

Gold — Finn Christian Jagge, Norway.
Silver — Alberto Tomba.
Bronze — Michael Tritscher, Austria.

Olympics-Cross-Country Skiing

Women's 5k

Gold — Marjut Lukkarinen, Finland.
Silver — Lyubov Yegorova, Unified Team.
Bronze — Yelena Valbe, Unified Team.

Women's 10k

Gold — Lyubov Yegorova.
Silver — Stefania Belmondo, Italy.
Bronze — Yelena Valbe.

Women's 15k

Gold — Lyubov Yegorova.
Silver — Marjut Lukkarinen.
Bronze — Yelena Valbe, Unified Team.

Women's 20k Relay

Gold — Unified Team.
Silver — Norway.
Bronze — Italy.

Women's 30k

Gold — Stefania Belmondo.
Silver — Lyubov Yegorova.
Bronze — Yelena Valbe.

Men's 10k

Gold — Vegard Ulvang, Norway.
Silver — Marco Alvarello, Italy.
Bronze — Christer Majback, Sweden.

Men's 15k

Gold — Bjorn Dahlie, Norway.
Silver — Vegard Ulvang, Norway.
Bronze — Giorgio Vanzetta, Italy.

Men's 30k

Gold — Vegard Ulvang.
Silver — Bjorn Dahlie.
Bronze — Terje Langli, Norway.

Men's 40k, Relay

Gold — Norway.
Silver — Italy.
Bronze — Finland.

Men's 50k

Gold — Bjorn Dahlie.
Silver — Maurilio De Zolt, Italy.
Bronze — Giorgio Vanzetta.

Nordic Combined

Team

Gold — Japan.
Silver — Norway.
Bronze — Austria.

Individual

Gold — Fabrice Guy, France.
Silver — Sylvain Guillaume, France.
Bronze — Klaus Sulzenbacher, Austria.

RESULTS

Ski Jump

Team, 120m

Gold — Finland.
Silver — Austria.
Bronze — Czechoslovakia.

Individual, 120m

Gold — Toni Nieminen, Finland.
Silver — Martin Hollwarth, Austria.
Bronze — Heinz Kuttin, Austria.

Individual, Norman Hill

Gold — Ernst Vettori, Austria.
Silver — Martin Hollwarth.
Bronze — Toni Nieminen.

Freestyle Skiing

Women's Moguls

Gold — Donna Weinbrecht, United States.
Silver — Elizaveta Kojevnikova, Unified Team.
Bronze — Stine Hattestad, Norway.

Men's Moguls

Gold — Edgar Grospiron, France.
Silver — Olivier Allamand, France.
Bronze — Nelson Carmichael, United States.

Speed Skating

Men

Gold — Michael Prufer, France.
Silver — Phillippe Goitschel, France.
Bronze — Jeffrey Hamilton, United States.

Women

Gold — Tarja Mulari, Finland.
Silver — Liss Petterson, Norway.
Bronze — Renata Kolaarova, Switzerland.

SLED DOG RACING

Iditarod (Anchorage to Nome) — Martin Buser,
Two Rivers, Alaska.

SNOWMOBILE RACING

World — Greg Goodwin, United States.

SOAP BOX DERBY

Stock Car — Loren Hurst, Akron, Ohio.
Masters — Bonnie Thornton, Las Vegas, Nev.
Kit Car — Carolyn Fox, Salem, Ore.

SOCCER

Nations

America Cup (South American Championship)
— Argentina.
CONCACAF Gold Cup — United States.
European Championship — Denmark.
African Nations Cup — Ivory Coast.
Asian Cup — Saudi Arabia.
North American Nations Cup — Mexico.
Caribbean Cup — Trinidad and Tobago.
Central American Cup — Costa Rica.
Pan American Games (under 23) — United
States.
Olympic Games (under 23) — Spain.
FIFA World Youth Championship (under 20) —
Portugal.
FIFA Under-17 Championship — Ghana.
FIFA Women's Championship — United States.

U.S. Clubs

A.P.S.L. — San Francisco Bay.
M.I.S.L. — San Diego Sockers.
U.S. Open Cup — San Jose.
U.S. Amateur Cup — Madison (Wis.) 56ers.
U.S. Women's Amateur Cup — Ajax (Los
Angeles).

International Champions

Intercontinental Cup (World Club Championship)
— Red Star, Belgrade (Yugoslavia).
European Champions Cup — Barcelona
(Spain).

European Cup Winners Cup — Werder Bremen (Germany).

U.E.F.A. Cup — Ajax Amsterdam (Netherlands)

European SuperCup — Manchester United (England).

South American Liberators Cup — Sao Paulo (Brazil).

South American Super Cup — Cruzeiro (Brazil).

CONCACAF Champions Cup — Puebla (Mexico).

Interamerican Cup — Club America (Mexico).

Asian Cup Winners Cup — Nissan (Japan).

Collegiate

N.C.A.A. Division I — Virginia.

N.C.A.A. Division II — Florida Tech.

N.C.A.A. Divison III — University of California at San Diego.

N.C.A.A. Division I Women — North Carolina.

N.C.A.A. Division II Women — California State University at Dominguez Hills.

N.C.A.A. Division III Women — Ithaca, N.Y.

N.A.I.A. — Lynn, Fla.

N.A.I.A Women — Pacific Lutheran.

International Leagues and Cups

Albanian League — Vllaznia Shkoder.

Albanian Cup — SK Elbasan.

Austrian League — Austria Vienna.

Austrian Cup — Austria Vienna.

Belgian League — FC Bruges.

Belgian Cup — FC Royal Antwerp.

Bulgarian League — CSKA Sofia.

Bulgarian Cup — Levsky Sofia.

CIS League — CSKA Moscow.

CIS CUP — Spartak Moscow.

Croatian League — Hajduk Split.

Croatian Cup — Inker Zapresic.

Cyprus League — Apoel Nicosia.

Cyprus Cup — Apollon Limassol.

Czechoslovak League — Slovan Bratislava.

Czechoslovak Cup — Sparta Prague.

Danish Cup — Lyngby Boldklub.

Danish Cup — Aarhus GF.

English League — Leeds United.

English Football Association Cup — Liverpool.

Faroe Islands League — KI Klakksvik.

Faroe Islands Cup — B 36 Thorshavn.

Finnish League — Kuusysi Lahti.

Finnish Cup — Turku Palloseura.

French League — Olympique Marseille.

French Cup — Abandoned.

German League — VFB Stuttgart.

German Cup — Hanover 96.

Greek League — AEK Athens.

Greek Cup — Olymplakos Plraeus.

Hungarian League — Ujpest Budapest.

Hungarian Cup — Ujpest Budapest.

Iceland League — Vikingur.

Iceland Cup — Valur Reykjavik.

Irish League — FC Shelbourne.

Irish Cup — Bohemians.

Israeli League — Maecabi Tel Aviv.

Israeli Cup — Hapoel Petach Tikva.

Italian League — AC Milan.

Italian Cup — Parma.

Luxembourg League — Union Luxembourg.

Luxembourg Cup — Avenir Beggen.

Malta League — FC Valletta.

Malta Cup — Hamrun Spartans.

Netherlands League — PSV Eindhoven.

Netherlands Cup — Feyenoord of Rotterdam.

Northern Ireland League — Glentoran.

Northern Ireland Cup — Glenavon.

Norwegian League — Viking Stavanger.

Norwegian Cup — Stroemgodset Drammen.

Polish League — Lech Poznan.

Polish Cup — Miedz Legnica.

Portugese League — FC Porto.

Portugese Cup — Boavista Porto.

Romanian League — Dinamo Bucharest.

Romanian Cup — Steaua Bucharest.

Scottish League — Glasgow Rangers.

Scottish Football Association Cup — Glasgow Rangers.

Slovenian League — Olimpija Ljubljana.

Slovenian Cup — Branik Maribor.

Soviet Cup — CSKA Moscow.

Spanish League — Barcelona.

Spanish Cup — Atletico Madrid.

Swedish League — IFK Goteborg.

Swedish Cup — AIK Stockholm.

Swiss League — FC Sion.

Swiss Cup — FC Lucerne.

Turkish League — Besiktas.

Turkish Cup — Trabzonspor.

Ukraine League — Tavria Simferopol.

Ukraine Cup — Chernomorets Odessa.

Welsh Cup — Cardiff City.

Willard Cup — Helena.

Yugoslavian League — Red Star Belgrade.

Yugoslavian Cup — Partizan Belgrade.

Olympics

Gold — Spain.

Silver — Poland.

Bronze — Ghana.

SOFTBALL

U.S. Men's Fast Pitch — Guanella Brothers, Rohnert Park, Calif.

U.S. Women's Fast Pitch — Raybestos Brak Ettes, Stratford, Conn.

U.S. Men's Super-Slow Pitch — Ritch's/Superior, Windson Locks, Conn.

U.S. Men's Major-Slow Pitch — Vernon's, Jacksonville, Fla.

U.S. Women's Major-Slow Pitch — Universal Plastics, Cookeville, Tenn.

U.S. College Women — Arizona.

SPEED SKATING

U.S. Long-Track Champions

Women's Sprint Champion — Bonnie Blair, Champaign, Ill.

Men — Dan Jansen, Milwaukee.

All-Around, Women — Michelle Kline, Circle Pines, Minn.

All-Around Men — Brian Waanek, Milwaukee, Wisc.

US Short-Track Champions

Women's All-Around — Cathy Turner, Rochester, N.Y.

Men's All-Around — Andy Gabel, Franklin, Wisconsin.

Olympics

Long Track — Women's 500 M

Gold — Bonnie Blair, United States.

Silver — Ye Qiaobo, China.

Bronze — Christa Luding, Germany.

Long Track — Women's 1,000 M

Gold — Bonnie Blair.

Silver — Ye Qiaobo.

Bronze — Monique Gatbrecht, Germany.

Long Track Women's 1,500 M

Gold — Jacqueline Borner, Germany.

Silver — Gunda Niemann, Germany.

Bronze — Seiko Hashimoto, Japan.

Long Track Women's 3,000 M

Gold — Gunda Niemann.

Silver — Heike Warnicke, Germany.

Bronze — Emese Hunyady, Austria.

Long Track Women's 5,000 M

Gold — Gunda Niemann.

Silver — Heike Warnicke.

Bronze — Claudia Pechstein, Germany.

Long Track Men's 500 M

Gold — Uwe-Jens Mey, Germany.

Silver — Toshiyuki Kuroiwa, Japan.

Bronze — Junichi Inoue, Japan.

Long Track Men's 1,000 M

Gold — Olaf Zinke, Germany.

Silver — Kim Yoon Man, South Korea.

Bronze — Yukinori Miyabe, Japan.

Long Track Men's 1,500 M

Gold — Johann Koss, Norway.

Silver — Adne Sondral, Norway.

Bronze — Leo Visser, the Netherlands.

Long Track Men's 5,000 M

Gold — Geir Karlstad, Norway.

Silver — Falco Zandstra, the Netherlands.

Bronze — Leo Visser, the Netherlands.

Long Track Men's 10,000 M

Gold — Bart Veldkamp, the Netherlands.

Silver — Johann Koss, Norway.

Bronze — Geir Karlstad, Norway.

Short Track Women's 3,000 M Relay

Gold — Canada.

Silver — United States.

Bronze — Unified Team.

Short Track Women's 500 M

Gold — Cathy Turner, United States.

Silver — Li Yan, China.

Bronze — Hwang Ok Sil, North Korea.

Short Track Men's 1,000 M

Gold — Kim Ki Hoon, South Korea.

Silver — Frederic Blackburn, Canada.

Bronze — Lee Yoon Ho, South Korea.

Short Track Women's 5,000 M Relay

Gold — South Korea.

Silver — Canada.

Bronze — Japan.

SQUASH RACQUETS

U.S. Champions

U.S. Open Softball — Rodney Martin.

Men's Softball — Hector Barragan, Mexico.

Women's Softball — Ellie Pierce, New York City.

Men's Hardball — Hector Barragan.

Women's Hardball — Demer Holleran, Hanover, N.H.

Men's College — Jeremy Fraiberg, Harvard.

Women's College — Jordana Fraiberg, Harvard.

World Champions

Men's Softball — Rodney Martin, Australia.

Women's Softball — Susan Devoy, England.

North American Open Hardball — Mark Talbott, United States.

British Open — Jansher Khan, Pakistan.

SQUASH TENNIS

U.S. Champion

Men — Gary Squires, Darien, Conn.

SURFING

World Championship

Ocean Pacific Pro Tag Team — United States.

SWIMMING

Phillips 66 National Championships

Men

50-Meter Free — Todd Pace, Ft. Lauderdale.

100 Free — Alyn Towne, Ft. Lauderdale.

200 Free — John Piersman, Huntsville.

400 Free — Peter Wright, Jersey Wahoos.

800 Free — Lars Jorgensen, Blue Fins.

1,500 Free — Carlton Bruner, Florida Aquatics.

100 Back — Derek Weatherford, Swim Florida.

200 Back — Derek Weatherford.

100 Breast — Mike Barrowman, Curl-Burke.

200 Breast — Mike Barrowman.

100 Butterfly — Mike Merrell, Mecklenburg Aquatics.

200 Butterfly — Ray Carey, Reno Aquatic Club.

200 Individual Medley — Ron Karnaugh, Mission Viejo.

400 Individual Medley — Matt Hooper, Alamo Area Aquatics.

400 Free Relay — Ft. Lauderdale 'A'.

800 Free Relay (Team) — Santa Clara 'A'.

400 Medley Relay (Team) — Ft. Lauderdale 'A'.

RESULTS

Women

50-Meter Free — Angel Martino, Americus Blue Tide.

100 Free — Angel Martino.

200 Free — Michelle Jesperson, Badger Dolphins.

400 Free — Tobie Smith, Badger Swimming.

800 Free — Sarah L. Anderson, San Ramon Valley.

1,500 — Alexis Larsen, CLASS Aquatics.

100 Back — Kerry O'Hanlon, Nova Virginia.

200 Back — Paige Wilson, Athens Bulldogs.

100 Breast — Kristine Quance, CLASS Aquatics.

200 Breast — Kristine Quance.

100 Butterfly — Angie Wester-Krieg, Stanford Swimming.

200 Butterfly — Angie Wester-Krieg.

200 Individual Medley — Kristine Quance.

400 Individual Medley — Kristine Quance.

400 Free Relay — Fort Lauderdale 'A'.

800 Free Relay — Fort Lauderdale 'A'.

400 Medley Relay — Americus Blue Tide 'A'.

N.C.A.A. Men

50-Yard Free — Erik Maurer, Stanford.

100 Free — Gustavo Borges, Michigan.

200 Free — Gustavo Borges.

500 Free — Artur Wojdat, Iowa.

1,650 Free — Artur Wojdat.

100 Back — Jeff Rouse, Stanford.

200 Back — Jeff Rouse.

100 Breast — Andrea Cecchi, U.C.L.A.

200 Breast — Andrea Cecchi.

100 Butterfly — Anthony Nesty, Florida.

200 Butterfly — Rasal Szukala, Iowa.

200 Individual Medley — Jeff Rouse.

400 Individual Medley — Jeff Vance, Southern Methodist.

One-Meter Diving — Dean Panaro, Miami (Fla.).

Three-Meter Diving — Jason Rhodes, Texas.

200-Medley Relay — Stanford.

400-Medley Relay — Stanford.

200-Freestyle Relay — Stanford.

400-Freestyle Relay — Stanford.

800-Freestyle Relay — Stanford.

Division I Team — Stanford.

Division II Team — Cal. State Bakersfield.

Division III Team — Kenyon, Ohio.

N.C.A.A. Women

50-Yard Free — Jenny Thompson, Stanford.

100-Free — Jenny Thompson.

200-Free — Nicole Haislett, Florida.

500-Free — Erika Hansen, Texas.

1650 Free — Katy Arris, Texas.

100 Back — Lea Loveless, Stanford.

200 Back — Whitney Hedgeteth, Texas.

100 Breast — Susan Lipscomb, Southern Methodist.

200 Breast — Lisa Flood, Villanova.

100 Butterfly — Cris Ahmann-Leighton, Arizona.

400 Butterfly — Summer Sanders, Stanford.

200-Yard Individual Medley — Summer Sanders.

400-Yard Individual — Summer Sanders.

One-Meter Diving — Cheril Santini, Southern Methodist.

Three-Meter Diving — Eileen Richetelli, Stanford.

200-Medley Relay — Stanford.

400-Medley Relay — Stanford.

200-Freestyle Relay — Texas.

400-Freestyle Relay — Stanford.

800-Freestyle Relay — Stanford.

Division I Team — Stanford.

Division II Team — Oakland.

Division III Team — Kenyon, Ohio.

Olympics

Men's 50 Freestyle

Gold — Alexandre Popov, Unified Team.

Silver — Matt Biondi, United States.

Bronze — Tom Jager, United States.

Men's 100 Freestyle

Gold — Alexandre Popov, Unified Team.

Silver — Gustavo Borges, Brazil.

Bronze — Stephan Caron, France.

Men's 200 Freestyle

Gold — Evgueni Sadovyi, Unified Team.

Silver — Anders Holmertz, Sweden.

Bronze — Antti Kasvio, Finland.

Men's 400 Freestyle

Gold — Evgueni Sadovyi, Unified Team.

Silver — Kieren Perkins, Australia.

Bronze — Anders Holmertz, Sweden.

Men's 1,500 Freestyle

Gold — Kieren Perkins, Australia.

Silver — Glen Housman, Australia.

Bronze — Joerg Hoffmann, Germany.

Men's 100 Backstroke

Gold — Mark Tewksbury, Canada.

Silver — Jeff Rouse, United States.

Bronze — David Berkoff, United States.

Men's 200 Backstroke

Gold — Martin Lopez-Zubero, Spain.

Silver — Vladimir Selkov, Unified Team.

Bronze — Stefano Battistelli, Italy.

Men's 100 Breaststroke

Gold — Nelson Diebel, United States.

Silver — Norbert Rozsa, Hungary.

Bronze — Philip Rogers, Australia.

Men's 200 Breaststroke

Gold — Mike Barrowman, United States.

Silver — Norbert Rozsa, Hungary.

Bronze — Nick Gillingham, Britain.

Men's 100 Butterfly

Gold — Pablo Morales, United States.

Silver — Rafal Szukala, Poland.

Bronze — Anthony Nesty, Surinam.

Men's 200 Butterfly

Gold — Mel Stewart, United States.

Silver — Danyon Loader, New Zealand.

Bronze — Franck Esposito, France.

Men's 200 Individual Medley

Gold — Tamas Darnyi, Hungary.

Silver — Greg Burgess, United States.

Bronze — Attila Czene, Hungary.

Men's 400 Individual Medley

Gold — Tamas Darnyi, Hungary.

Silver — Eric Namesnik, United States.

Bronze — Luca Sacchi, Italy.

Men's 400 Freestyle Relay

Gold — United States (Joseph Hudepohl, Matt Biondi, Tom Jager, Jon Olsen).

Silver — Unified Team (Pavel Khnykine, Guennadi Prigoda, Iouri Bashkatov, Alexandre Popov).

Bronze — Germany (Christian Troeger, Dirk Richter, Steffen Zesner, Mark Pinger).

Men's 400 Medley Relay

Gold — United States (Jeff Rouse, Nelson Diebel, Pablo Morales, Jon Olsen).

Silver — Unified Team (Vladimir Selkov, Vassili Ivanov, Pavel Khnykine, Alexandre Popov).

Bronze — Canada (Mark Tewksbury, Jonathan Cleveland, Marcel Gery, Stephen Clarke).

Men's 800 Freestyle Relay

Gold — Unified Team (Dmitri Lepikov, Vladimir Pychnenko, Veniamin Taianovitch, Evgueni Sadovyi).

Silver — Sweden (Christer Wallin, Anders Holmertz, Tommy Werner, Lars Frolander).

Bronze — United States (Joseph Hudepohl, Mel Stewart, Jon Olsen, Doug Gjertsen).

Women's 50 Freestyle

Gold — Yang Wenyi, China.

Silver — Zhuang Yong, China.

Bronze — Angel Martino, United States.

Women's 100 Freestyle

Gold — Zhuang Yong, China.

Silver — Jenny Thompson, United States.

Bronze — Franziska Van Almsick, Germany.

Women's 200 Freestyle

Gold — Nicole Haislett, United States.
Silver — Franziska Van Almsick, Germany.
Bronze — Kerstin Kielgass, Germany.

Women's 400 Freestyle

Gold — Dagmar Hase, Germany.
Silver — Janet Evans, United States.
Bronze — Hayley Lewis, Australia.

Women's 800 Freestyle

Gold — Janet Evans, United States.
Silver — Hayley Lewis, Australia.
Bronze — Jana Henke, Germany.

Women's 100 Backstroke

Gold — Kristina Egerszegi, Hungary.
Silver — Tunde Szabo, Hungary.
Bronze — Lea Loveless, United States.

Women's 200 Backstroke

Gold — Kristina Egerszegi, Hungary.
Silver — Dagmar Hase, Germany.
Bronze — Nicole Stevenson, Australia.

Women's 100 Breaststroke

Gold — Elena Roudkovskaia, Unified Team.
Silver — Anita Nall, United States.
Bronze — Samantha Riley, Australia.

Women's 200 Breaststroke

Gold — Kyoko Iwasaki, Japan.
Silver — Lin Li, China.
Bronze — Anita Nall, United States.

Women's 100 Butterfly

Gold — Qian Hong, China.
Silver — Christine Ahmann-Leighton, United States.
Bronze — Catherine Plewinski, France.

Women's 200 Butterfly

Gold — Summer Sanders, United States.
Silver — Wang Xiaohong, China.
Bronze — Susan O'Neill, Australia.

Women's 200 Individual Medley

Gold — Lin Li, China.
Silver — Summer Sanders, United States.
Bronze — Daniela Hunger, Germany.

Women's 400 Individual Medley

Gold — Krisztina Egerszegi, Hungary.
Silver — Lin Li, China.
Bronze — Summer Sanders, United States.

Women's 400 Freestyle Relay

Gold — United States (Nicole Haislett, Dara Torres, Angel Martino, Jenny Thompson).
Silver — China (Zhuang Yong, Lu Bin, Yang Wenyi, Le Jingyi).
Bronze — Germany (Franziska Van Almsick, Simone Osygus, Daniela Hunger, Manuela Stellmach).

Women's 400 Medley Relay

Gold — United States (Lea Loveless, Anita Nall, Crissy Ahmann-Leighton, Jenny Thompson).
Silver — Germany (Dagmar Hase, Jana Doerries, Franziska Van Almsick, Daniela Hunger).
Bronze — Unified Team (Nina Jivanevskaia, Elena Roudkovskaia, Olga Kiritchenko, Natalia Mechtcheriakova).

SYNCHRONIZED SWIMMING

National Champions

Solo — Kristen Babb-Sprague, Pleasanton, Calif.
Duet — Karen and Sarah Josephson, Bristol, Conn.
Team — Walnut Creek, Calif.

Olympics

Solo

Gold — Kristen Babb-Sprague, United States.
Silver — Sylvie Frechette, Canada.
Bronze — Fumiko Okuno, Japan.

Duet

Gold — Karen Josephson and Sarah Josephson, United States.

Silver — Penny Vilagos and Vicky Vilagos, Canada.

Bronze — Fumiko Okuno and Aki Takayama, Japan.

TABLE TENNIS

Olympics

Men's Singles

Gold — Jan Waldner, Sweden.

Silver — Jean Philippe Gatien, France.

Bronze — Kim Taek Soo, South Korea.

Men's Doubles

Gold — Lu Lin and Wang Tao, China.

Silver — Steffen Fetzner and Jorg Rosskopf, Germany.

Bronze — Kang Hee Chan and Lee Chul Seung, South Korea, and Kim Taek Soo and Yoo Nam Kyu, South Korea.

Women's Singles

Gold — Deng Yaping, China.

Silver — Qiao Hong, China.

Bronze — Hyun Jung Hwa, South Korea, and Li Bun Hui, North Korea.

Women's Doubles

Gold — Deng Yaping and Qiao Hong, China.

Silver — Chen Zihe and Gao Jun, China.

Bronze — Li Bun Hui and Yu Sun Bok, North Korea, and Hong Cha Ok and Hyun Jung Hwa, South Korea.

TAE KWON DO

U.S. Men's Heavyweight — Paris Amani, Colorado Springs, Colo.

U.S. Women's Heavyweight — Lynette Love, Detroit.

TEAM HANDBALL

National Champions

U.S. Men — Garden City, L.I.

U.S. Women — Colorado Springs Stars.

Women's U.S.A. Cup — Austria.

College Men — West Point.

College Women — Slippery Rock (Pa.).

Olympics

Men

Gold — Unified Team.

Silver — Sweden.

Bronze — France.

Women

Gold — South Korea.

Silver — Norway.

Bronze — Unified Team.

TENNIS

N.C.A.A.

Men's Division I — Wade Mcguire, Georgia.

Men's Division I Team — Stanford.

Women's Division I — Lisa Raymond, Fla.

Women's Division I Team — Florida.

Men's Division II — Philipp Schertel, Armstrong.

Men's Division II Team — U.C. Davis.

Women's Division II — Michelle King, Abilene Christian.

Women's Division II Team — Cal Poly, Pomona.

Men's Division III — Lew Miller, Kalamazoo.

Men's Division III Team — Kalamazoo.

Women's Division III — Shelley Keeler, Pomona-Pitzer (Claremont, Calif.).

Women's Division III Team — Pomona Pitzer.

N.A.I.A. Men's Champion — Niclas Nilsson, Lander.

N.A.I.A. Men's Team — Lander, Greenwood, S.C.

N.A.I.A. Women's Champion — Helena Dahlstrom, Flagler.

N.A.I.A. Women's Team — Auburn-Montgomery, Ala.

RESULTS

U.S. Open Champions

Men's Singles — Stefan Edberg, Sweden.

Women's Singles — Monica Seles, United States.

Men's Doubles — Jim Grabb and Richey Reneberg, United States.

Women's Doubles — Gigi Fernandez, United States, and Natalya Zvereva, Belarus.

Mixed Doubles — Nicole Provis and Mark Woodforde, Australia.

Senior Men's Singles — Hank Pfister, United States.

Senior Men's Doubles — Paul McNamee, Australia and Tomas Smid, Czechoslovakia.

Senior Women's Doubles — Wendy Turnball, Australia and Virginia Wade, Great Britian.

Senior Mixed Doubles — Wendy Turnbull, Australia and Marty Riessen, United States.

Boys' Junior Singles — Brian Dunn, United States.

Girls' Junior Singles — Lindsay Davenport, United States.

Boys' Doubles — J.J. Jackson and Eric Taino, United States.

Girls' Doubles — Lindsay Davenport and Nicole London, United States.

Wimbledon

Men — Andre Agassi, United States.

Women — Steffi Graf, Germany.

French Open

Men — Jim Courier, United States.

Women — Monica Seles, United States.

Australian Open

Men — Jim Courier, United States.

Women — Monica Seles, United States.

Virginia Slims Championship

Singles — Monica Seles, United States.

Doubles — Monica Seles, and Martina Navratilova, United States.

Olympics

Men's Singles

Gold — Marc Rosset, Switzerland.

Silver — Jordi Arrese, Spain.

Bronze — Goran Ivanisevic, Croatia, and Andrei Cherkasov, Unified Team.

Men's Doubles

Gold — Boris Becker and Michael Stich, Germany.

Silver — Wayne Ferreira and Piet Norval, South Africa.

Bronze — Goran Ivanisevic and Goran Prpic, Croatia, and Javier Frana and Christian Carlos Miniussi, Argentina.

Women's Singles

Gold — Jennifer Capriati, United States.

Silver — Steffi Graf, Germany.

Bronze — Aranxta Sanchez-Vicario, Spain, and Mary Joe Fernandez, United States.

Women's Doubles

Gold — Gigi Fernandez and Mary Joe Fernandez, United States.

Silver — Conchita Martinez and Arantxa Sanchez-Vicario, Spain.

Bronze — Natalia Zvereva and Leila Meskhi, Unified Team, and Rachel McQuillan and Nicole Provis, Australia.

TRACK AND FIELD

U.S. Champions — Olympic Track and Field Trials

Men

100-Meter — Dennis Mitchell, Gainesville, Fla.

200 — Michael Johnson, Waco, Tex.

400 — Danny Everet, Santa Monica, Calif.

800 — Johnny Gray, Santa Monica Calif.

1,500 — Jim Spivey, Glen Ellyn, Ill.

3,000 Steeplechase — Brian Diemer, Kentwood, Mich.

5,000 — John Trautmann, Washington.

10,000 — Todd Williams, Knoxville, Tenn.

110 Hurdles — Jack Pierce, Marlton, N.J.

400 Hurdles — Kevin Young, Los Angeles.

20K Walk — Allen James, Mission Viejo, Calif.

High Jump — Hollis Conway, Lafayette, La.

Pole Vault — Tim Bright Milwaukie, Ore.

Long Jump — Mike Powell, Alta Loma.

Triple Jump — Charlie Simpkins, Murfreesboro, Tenn.

Shot-Put — Mike Stulce, College Station, Texas.

Discus — Kamy Keshmiri, Reno, Nev.

Hammer Throw — Jud Logan, North Canton, Ohio.

Javelin — Tom Pukstys, Hickory Hills, Ill.

Decathlon — Dave Johnson, Pomona, Calif.

Women

100-Meter — Gwen Torrence, Decatur, Ga.

200 M — Gwen Torrence.

400 M — Rochelle Stevens, Memphis, Tenn.

800 M — Joetta Clark, Columbia, N.J.

1,500 M — Regina Jacobs, Oakland, Calif.

3,000 M — Patti Sue Plumer, Palo Alto, Calif.

10,000 M — Lynn Jennings, Newmarket, N.H.

100 M Hurdles — Gail Devers, Van Nuys, Calif.

400 M Hurdles — Sandra Farmer-Patrick, Pflugerville, Texas.

10 K Walk — Debbi Lawrence, Kenosha, Wisc.

High Jump — Tanya Hughes, Tucson, Ariz.

Long Jump — Jackie Joyner-Kersee, Canoga Park, Calif.

Shot Put — Connie Price-Smith, Hobart, Ind.

Discus — Connie Price-Smith.

Javelin — Donna Mayhew, Glendale, Calif.

Heptathlon — Jackie Joyner-Kersee.

Mobil Indoor Championships

Men

60-Meter Hurdles — Leroy Burrell, Houston, Texas.

400 M — Willie Caldwell, Tucson, Ariz.

500 M — Mark Everett Gainesville, Fl.

800 M — Fred Williams, Canada.

Mile — Noureddine Morceli, Algeria.

3,000 M — Doug Padilla, Orem, Utah.

5,000 M Walk — Gary Morgan, Clarkston, Mich.

High Jump — Hollis Conway, Shreveport, La.

Pole Vault — Dean Starkey, Atascadero, Calif.

Long Jump — Carl Lewis, Houston, Tex.

Triple Jump — Mike Conley, Fayetteville, Ark.

Shot-Put — Ron Backes, Minneapolis, Mn.

35-lb. Weight Throw — Lance Deal, Casper, Wyo.

Men's 4 x 800 M Relay — New York Athletic Club, Manhattan.

Men's 4 x 400 M Relay — Seton Hall University.

Women

60-Meter Dash — Michelle Finn, Houston, Tex.

200 M Dash — Dyan Webber, Houston, Tex.

400 M Run — Diane Dixon, Brooklyn.

800 M Run — Maria Mutola, Mozambique.

Mile — Lynn Jennings, Newmarket N.H.

3,000 M Walk — Debbi Lawrence, Kenosha, Wi.

60-Meter Hurdles — Jackie Joyner-Kersee, Canoga Park, Ca.

3,000 M Run — Shelly Steely, Albuquerque, N.M.

High Jump — Angela Bradburn, Austin, Texas.

Long Jump — Jackie Joyner-Kersee.

Triple Jump — Claudia Haywood, Houston, Texas.

Shot Put — Connie Price-Smith, Hobart, Ind.

20 lb Weight-throw — Sonia Fitts, Rochester, N.Y.

4x400 Meter Relay — Seton Hall University.

N.C.A.A.

Men's Outdoor

100 Meters — Olapade Adeniken, Texas El Paso.

200 M — Olapade Adeniken.

400 M — Quincy Watts, Southern California.

800 M — Tony Parilla, Tennessee.

1,500 M — Steve Holman, Georgetown.

3,000 Steeplechase M — Marc Davis, Arizona.

5,000 Run M — John Dennis, South Florida.

10,000 Run M — Sean Dollman, Western Kentucky.

110 High Hurdles — Mark Crear, Southern California.

400 M Hurdles — Dan Steele, Eastern Illinois.

4 x 100 M Relay Team — Louisiana State.

4 x 400 M Relay Team — Georgia Tech.

High Jump — Darrin Plab, Southern Illinois.

Pole Vault — Istvan Bagyula, George Mason.

Long Jump — Erick Walder, Arkansas.

Triple Jump — Brian Wellman, Arkansas.

Shot-Put — Brent Noon, Georgia.

Discus — Kamy Keshmiri, Nevada-Reno.

Javelin — Art Skipper, Oregon.

Hammer Throw — Mika Laaksonen, Texas-El Paso.

Decathlon — Brian Brophy, Tennessee.

Team Champion — Arkansas.

Women's Outdoor

100 Meter Dash — Chryste Gaines, Stanford.

200 M Dash — Dahlia Duhaney, L.S.U.

400 M Dash — Anita Howard, Florida.

800 M Run — Nekita Beasley, Florida.

1,500 M Run — Sue Gentes, Wisconsin.

3,000 M Run — Nnenna Lyncb, Villanova.

5,000 M Run — Monique Ecker, Oklahoma.

10,000 M Run — Kim Saddic, George Mason.

100 M Hurdles — Michelle Freeman, Florida.

400 M Hurdles — Tonja Buford, Illinois.

400 M Relay Team — L.S.U.

1,600 M Relay Team — Florida.

High Jump — Tanya Hughes, Arizona.

Long Jump — Jackie Edwards, Stanford.

Triple Jump — Leah Kirkland, Florida.

Shot Put — Katrin Koch, Indiana.

Discus Throw — Anna Mosdell, Brigham Young.

Javelin Throw — Valerie Tulloch, Rice.

Heptathlon — Anu Kaljurand, Brigham Young.

Team Champion — L.S.U.

Men's Indoor

55 Meter Dash — Michael Green, Clemson.

55 M Hurdles — Allen Johnson, North Carolina.

200 M Dash — James Trapp, Clemson.

400 M Dash — Deon Minor, Baylor.

800 M Run — Rich Kenah, Georgetown.

Mile M Run — Andrew Keith, Providence College.

3,000 M Run — Josephat Kapkory, Washington.

5,000 M Run — Jon Brown, Iowa St.

1,600 M Relay — Baylor.

3,200 M Relay — Florida.

High Jump — Tom Lange, L.S.U.

Long Jump — Erick Walder, Arkansas.

Triple Jump — Erick Walder.

Pole Vault — Istvan Bagyula, George Mason.

Shot-Put — Kevin Coleman, Nebraska.

35-Pound Weight Throw — Mika Laaksonen, Texas El Paso.

Team Champion — Arkansas.

Women's Indoor

55-Meter Dash — Chryste Gaines, Stanford.

55 M Hurdles — Gillian Russell, Miami.

200 M Dash — Michelle Collins, Houston.

400 M Dash — Maicel Malone, Arizona St.

800 Run — Mareille Sankatsing, Eastern Michigan University.

1 Mile Run — Karen Glerum, Iowa St.

3,000 M Run — Geraldine Hendricken, Providence.

5,000 M Run — Tracy Dahl, Iowa.

1,600 M Relay Team — Florida.

3,200 M Relay Team — Wisconsin.

High Jump — Natasha Alleyne, Georgia Tech.

Long Jump — Jackie Edwards, Stanford.

Triple Jump — Leah Kirklin, Florida.

Shot-Put — Don Dumble, U.C.L.A.

Team Champion — University of Florida.

Olympics — Men

100 Meter Dash

Gold — Linford Christie, Britain.

Silver — Frankie Fredericks, Namibia.

Bronze — Dennis Mitchell, United States.

200 Meter Dash

Gold — Mike Marsh, United States.
Silver — Frankie Fredericks, Namibia.
Bronze — Michael Bates, United States.

400 Meter Dash

Gold — Quincy Watts, United States.
Silver — Steve Lewis, United States.
Bronze — Samson Kitur, Kenya.

800 Meter Dash

Gold — William Tanui, Kenya.
Silver — Nixon Kiprotich, Kenya.
Bronze — Johnny Gray, United States.

1,500 Meter Dash

Gold — Fermin Cacho Ruiz, Spain.
Silver — Rachid El-Basir, Morocco.
Bronze — Mohamed Ahmed Sulaiman, Qatar.

5,000 Meter Dash

Gold — Dieter Baumann, Germany.
Silver — Paul Bitok, Kenya.
Bronze — Fita Bayisa, Ethiopia.

10,000 Meter Dash

Gold — Khalid Skah, Morocco.
Silver — Richard Chelimo, Kenya.
Bronze — Addis Abebe, Ethiopia.

110 Meter Hurdles

Gold — Mark McKoy, Canada.
Silver — Tony Dees, United States.
Bronze — Jack Pierce, United States.

400 Meter Hurdles

Gold — Kevin Young, United States.
Silver — Winthrop Graham, Jamaica.
Bronze — Kriss Akabusi, Britain.

400 Meter Relay

Gold — United States (Mike Marsh, Leroy Burrell, Dennis Mitchell, and Carl Lewis).

Silver — Nigeria (Oluyemi Kayode, Chidi Imoh, Olapade Adeniken, and Davidson Ezinwa).
Bronze — Cuba (Andres Simon, Joel Lamela, Joel Isasi, and Jorge Aguilera).

1,600 Meter Relay

Gold — United States (Andrew Valmon, Quincy Watts, Michael Johnson, and Steve Lewis).
Silver — Cuba (Lazaro Martinez, Hector Herrera, Norberto Tellez, and Roberto Hernandez).
Bronze — Britain (Roger Black, David Grindley, Kriss Akabusi, and John Regis).

3,000 Meter Steeplechase

Gold — Mathew Birir, Kenya.
Silver — Patrick Sang, Kenya.
Bronze — William Mutwol, Kenya.

20 Km Walk

Gold — Daniel Plaza Montero, Spain.
Silver — Guillaume Leblanc, Canada.
Bronze — Giovanni De Benedictis, Italy.

50 Km Walk

Gold — Andrei Perlov, Unified Team.
Silver — Carlos Mercenario Carbajal, Mexico.
Bronze — Ronald Weigel, Germany.

Marathon

Gold — Hwang Young-Cho, South Korea.
Silver — Koitchi Morishita, Japan.
Bronze — Stephan Freigang, Germany.

Decathlon

Gold — Robert Zmelik, Czechoslovakia.
Silver — Antonio Penalver, Spain.
Bronze — Dave Johnson, United States.

Discus

Gold — Romas Ubartas, Lithuania.
Silver — Jurgen Schult, Germany.
Bronze — Roberto Moya, Cuba.

Hammer Throw

Gold — Andrey Abduvaliyev, Unified Team.
Silver — Igor Astapkovich, Unified Team.
Bronze — Igor Nikulin, Unified Team.

RESULTS

High Jump

Gold — Javier Sotomayor, Cuba.

Silver — Patrik Sjoeberg, Sweden.

Bronze — Artur Partyka, Poland; Timothy Forsythe, Australia; and Hollis Conway, United States.

Javelin

Gold — Jan Zelezny, Czechoslovakia.

Silver — Seppo Raty, Finland.

Bronze — Steve Backley, Britain.

Long Jump

Gold — Carl Lewis, United States.

Silver — Mike Powell, United States.

Bronze — Joe Greene, United States.

Pole Vault

Gold — Maxim Tarassov, Unified Team.

Silver — Igor Trandenkov, Unified Team.

Bronze — Javier Garcia Chico, Spain.

Shot Put

Gold — Michael Stulce, United States.

Silver — James Doehring, United States.

Bronze — Viacheslav Lykho, Unified Team.

Triple Jump

Gold — Mike Conley, United States.

Silver — Charles Simpkins, United States.

Bronze — Frank Rutherford, Bahamas.

Olympics — Women

100 Meter Dash

Gold — Gail Devers, United States.

Silver — Juliet Cuthbert, Jamaica.

Bronze — Irina Privalova, Unified Team.

200 Meter Dash

Gold — Gwen Torrence, United States.

Silver — Juliet Cuthbert, Jamaica.

Bronze — Merlene Ottey, Jamaica.

400 Meter Dash

Gold — Marie-Jose Perec, France.

Silver — Olga Bryzgina, Unified Team.

Bronze — Ximena Restrepo Gaviria, Colombia.

800 Meter Dash

Gold — Ellen Van Langen, Netherlands.

Silver — Lilia Nurutdinova, Unified Team.

Bronze — Ana Quirot, Cuba.

1,500 Meter Dash

Gold — Hassiba Boulmerka, Algeria.

Silver — Lyudmila Rogacheva, Unified Team.

Bronze — Qu Yunxia, China.

3,000 Meter Dash

Gold — Elena Romanova, Unified Team.

Silver — Tatiana Dorovskikh, Unified Team.

Bronze — Angela Chalmers, Canada.

10,000 Meter Dash

Gold — Derartu Tulu, Ethiopia.

Silver — Elana Meyer, South Africa.

Bronze — Lynn Jennings, United States.

100 Meter Hurdles

Gold — Paraskevi Patoulidou, Greece.

Silver — LaVonna Martin, United States.

Bronze — Yordanka Donkova, Bulgaria.

400 Meter Hurdles

Gold — Sally Gunnell, Britain.

Silver — Sandra Farmer-Patrick, United States.

Bronze — Janeene Vickers, United States.

400 Meter Relay

Gold — United States (Evelyn Ashford, Esther Jones, Carlette Guidry, Gwen Torrence).

Silver — Unified Team (Olga Bogoslovskaya, Galina Malchugina, Marina Trandenkova, Irina Privalova).

Bronze — Nigeria (Beatrice Utondu, Faith Idehen, Christy Thompson, Mary Onyali).

1,600 Meter Relay

Gold — Unified Team (Yelena Ruzina, Lioudmila Dzhigalova, Olga Nazarova, Olga Bryzgina).

Silver — United States (Natasha Kaiser, Gwen Torrence, Jearl Miles, Rochelle Stevens).

Bronze — Britain (Phylis Smith, Sandra Douglas, Jennifer Stoute, Sally Gunnell).

10 Km Walk

Gold — Chen Yueling, China.

Silver — Elena Nikolaeva, Unified Team.

Bronze — Li Chunxiu, China.

Marathon

Gold — Valentina Yegorova, Unified Team.

Silver — Yuko Arimori, Japan.

Bronze — Lorraine Moller, New Zealand.

Discus

Gold — Maritza Marten, Cuba.

Silver — Tzvetanka Khristova, Bulgaria.

Bronze — Daniela Costian, Australia.

Heptathlon

Gold — Jackie Joyner-Kersee, United States.

Silver — Irina Belova, Unified Team.

Bronze — Sabine Braun, Germany.

High Jump

Gold — Heike Henkel, Germany.

Silver — Galina Astafei, Romania.

Bronze — Joanet Quintero, Cuba.

Javelin

Gold — Silke Renk, Germany.

Silver — Natalia Shikolenko, Unified Team.

Bronze — Karen Forkel, Germany.

Long Jump

Gold — Heike Drechsler, Germany.

Silver — Inessa Kravets, Unified Team.

Bronze — Jackie Joyner-Kersee, United States.

Shot Put

Gold — Svetlana Kriveleva, Unified Team.

Silver — Huang Zhihong, China.

Bronze — Kathrin Neimke, Germany.

TRIATHLON

Ironman Men — Mark Allen, Cardiff, Calif.

Ironman Women — Paula Newby-Fraser, Encinitas, Calif.

TUMBLING

U.S. Men's Tumbling — Rashaan Sampson, Newark, N.J.

U.S. Women's Tumbling — Michelle Mara, Rockford, Ill.

U.S. Men's Trampoline — Karl Heger, Manhattan, Kansas.

U.S. Women's Trampoline — Jennifer Sans, Apple Valley, Minnesota.

VOLLEYBALL

National

U.S. Open

1st Place - Men — Creole Six Pack, Elmhurst, N.Y.

1st Place - Women — Nick's Kronies, Chicago, Ill.

International

World League Championship — Italy

Collegiate

N.A.I.A. — Brigham Young, Hawaii campus.

N.J.C.A.A. — Eastern Arizona College.

N.C.A.A.

Division I Men — Pepperdine.

Division I Women — U.C.L.A.

Division II Women — West Texas State.

Division III Women — Washington (Missouri).

Olympics

Men

Gold — Brazil.
Silver — Netherlands.
Bronze — United States.

Women

Gold — Cuba.
Silver — Unified Team.
Bronze — United States.

WATER POLO

U.S. Champions

U.S. Men's Outdoor — The Olympic Club.
U.S. Women's Outdoor — Cal-Berkeley.
U.S. Men's Indoor — Harvard WP Foundation, Los Angeles.
U.S. Women's Indoor — Beach.
N.C.A.A. — California (University of Berkeley).

Olympics

Gold — Italy.
Silver — Spain.
Bronze — Unified Team.

WATER SKIING

U.S. Open

Men's Over All — Patrice Martin, France.
Women's Over All — Julie Petrus, United States.

World

Men's Over All — Patrice Martin, France.
Women's Over All — Karen Neville, Australia.

WINDSURFING

U.S. National Champions

Men — Andy Morrell, Virgin Islands.
Women — Blanche Montelongo, Corpus Christi, Tex.

Junior Men's — Paul Stoeken, Virgin Islands.
Master's Men — Derek Escher, Ipswich, Mass.
Grand Master's Men — Ed Cannon, Wayland, Mass.

U.S. Production National Champions

Men — Alf Imperato, Rochester, N.Y.
Women — Jayne Fenner, Sarasota, Fla.
Corpus Christi Bay Trophy — Jayne Fenner.
Junior Men's — James Ford, Darien, Conn.
Master's Men — Platt Johnson, Middletown, R.I.
Grand Master's — Richard Collins, Ocean City, Maryland.

Olympics

Men's Final Standings

Gold — Frank David, France.
Silver — Michael Gebhardt, United States.
Bronze — Lars Klappich, Australia.

Women's Final Standings

Gold — Barbara Anne Kendall, New Zealand.
Silver — Xlaodong Zhang, China.
Bronze — Dorien De Vries, Netherlands.

WEIGHT LIFTING

U.S. Weightlifting Federation

Men

52 Kgs. — Brian Okada, Wailuku, Hawaii.
56 — Robert "Gene" Gilsdorf, Onaga, Kansas.
60 — Bryan Jacob, Norcross, Ga.
67.5 — Vernon Patao, Kahului, Hawaii.
75 — David Santillo, Runnemede, N.J.
82.5 — Roberto Tony Urrutia, Hollywood, Fla.
90 — Bret Brian, Baton Rouge, La.
100 — Wesley Barnett, St. Joseph, Missouri
110 — Rich Schutz, Mt. Prospect, Ill.
Plus 110 — Mario Martinez, South San Francisco, Calif.

Women

44 Kgs. — Sibby Flowers, Carrollton, Ga.
48 — Misha Utley, Lawrenceburg, Ind.
52 — Robin Byrd, Newnan, Ga.
56 — Ursula Garza, Austin, Texas.
60 — Giselle Shepatln, San Francisco.
67.5 — Dianna Fuhrman, Simi Valley, Calif.
75 — Arlys Johnson, Seattle.
82.5 — Mary Hyder, Dallas.
Plus 82.5 — Carla Garrett, Tucson, Ariz.

Women's World Champions

44 Kgs. — Hong Guan, China.
48 — Xiuhua Liu, China.
52 — Liping Peng, China.
56 — Caiyan Sun, China.
60 — Hongyun Li, China.
67.5 — Lijuan Gal, China.
75 — Ju Hua, China.
82.5 — Xiaoli Zhang, China.
Women's heavyweight — Li Yajuan, China.
Women's team — China.

Olympics

52 Kg (115 pounds)

Gold — Ivan Ivanov, Bulgaria.
Silver — Lin Qisheng, China.
Bronze — Traian Ciharean, Romania.

56 Kg (123 pounds)

Gold — Chun Byung-Kwan, South Korea.
Silver — Liu Shoubin, China.
Bronze — Luo Jianming, China.

60 Kg (132 pounds)

Gold — Naim Suleymanoglu, Turkey.
Silver — Nikolai Peshalov, Bulgaria.
Bronze — He Yingqiang, China.

67.5 Kg (148 pounds)

Gold — Israel Militossian, Unified Team.
Silver — Yoto Yotov, Bulgaria.
Bronze — Andreas Behm, Germany.

75 Kg (165 pounds)

Gold — Fedor Kassapu, Unified Team.
Silver — Pablo Lara, Cuba.
Bronze — Kim Myong Nam, North Korea.

81.5 Kg (181 pounds)

Gold — Pyrros Dimas, Greece.
Silver — Krzysztof Siemion, Poland.
Bronze — None Awarded (Ibragim Samadov of
Unified Team refused medal).

90 Kg (198 pounds)

Gold — Kakhi Kakhiachvili, Unified Team.
Silver — Serguei Syrtsov, Unified Team.
Bronze — Sergiusz Wolczaniecki, Poland.

100 Kg (220 pounds)

Gold — Victor Tregoubov, Unified Team.
Silver — Timour Taimazov, Unified Team.
Bronze — Waldemar Malak, Poland.

110 Kg (243 pounds)

Gold — Ronny Weller, Germany.
Silver — Artour Akoev, Unified Team.
Bronze — Stefan Botev, Bulgaria.

110 Kg-plus (243-plus pounds)

Gold — Alexandre Kourlovitch, Unified Team.
Silver — Leonid Taranenko, Unified Team.
Bronze — Manfred Nerlinger, Germany.

WRESTLING

Men's National Champions

Freestyle

105.5 lbs. — Rob Eiter, Scottsdale, Ariz.
114.5 — Jack Griffin, Iowa City, Iowa.
125.5 — Kendall Cross, Stillwater, Okla.
136.5 — John Fisher, Ann Arbor, Mich.
149.5 — Matt Demaray, Madison, Wisc.
163 — Greg Elinsky, Philadelphia.
180.5 — Royce Alger, Iowa City, Iowa.
198 — Dan Chaid, Newtown Square, Pa.

220 — Bill Scherr, Evanston, Ill.

286 — Bruce Baumgartner, Cambridge Springs, Pa.

Div. I Team — Sunkist Kids.

Div. II Team — Foxcatcher.

Greco-Roman

105.5 lbs. — Eric Wetzel, Quantico, Va.

114.5 — Mark Fuller, Gilert, Ariz.

125.5 — Dennis Hall, Neosho, Wisc.

136.5 — Buddy Lee, Woodbridge, Va.

149.5 — Rodney Smith, Fort Benning, Ga.

163 — Travis West, Portland, Ore.

180.5 — John Morgan, Minneapolis, Minn.

198 — Michial Foy, Brooklyn Park, Minn.

220 — Dennis Koslowski, St. Louis Park, Minn.

286 — Matt Ghaffari, Chandler, Ariz.

Div. I Team — N.Y. Athletic Club.

Div. II Team — Sunkist Kids.

Women's National Champions

Freestyle

97 lbs. — Cheryl Meyer, Morrill, Ka.

103.5 — Afsoon Roshanzimir, Davis, Caif.

110 — Tricia Saunders, Phoenix, Ariz.

116.5 — Jennifer Ottiano, Orelo, Conn.

125.5 — Lee Ann Gonzalez, Hanford, Calif.

134 — Diana Wesendunk, Hillsbrough, Calif.

143 — Grace Jividen, Colorado Springs, Colo.

Olympics — Freestyle

48 Kg (105.5 pounds)

Gold — Kim Il, North Korea.

Silver — Kim Jong-Shin, South Korea.

Bronze — Vougar Oroudjov, Unified Team.

52 Kg (114.5 pounds)

Gold — Li Hak-Son, South Korea.

Silver — Zeke Jones, United States.

Bronze — Valentin Jordanov, Bulgaria.

57 Kg (125.5 pounds)

Gold — Alejandro Puerto, Cuba.

Silver — Serguei Smal, Unified Team.

Bronze — Kim Yong Sik, North Korea.

62 Kg (136.5 pounds)

Gold — John Smith, United States.

Silver — Asgari Mohammadian, Iran.

Bronze — Lazaro Reinoso, Cuba.

68 Kg (149.5 pounds)

Gold — Arsen Fadzaev, Unified Team.

Silver — Valentin Getzov, Bulgaria.

Bronze — Kosei Akaishi, Japan.

74 Kg (163 pounds)

Gold — Park Jang-Soon, South Korea.

Silver — Kenny Monday, United States.

Bronze — Amir Reza Khadem Azghadi, Iran.

82 Kg (181.5 pounds)

Gold — Kevin Jackson, United States.

Silver — Elmadi Jabraijlov, Unified Team.

Bronze — Rasul Azghadi, Iran.

90 Kg (198 pounds)

Gold — Makharbek Khadartsev, Unified Team.

Silver — Kenan Simsek, Turkey.

Bronze — Chris Campbell, United States.

100 Kg (220 pounds)

Gold — Leri Khabelov, Unified Team.

Silver — Heiko Balz, Germany.

Bronze — Ali Kayali, Turkey.

130 Kg (286 pounds)

Gold — Bruce Baumgartner, United States.

Silver — Jeff Thue, Canada.

Bronze — David Gobedjichvili, Unified Team.

Olympics — Greco-Roman

48 Kg (105.5 pounds)

Gold — Oleg Koutherenko, Unified Team.

Silver — Vincenzo Maenza, Italy.

Bronze — Wilber Sanchez, Cuba.

52 Kg (114.5 pounds)

Gold — Jon Ronningen, Norway.

Silver — Alfred Ter-Mkrttchian, Unified Team.

Bronze — Min Kyung-Kap, South Korea.

57 Kg (125.5 pounds)

Gold — An Han-Bong, South Korea.

Silver — Rifat Yildiz, Germany.

Bronze — Sheng Zetian, China.

62 Kg (136.5 pounds)

Gold — M. Akif Pirim, Turkey.

Silver — Serguei Martynov, Unified Team.

Bronze — Juan Maren, Cuba.

68 Kg (149.5 pounds)

Gold — Attila Repka, Hungary.

Silver — Islam Dougoutchiev, Unified Team.

Bronze — Rodney Smith, United States.

74 Kg (163 pounds)

Gold — Mnatsakan Iskandarian, Unified Team.

Silver — Jozef Tracz, Poland.

Bronze — Torbjorn Johansson, Sweden.

82 Kg (181.5 pounds)

Gold — Peter Farkas, Hungary

Silver — Piotr Stepien, Poland

Bronze — Daoulet Tourlykhanov, Unified Team.

90 Kg (198 pounds)

Gold — Maik Bullmann, Germany.

Silver — Hakki Basar, Turkey.

Bronze — Gogui Kogouachvili, Unified Team.

110 Kg (220 pounds)

Gold — Hector Milian, Cuba.

Silver — Dennis Koslowski, United States.

Bronze — Serguei Demiachkievitch, Unified Team.

130 Kg (286 pounds)

Gold — Alexander Karelin, Unified Team.

Silver — Tomas Johansson, Sweden.

Bronze — Ioan Grigoras, Romania.

N.C.A.A. Champions

118 lbs. — Jeff Prescott, Penn State.

126 — Terry Brands, Iowa.

134 — Tom Brands, Iowa.

142 — Troy Steiner, Iowa.

150 — Matt Demaray, Wisconsin.

158 — Pat Smith, Oklahoma St.

167 — Charles Jones, Purdue.

177 — Kevin Randleman, Ohio St.

190 — Mark Kerr, Syracuse.

Heavyweight — Kurt Angle, Clarion.

Team — Iowa.

YACHTING

America's Cup

Winner — America Team, Bill Koch d. Italy.

Olympics

Men's Lechner

Gold — Franck David, France.

Silver — Mike Gebhardt, United States.

Bronze — Lars Kleppich, Australia.

Women's Lechner

Gold — Barbara Kendall, New Zealand.

Silver — Zhang Xiaodong, China.

Bronze — Dorien De Vries, Netherlands.

Men's 470

Gold — Spain (Jordi Calafat and Francisco Sanchez).

Silver — United States (Morgan Reeser and Kevin Burnham).

Bronze — Estonia (Tonu Toniste and Toomas Toniste).

Women's 470

Gold — Spain (Theresa Zabell and Patricia Guerra).

Silver — New Zealand (Leslie Jean Egnot and Janet Shearer).

Bronze — United States (Jennifer Isler and Pamela Healy).

RESULTS

Finn

Gold — Jose Van Der Ploeg, Spain.

Silver — Brian Ledbetter, United States.

Bronze — Craig Monk, New Zealand.

Europe

Gold — Linda Anderson, Norway.

Silver — Natalia Via Dufresne, Spain.

Bronze — Julia Trotman, United States.

Flying Dutchman

Gold — Spain (Luis Doreste and Domingo Manrique).

Silver — United States (Paul Foerster and Stephen Bourdow).

Bronze — Denmark (Jorgen Bojsen and Jens Bojsen).

Soling

Gold — Denmark (Jesper Bank, Steen Secher, and Jesper Seier).

Silver — United States (Kevin Mahaney, James Brady, and Doug Kern).

Bronze — Britain (Lawrence Smith, Robert Cruikshank, and Simon Stewart).

Star

Gold — United States (Mark Reynolds, Hal Haenel).

Silver — New Zealand (Roderick Davis, Donald Cowie).

Bronze — Canada (D. Ross MacDonald, Eric Jespersen).

Tornado

Gold — France (Yves Loday, Nicolas Henard).

Silver — United States (Randy Smyth, Keith Notary).

Bronze — Australia (Mitch Booth, John Forbes).

The following is a list of events for the 1993 calendar year.

AUTO RACING

Daytona 500 — Daytona Beach, FL; February 14.

Winston 500 — Tallageda, Al; Early May.

Coca-Cola 600 — Charlotte, NC; Late May.

Indianapolls 500 — Indianapolis, IN; May 30.

LeMans — France; June 19-20.

Heinz Southern — Darlington, SC; Last week of September.

BASEBALL

Major League

All Star Game — Camden Yards, Baltimore, MD; July 13.

American League Championship Series — Early October.

National League Championship Series — Early October.

World Series — Mid-October.

College World Series — Early June.

Little League Championship — Williamsport, PA; Late August.

BASKETBALL

NBA

All Star Game — Delta Center, Salt Lake City, UT; February 21.

Playoffs — Begin April 29.

NCAA

Men's Final Four — Superdome, New Orleans, LA; April 3-5.

Women's Final Four — The Omni, Atlanta, GA; April 3-4.

BOWLING

PBA National Championship — Imperial Lanes, Toledo, OH; February 21-27.

BPAA U.S. Open — Roseland Bowl; Canandiagua, NY; April 4-10.

Firestone Tournament of Champions — Riveria Lanes, Fair Lawn, OH; April 20-24.

WIBC Open Singles Championship — Don Carter All-Star Lanes, Baton Rouge, LA; April 1 to May 23 (could be extended).

CYCLING

Tour Du Pont — Eastern United States; May 6-16.

Tour de France — Mid-July.

DARTS

North American Open — Las Vegas, NV; August 12-15.

DOG SHOW

Westminster — Madison Square Garden, New York, NY; February 8-9.

FOOTBALL

NFL

Wild Card — January 2 & 3.

Division Playoffs — January 9 & 10.

Conference Playoffs — January 17.

Super Bowl — Rose Bowl, Pasadena, CA; January 31.

Pro Bowl — Aloha Stadium, Honolulu, HI; February 7.

NCAA Bowl Games — 1 January

Blockbuster — Joe Robbie Stadium, Miami, FL.

Cotton — Cotton Bowl, Dallas, TX.

Florida Citrus — Citrus Bowl, Orlando, FL.

Fiesta — Sun Devil Stadium, Tempe, AZ.

Gator — Gator Bowl, Jacksonville, FL.

Hall of Fame — Tampa Stadium, Tampa, FL.

Rose — Rose Bowl, Pasadena, CA.

Orange — Orange Bowl, Miami, FL.

Peach — Georgia Dome, Atlanta, GA (Jan. 2).

Sugar — Louisiana Superdome, New Orleans, LA.

NCAA Bowl Games — Late December

Holiday — Jack Murphy Stadium, San Diego, CA.

John Hancock — Sun Bowl, El Paso, TX.

Liberty — Memorial Stadium, Memphis, TN.

FIGURE SKATING

U.S. Championships — Phoenix, AZ; January 17-24.

World Championships — Prague, Czechoslovakia; March 9-14.

GOLF

The Masters — Augusta National, Georgia; April 8-11.

LPGA Championship — Bethesda Country Club, Maryland; June 7-13.

U.S. Open — Baltusrol Golf Club, Springfield, NJ; June 17-20.

U.S. Senior Open — Cherry Hills Country Club, Engelwood, CO; July 8-11.

U.S. Women's Open — Crooked Stick Golf Club, Carmel, IN; July 22-25.

British Open — Royal St. George Golf Club, Sandwich, England; July 15-18.

PGA Championship — Inverness Club, Toledo, OH; Augst 12-15.

Nabisco Dinah Shore — Mission Hills Country Club, Rancho Mirage, CA; Late March.

GYMNASTICS

McDonald's American Cup — Orlando, FL; March 5-6.

World Championships — Birmingham, England; April 13.

U.S. Championships — Salt Lake City, UT; August 26-29.

HARNESS RACING

Yonkers Trot — Yonkers Raceway, NY; July 10.

Hambleton — Meadowlands, NJ; August 7.

Little Brown Jug Pace — Delaware, OH; Late September.

Kentucky Futurity — The Red Mile, KY; October 8.

NHL HOCKEY

All Star Game — Montreal Forum, Canada; February 6.

Division Semifinals — Wales: April 18; Campbell: April 19.

Division Finals — Wales: May 2; Campbell: May 3.

Conference Championship — Wales; May 16, Campbell; May 17.

Stanley Cup Playoffs — June 1.

HORSE RACING

Kentucky Derby — Churchill Downs, Louisville, KY; May 1.

Preakness Stakes — Pimlico Race Course, Baltimore, MD; May 15.

Belmont Stakes — Belmont Park, Elmont, NY; June 5.

Breeder's Cup — Santa Anita Park, Arcadia, CA; November 6.

LACROSSE

M.I.L.L. World Championship — Mid-April.

MARATHON

Boston — April 5.

New York — November 14.

MISCELLANEOUS

The World University Games — Buffalo, NY; July 8-18

ROLLER HOCKEY

U.S. Championships — Fort Smith, AR; July.

World Games — The Hague, NED; July 22-28.

ROWING

Collegiate National Championships — Cincinnati, OH; June 12-13.

National Championships — Indianapolis, IN; June 24-27.

Henley Royal Regatta — Henley-on-Thames, England; June 30-July 4.

International Rotsee Regatta — Lucerne, Switzerland; July 9-11.

RUGBY

Seven-A-Side World Cup — Edinburgh, Scotland; April 16-18.

National Club Championships — Site not Announced; May 8-9.

SKIING

World Championships — Shizukuishi, Japan; February 3-14.

Men's Alpine World Cup — Aspen, CO; March 6-7.

SOCCER

European Cup Winners Final — Site Not Announced; May 12.

U.E.F.A. Cup Finals — Sites Not Announced; May 5 and May 19.

European Champions Cup Final — Site Not Announced; May 26.

America Cup — Ecuador; June 19 - July 4.

World Cup Draw — Las Vegas, NE; September 18 or 19.

SOFTBALL

Women's Major Fast Pitch — Stratford, CT; August 13-20.

Women's Major Slow Pitch — Albany, GA; September 3-6.

Men's Major Slow Pitch — Tifton, GA; September 3-6.

Men's Major Fast Pitch — Decatur, IL; September 10-18.

SWIMMING

Phillips 66 National Championships — Nashville, TE; March 31 - April 4.

Pan Pacific Championships — Kobe, Japan; August 12-15.

TENNIS

Australian Open — Flinders Park, Melbourne; January 18-31.

French Open — Roland Garros Stadium, Paris; May 24 - June 6.

Wimbledon — All-England Club, London; June 28 - July 4.

U.S. Open — National Tennis Center, New York, NY; August 30 - September 12.

TRACK AND FIELD

Milrose Games — Madision Square Garden, New York, NY; February 5.

Mobil Indoor Championships — Madison Square Garden, New York, NY; February 26.

World Indoor Championships — Toronto, Canada; March 12-14.

World Outdoor Championships — Eugene, OR; June 18-20.

World Track and Field Championships — Stuttgart, Germany; August 13-22.

TRIATHLON

Iron Man — Kuilua-Kona, HI; October 30.

VOLLEYBALL

U.S. Open — Memphis,TE; May 29 - June 6.

WEIGHT LIFTING

National Championships — Peoria, IL; April 30 - May 2, or May 7-9.

National Junior Championships — Blaine, MN; April 3-4.

World Championships — Melbourne, Australia; November 12-21.

WRESTLING

U.S. National Championships — Las Vegas, NV; April 28 - May 1.

World Free-Style Championships — Toronto, Canada; August 25 - 28.

World Greco-Roman Championships — Stockholm, Sweden; September 16-19.

YACHTING

Key West Race Week — Key West, FL; January 17-22.

Storm Trysail — Royal Ocean Racing Club, NY to U.K.; Starts July 3.

Admiral's Cup — Cowes, England; Late July.

MASTERS PRESS

DEAR VALUED CUSTOMER,

Masters Press is dedicated to bringing you timely and authoritative books for your personal and professional library. As a leading publisher of sports and fitness books, our goal is to provide you with easily accessible information on topics that interest you written by the most qualified authors. You can assist us in this endeavor by checking the box next to your particular areas of interest.

We appreciate your comments and will use the information to provide you with an expanded and more comprehensive selection of titles.

Thank you very much for taking the time to provide us with this helpful information.

Cordially,
Masters Press

Areas of interest in which you'd like to see Masters Press publish books:

☐ COACHING BOOKS
    Which sports? What level of competition?

☐ INSTRUCTIONAL/DRILL BOOKS
    Which sports? What level of competition?

☐ FITNESS/EXERCISE BOOKS
    ☐ Strength—Weight Training
    ☐ Body Building
    ☐ Other

☐ REFERENCE BOOKS
    what kinds?

☐ BOOKS ON OTHER
    Games, Hobbies
    or Activities

Are you more likely to read a book or watch a video-tape to get the sports information you are looking for?

I'm interested in the following sports as a participant:

I'm interested in the following sports as an observer:

Please feel free to offer any comments or suggestions to help us shape our publishing plan for the future.

Name _____ Age _____

Address _____

City _____ State _____ Zip _____

Daytime phone number _____

BUSINESS REPLY MAIL

FIRST CLASS MAIL   PERMIT NO. 1317   INDIANAPOLIS IN

POSTAGE WILL BE PAID BY ADDRESSEE

MASTERS PRESS

2647 WATERFRONT PKY EAST DR DEPT WF
INDIANAPOLIS IN 46209-1418

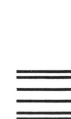

NO POSTAGE
NECESSARY
IF MAILED
IN THE
UNITED STATES